RISE AND WALK

RISE AND WALK

THE TRIAL AND TRIUMPH OF
DENNIS BYRD

DENNIS BYRD

WITH MICHAEL D'ORSO

HarperCollins*Publishers*
•
Zondervan

HarperCollins books may be purchased for educational, business, or sales promotional use. For information, please write: Special Markets Department, HarperCollins Publishers, Inc., 10 East 53rd Street, New York, NY 10022.

FIRST EDITION

Designed by Jessica Shatan

LIBRARY OF CONGRESS CATALOG CARD NUMBER 93-32004
ISBN: 0-06-017783-7

93 94 95 96 97 ❖/HC 10 9 8 7 6 5 4 3 2 1

CONTENTS

REBIRTH

COMING HOME

ACKNOWLEDGMENTS

A year ago it would have been impossible for me to imagine the journey that lay just around the corner. That's what the past year has been, an incredible journey, a trip that's taken me through the range of every human emotion. From pain, fear, and doubt to courage, compassion, and faith, reliving that journey has been an experience in itself. There are many people to thank for helping me tell this story.

First, of course, there is the Jets medical staff, especially Jim and Steve Nicholas, Elliott Hershman, and Pepper Burruss, who helped me piece together the details of those first ten hours, as well as the next ten days. At Lenox Hill Hospital, Dr. Marty Camins helped immensely with his insights into the acute stage of my treatment there. The staff at Mount Sinai Medical Center, especially Dr. Kristjan Ragnarsson, were behind me again, just as they were during my two-month stay there. And once again, Joanne Giammetta and Lawrence Harding came through beyond the call of duty.

In terms of my football memories, Mustang High School head coach Charlie Carpenter answered the call, as did Don Tomkalski, sports information director for the University of Tulsa. I also have Frank Ramos to thank for his tremendous dedication and help in compiling facts and photo information, along with Doug Miller and Ken Ilchuk of the New York Jets' public relations office.

I would not be where I am today without the wisdom and guidance of my agent and attorney, Rick Schaeffer, and the constant coaxing of my co-author, Mike D'Orso. Mike and I both have to thank our literary agent, David Black, and our editors, Rick Horgan and Chris McLaughlin of HarperCollins and John Sloan and Scott Bolinder of Zondervan. We would also like to thank Randy Jessee of the *Virginian-Pilot* for his technical support.

I'd like to thank my teammates, the men I've shared a relationship with through triumph and tears. There is a love that develops between players in the truly tough times that no one else can share. Thanks, guys — for the lights, the fields, this game of football. I feel especially privileged to have had as teammates Marvin Washington, Jeff Lageman, Scott Mersereau, Paul Frase, Bill Pickel, and Mark Gunn, and as a coach, Greg Robinson. You hold a special place in my heart.

I must thank Steve Gutman, president of the New York Jets, for his caring support of me and my family when no one knew that this story would have a happy ending.

Mr. Leon Hess has my special gratitude. I first knew him as the quiet, reclusive owner of the New York Jets, but after my injury he dedicated all he had to my recovery. He gave not only financially but also of himself, sharing stories late at night of failure turning into success. He talked to me much the way a grandfather would. To Mr. Hess, let me say, "I love you."

I also can't thank enough Angela's family—her parents, David and Betty Hales, and her brother, Chris—who've been beside me as if I were one of their own. I love all of you, too.

To my family—Dan and Nancy Byrd, my brothers, Dan and Doug, and my sisters, Jeni and Dawn: You are what Dennis Byrd learned from, what I am. I can only pray that I have positively affected your lives half as much as you have mine. Thank you for me. I will love you always.

Angela, I can hardly write this because of the emotion that wells inside me. Few men have had the chance to learn about their wives' courage. I laid there helpless, and you were my strength. The world thinks I'm a courageous man, but you are my courage. You are also my best friend. Thank you for never leaving my side. It will take the rest of my life to return to you the love you gave me those first nights, and that's how long I'll try.

And to my girls, Ashtin and Haley, you showed me it doesn't

take six-foot-five and 270 pounds to be a man, all I had to be was Daddy.

P.S. That size will help when you girls turn sixteen. I love you both so much.

Most of all, I'm grateful to Jesus Christ, who was there when no one else could be. I thank Him for my salvation and for the strength He gave me in my darkest hour. I was only able to receive it by turning it all over to Him.

Because of Christ and the many, many others who supported me in the darkness of night, I now stand in the bright light of day ... in triumph.

—Dennis Byrd
August 1993

Now Peter and John went up together into the temple at the hour of prayer, being the ninth hour.

And a certain man lame from his birth was carried, whom they laid daily at the gate of the temple which is called Beautiful, to ask alms of them that entered into the temple;

Who, seeing Peter and John about to go into the temple, asked an alms.

And Peter, fastening his eyes upon him, with John, said, "Look on us."

And he gave heed unto them, expecting to receive something from them.

Then Peter said, "Silver and gold have I none, but, such as I have, give I thee. In the name of Jesus Christ of Nazareth, rise up and walk."

And he took him by the right hand, and lifted him up; and immediately his feet and ankle bones received strength.

And he, leaping up, stood and walked, and entered with them into the temple, walking, and leaping, and praising God.

ACTS 3:1–8

PROLOGUE

Now I know exactly how fragile life is and how close to the edge we live. In an instant, the one it takes to turn out the lights or close the door, in that instant our lives can change forever. We all face this crisis at some point, but unlike most, my instant was witnessed by millions and millions of people.

I remember lying there and looking up at the sky, the tingling in my body slowly subsiding, my eyes and mind gradually regaining their focus on the gray New Jersey sky above me, a sky that was turning toward twilight, with a few thin clouds breaking it up.

The buzzing inside my body gradually slipped away, replaced by a new, more terrifying feeling—nothing. I had to get to my feet, to stand upright, to prove to myself that everything was all right. All I needed to do was push myself off the turf, as I had a thousand times before, then look to our sideline for approval of my performance and to gather in the signals for the next play. But for me, there would never be another play.

I tried to get up. My head raised off the ground just enough for its weight to dislodge the bone chips randomly filling the space that had been my C-5 vertebra. I felt something give way. I heard it, too, a grinding and crunching at the top of my spine. And I knew then. I'd broken my neck.

No one else knew. Not yet. It was Mers the guys were worried about at first. He'd taken the hit in his sternum, his body violently recoiling from the blow, then going limp. He was down a long time, fighting to breathe as some of my teammates went over to help.

I slowly settled my head back to the ground. Then I raised my right arm to unsnap my helmet. But instead of going where I willed it, my hand hit my face mask with a sickening clank. The sound of it, that hand hitting my helmet, is a sound I'll hear the rest of my life. It was like the sound of something landing on a tin roof. It reminded me of the sound of the rain and hail that pounded the ventilation pipe of my granny's storm cellar back in Oklahoma as we all huddled in the glow of lantern light, waiting out the violence passing overhead. I'll never forget the sound in that cellar, that haunting, hollow sound. And I'll never forget the sound of my hand hitting that face mask.

Thoughts were beginning to tumble through my head. And one thought kept repeating itself: "Don't move. Don't move *anything*."

Kyle Clifton, our middle linebacker, was the first to come over.

"Let's go, buddy," he said, expecting me to just jump to my feet. "Get up. Let's go."

"Kyle," I said. "I can't. I'm paralyzed."

His face turned pale, almost blank. It was as if everything that meant anything to him had drained from his body in that instant. It was in his eyes, such a lonely look, like he was the only man left on earth. He realized I was lying there powerless, paralyzed, and he didn't know how to deal with it. He couldn't say a word. There was nothing to say.

Then Marvin kneeled by my side. Marvin Washington, my roommate and closest friend.

"Dennis," he said softly, "what's the matter?"

"I don't have any feeling in my legs, Marvin," I said. "I can't feel my legs."

He lowered his voice, almost to a whisper.

"Just try, baby," he hissed. "*Try.*"

He turned away. He had to. He didn't want me to see the pain he felt, the tears he was already wiping from his eyes.

Marvin knew. They all knew by then. All my teammates, and the Chiefs, too. Without hearing what I'd said to Kyle or Marvin, they had this realization that I was really hurt. I wasn't grabbing a knee. I wasn't squealing in pain about my shoulder or arm. I wasn't moving a muscle. That's the most frightening sight in sports, an athlete who's down and not moving.

By now Pepper Burruss, our assistant trainer, was beside me. Pepper, always goofing, always pranking, always one of the guys, laughing and joking around in the locker room. But now he was somebody I'd never seen before. His voice had taken on a completely different tone, one I'd never heard, one I'd never had to hear. The tone was totally calm, totally in control, totally professional.

"Hey, buddy," he said. "Just be still here. I got you. I'm gonna stabilize your neck."

Then he began reciting the things he was going to do to keep me from hurting myself more. He locked his hands on the sides of my helmet, holding my head in place. And that's the way it would stay for the next nine hours, someone else's hands locked on my head, as if they had become a part of my body.

Within seconds Bob was there, too. Bob Reese, our head trainer, came rushing over as quickly as he could, tumbling and stumbling and finally coming to a skid by my side. And Steve Nicholas and Elliot Hershman, two of our team's doctors. They were by my shoulder, with Pepper at my head as Bob asked me how I felt, what I could feel, and I told him.

"Bob, my neck's broken. I'm scared. Am I going to be paralyzed?"

He asked me what happened. I told him I didn't know. I'd run into someone, but I didn't know who. I'd hit someone, but I didn't know how.

My teammates were crowding in now, trying to see how I was, trying to say something. Mario Johnson, Mers's backup, leaned over and told me he loved me. "I love you, too," I said. He took my hand and caressed it. Tears were coming out of his eyes. He didn't want to look at this, but he didn't want to leave me either. "Hang in there, man," he said. "Be strong, D."

I caught a glimpse of all the Chiefs players sitting off a ways, some with their helmets off, all with these forlorn expressions that said, "Man, look what this game has done to this guy."

James Hasty, one of our cornerbacks, as tough and hard on the exterior as any player you'll see in this game, was now kneeling beside me, doing his best to comfort me. "Okay, D.," he said, "you're gonna be all right. Just relax, man. Be calm. Just relax."

I was relaxed by then. I had to fight to stay that way, but I was calm. I could feel the coolness coming up off the turf and crawling across the back of my neck and shoulders. I couldn't feel that cool anywhere else on my body.

I could smell the turf dust, the light green powder that comes off the fibers of artificial grass from the trampling it takes during a game. By the end of an afternoon, the stuff is all over your shoes and your pants and your jersey. I could smell the turf, along with the smell of sweat and fear. I certainly smelled the fear.

And I could hear feet shuffling around. Not on the field but up in the stands. A hush had settled over the stadium. That was eerie, real strange. No loud noises, no shouting. A kind of reverence had settled over the crowd, and I could feel them all looking at me.

It's a naked feeling, lying there like that, out in the middle of a football field, in front of fifty-some thousand people. Every eye is focused on you, and you can't do *any*thing. You're just lying there, helpless.

None of the other players on the field were doing anything either. They looked lost, which is abnormal in this totally organized world of professional football, where every play is programmed, every movement is rehearsed and drilled over and over again, everyone is trained how to act and react to every imaginable possibility.

But no one is trained for this. Players aren't prepared for something like this. And when it happens, they don't know what to do. They stand there asking themselves, What's next? And no one knows the answer. They feel helpless, just as helpless as the guy they're looking at.

But the trainers know. And the doctors. Dr. Jim Nicholas— Steve's dad—was there now, too, and everything started clicking like clockwork. Things were under control. Every move counted. It had to. These men all knew exactly what to do. This is what *they* are programmed for. Maybe fifteen minutes out of the four years I'd been with the Jets had I seen this professional demeanor kick in with these guys. The rest of the time they were just part of the team, trading quips and cutdowns along with the players.

But now Bob was barking orders, unbelievably organized, calling for a back board and telling someone to get the cart out here. And while he was whacking off these orders, Jim Nicholas was asking me question after question. "How do you feel? *What* do you feel? Can you feel *this?*" And he'd move my foot or tap it. My toes, knees, groin area, stomach, hands, arms, chest—he worked his way along my body, pushing it and poking it with a pin, seeing what I could feel. And I *could* feel, I could tell I was being touched, but not the way you normally feel something touching you. It was a dull sensation. There was no acuteness to it, just a feeling of pressure.

"Can you move your legs? Can you move your arms?" I tried, but I couldn't. I was intensely aware of what was going on from my shoulder pads up. Below there, everything felt different.

It occurred to me as I waited for the cart to arrive that this might mean the end of my football career, that this might be the injury that did it. I thought about that, but I never thought about the possibility that I might be paralyzed forever. I didn't consider that until I was in the ambulance.

I had been lying there seven minutes, on the Chiefs' eighteen-yard line, when they finally rolled me on my side, slid the yellow back board under me, cinched me down with ties, strapped down my helmet, and lifted me on to the cart, with Pepper still holding my head. Steve Nicholas and Dr. Hershman climbed on and we took off. Joe Patten was driving as we headed toward the west end of the stadium, bumping over the turf, the whirr of that little electric motor humming in my ears.

I took another look at the sky, not knowing it was the last look I'd get for a long time. And I began thinking beyond the moment. All sorts of thoughts. I wondered again if this would be the last time I wore this uniform on this field. I wondered when I'd get the feeling back in my legs. I wondered where Angela was, *how* she was. And our little girl, Ashtin. She'd waited up for me the week before, when we lost to the Patriots and I didn't get home till nearly midnight. Would she be waiting up tonight?

It seemed like there were a hundred people there as we turned into the tunnel, rounded the corner, and pulled up to the ambulance. Lots of commotion, lots of noise, and a sea of faces, including Jeff Lageman, one of my closest friends on the team, who was out for the year with a knee injury. He'd been watching the game from the press box.

"How do you feel?" Jeff asked, walking beside the cart.

"I can't move anything," I told him.

Jeff looked stunned. Then he started talking, as if the scariest thing right now was silence.

"You'll be all right," he said. "You'll be all right. It's not gonna last. You'll be all right."

Then Angela appeared. She was wearing her fur coat, the coyote fur I'd gotten her for her birthday, and she was crying hard, really sobbing. I knew how worried she must have been, watching me from up in her seat, seeing my legs motionless, not knowing how to get down to me, not knowing if she was allowed to be with me.

But now she was here, asking the emergency medical technicians if she could ride along. They said yes as I was being lifted into the ambulance. Pepper backed in, his hands still locked on my helmet as they slid me in behind him. Steve and Ange got in. Then somebody shut the doors, and suddenly everything was silent. That was another sound I'll never forget.

It was the sound of permanence.

BEGINNINGS

There was another set of doors that shut behind me dozens of times when I was a boy—the galvanized steel doors of my granny's storm cellar, where my entire family would flee whenever a tornado was coming.

It was an underground bunker dug out of the red Oklahoma clay, about twenty yards west of the trailer my granny lived in. Most of the time, that cellar was nothing but a dank, dark hole in the ground, a good place for Granny to store her canned goods. Its concrete walls were covered with cobwebs, and it had the musty smell of a basement mixed with the odor of kerosene. But when a twister hit, it was a place of protection, the safest place in the world as far as I was concerned.

I remember the first time the weather drove us down there. I was fourteen, and we'd just come back to Oklahoma after five years in California. We were staying on my grandmother's property, ten acres of land outside a little town called Mustang, at the southwest edge of Oklahoma City, almost exactly in the center of the state. My dad was looking for work, which wasn't easy to find in Oklahoma in the early eighties. The oil boom that had pumped up the state in the seventies was winding down, and businesses were pulling out. My dad was a builder, and there wasn't a lot of building going on.

So we were living in the RV we'd driven from California, stay- ing on my granny's land, which was far out in the country. Except for a family next door, our nearest neighbor was miles away. Oklahomans have a phrase for a place like this. They call it *Boga Cheetah*—the middle of nowhere. And I loved it. Some kids might have been bored, I guess, but to me it was paradise. Acres of corn and wheat fields, where you could wander to the horizon and not run into another soul. Miles of gullies and creeks, where my brothers, Doug and Dan, would team up against me and my cousin Dwayne in dirt-clod fights or slingshot wars. We'd turn old barns into castles, Dwayne and I huddled up in a loft hiding from my brothers, keeping still as shafts of sunlight sliced through the gaps in the roof, making patterns on the hay around us.

Animals were everywhere: deer, bobcats, raccoons, possums, armadillos. You heard them. You saw them. But the animal that attracted me most was one you rarely saw unless you knew what you were doing, and that was the coyote.

So many nights we'd be sitting down to dinner, just about twi- light, and suddenly there'd come a yip from off in the distance. Then a howl. Then another howl from a different direction. Then another. Then a whole chorus, one group of coyotes answering another.

I loved that sound. And I was fascinated by the fact that coy- otes are so hard to *see*. They're petrified of humans, and they're extremely intelligent—a combination that makes them practically invisible. You can see deer from your car as you're driving down a highway. Raccoons will come up to the back door of your house. But coyotes, they make their own way, and I liked that. There's something dignified about them, something almost regal.

I can't count the number of hours I spent out in the fields and prairies, calling coyotes. I learned to make the sound hunters used to lure the coyotes in. It's the sound of a rabbit in distress, a sound not too different from a baby crying. A coyote hears that sound, he figures a rabbit's been caught by something, and being the dominant predator in that region of the country, the coyote comes running to get that rabbit from whatever animal has snared it. Hunters use handmade calls to make the sound, little tubes of wood or metal they cup in their hands and blow into. I learned to make the same sound with a piece of cellophane.

I didn't have to go far to be alone enough to call coyotes— maybe a quarter-mile from our home. I'd huddle down in a bush and make myself as still as I could. For hours I'd sit that way, stock still, knowing that once everything settled down, the critters would start appearing. Sometimes you could see them coming in from as far as a mile away, weaving towards you through the brush and grass. Other times they'd just pop up ten yards away. One second there'd be nothing there, and the next second you'd be looking at a coyote, as if it had just appeared by magic.

Patience was never a problem for me. It was never even an issue. I *enjoy* the calmness, the serenity of simply sitting still, outdoors, away from everything. I love that feeling, and there is no better place to have it than out on the prairie, out in *Boga Cheetah*. I know better now than I did then how much my family didn't have, how hard my dad struggled to find work during those years. But as far as I was concerned, this was a great way to grow up, an ideal setting to be a boy.

Except for the weather, which I got my first taste of not a month after we'd settled in. It was a bright spring morning, calm and warm, everything green, with butterflies on the flowers and the sky so blue it almost hurt your eyes—a day made in heaven. Dwayne and I were playing in a creek bed about two hundred yards from the trailer. We had a rope tied to one of the trees back there, perfect for swinging out over—or into—the water. When there was water.

I hardly noticed when the wind came up that day. We were down in a gully, so we couldn't feel it. But the trees above us began rustling all of a sudden, which is how the weather changes in Oklahoma more than in any place I know of on earth—all of a sudden.

No sooner did I sense the wind picking up than I could feel the air getting chilly. In less than a minute the temperature plunged twenty degrees, from the eighties into the sixties.

Then it got dark, as if a black sheet were being pulled over us. I'd never heard of a wall cloud before, but that's what was coming at us—a giant, violent mass of rain and wind, sweeping across the land at sixty miles an hour, turning the sky from blue to black.

We had no warning. There is no warning for weather like this. You can't chart its approach on radar or computers, because it's not part of a general weather pattern. The wall clouds, tornadoes, and violent hailstorms so common in Oklahoma come literally out of nowhere. They are created right then and there, born of the volatile, unstable conditions unique to this part of the country.

It's really simple to understand. You've got the cold jet stream dipping down from Canada and slamming into the warm moisture coming up from the Gulf. They meet pretty much in the middle of Oklahoma, making for a roiling mix of wind, moisture, and temperature. Add in the fury of the weather coming out of the west, where Pacific coast conditions climb up over the Rockies then spill down into the Central Plains, and it's easy to see how this stuff all comes together and *explodes* seemingly out of nowhere.

That's what was bearing down on Dwayne and me as we scrambled up the side of that gully. The trees around us were beginning to bend. Leaves were swirling through the air and we could hear small branches snapping off in the rushing wind, which was growing stronger by the second.

By the time we came out of the tree line, we could see Granny and my parents across the field, about two hundred yards away, standing by the storm cellar, frantically waving their arms at us. The sky to our left was black, to our right, bright blue. But that would change in a minute or two. Then the wall cloud would be there. And with it maybe a tornado.

We were sprinting now. I'd never run that hard in my life. We had to lean into the wind as we ran, fighting to keep our footing. It felt strong enough to lift us up. By the time we reached the cellar, everyone else was already inside. Doug and Dan. My sisters, Dawn and Jeni. Dwayne's parents—my Aunt Rita and Uncle Tony. And Granny. And my mom and dad.

Dwayne and I were the last ones in, scrambling down those concrete steps and joining the others on the wooden benches pushed up against the walls. Everyone sat on those benches except Uncle Tony, who stayed on the steps and held the doors shut, in case the wind started pulling at them. Uncle Tony was a huge man—six-foot-five, about 280—so he was the natural choice to guard those doors.

Jeni, who was ten then, held the lantern. To this day, every time I smell kerosene, I think of sitting there, seeing my family in that lantern light, listening to the wind coming up outside, hearing it whistle through the metal ventilation pipe that brought us air from above. First I'd hear the wind, then the rain, as it pelted the pipe. Then the pinging sound of hailstones clattering off the pipe and echoing all through this subterranean cave, all around our heads.

It was always an eerie feeling being down there, but it was never frightening. Once you were in the cellar, you knew you were safe. We were never down there long—maybe twenty minutes at the most. That's all the time it takes for a tornado to pass through. Then, when it was silent outside, Uncle Tony would throw open those steel doors, and sunlight would stream in and it was day again—a bright, beautiful spring day. It was hard to believe anything had happened at all.

But it had. Water poured down the steps as the doors were pushed up, remnants of the torrent of rain dumped by that cloud. As much as four inches in twenty minutes—that's how fast it fell. The ground was covered with giant puddles and littered with the debris of the storm, mostly just tree branches—if we were lucky.

I know my parents were always terrified climbing out of that cellar, not knowing what damage the storm had done. But to us kids, it was unbelievably exciting. It was like stepping out into a new world. The light, the air, the trees, the sky—everything had this vividness to it, as if it had all just been created.

Yes, there was danger, but with that came a feeling of adventure, of truly, intensely being alive. And I loved that feeling.

There is no way to separate my life from the land, from the Oklahoma plains and prairies that framed the better part of my boyhood. It was on that land, through faith, family, and football, that I built the foundation of my life. For my first twenty-six years, that foundation was the source of my joy and strength; for my twenty-seventh, it became the basis for survival.

But then the Byrd clan has always known something about survival. Struggle and survival. We didn't get this far by caving in when times got tough, and there have been plenty of tough times in both my father's and mother's families.

Dad's grandparents, Jesse Cleveland Byrd and Dessa Bennett Byrd, moved down to Oklahoma from Illinois during the early thirties, driven by the Depression. They were doing the best they could to farm corn and raise their family, but those were the Dust Bowl days, when the soil that had been plowed up during the half-century since the Oklahoma land rush began drying up and blowing away. No sooner did the Byrds arrive than everyone was leaving. This was the great Okie migration west, when families piled everything they owned onto beat-up jalopies and headed toward California, picking crops as they went, looking for a fresh start. Jesse's family became part of that exodus. My dad says all you have to do is read *The Grapes of Wrath* and change the names—that was the Byrds in the thirties.

Jesse and his children, including a son named Delbert, became migrant workers, picking cotton and lettuce, peaches and plums, pears and prunes and apples, working their way through west Texas, New Mexico, Arizona, and on into California, which is where they finally settled, up around Stockton. That's where my father, Dan, was born in 1942, the first child of Delbert and Helen Brown Byrd.

Delbert had met Helen back in Oklahoma, married her in 1932, and brought her with him when the Byrds went west. Once they settled in Stockton, he got on full-time in the local orchards, pruning and studying the science of agronomy while Helen worked in the canneries to help make ends meet. He also studied sheet metal work at night, which got him a civil service job testing air force bombers at Stockton Field when the war started. A year after my dad was born, his father was transferred to Tinker Air Force Base in Oklahoma City, about a hundred miles from Wagner, where Helen's family lived.

The Browns were a religious family, much more so than the Byrds. They were charismatic Christians, members of the Pentecostal Holiness church, which teaches that the Holy Spirit dwells in each one of us and that that spirit can come out in prayer, through speaking in tongues. Both the Pentecostal Church and the closely related Assembly of God Church are based on this indwelling spirit coming out through testimony and witnessing, through miracle healings and through the kind of speaking in tongues described in the Bible. In Acts, the apostles are visited by a whirlwind not too different from the tornadoes so common in Oklahoma:

> And suddenly there came a sound from heaven, as of a rushing mighty wind, and it filled the whole house where they were sitting.
>
> Then there appeared to them divided tongues, as of fire, and *one* sat upon each of them.
>
> And they were all filled with the Holy Spirit and began to speak with other tongues, as the Spirit gave them utterance.

Some of my father's earliest memories are of being in church and watching men and women deep in prayer, delivering a message in a clearly enunciated, totally foreign language, an utterly unknown form of speech. My father remembers that when he was in third grade his mother received the Holy Spirit in church one Sunday, and it was three days before she got back to speaking English again. During those three days, he'd come through the door, say, "Hi, Mom," and she'd respond in this alien language, speaking precisely, enunciating perfectly. It wasn't gibberish at all. But it wasn't anything my dad could understand either.

My father and his parents stayed in Oklahoma City only until the war ended, but that was long enough to get to know their pastor at the First Pentecostal Holiness Church of Shawnee, a young minister named Oral Roberts.

Then they went back to California, where my grandfather worked first as a foreman on a wealthy man's ranch in the Sierra foothills, then as a landscaper in Stockton, then as an airplane mechanic down in Sacramento. That's where my father played his only year of football, going both ways as a freshman starting defensive tackle and offensive halfback for the San Juan Trojans.

Dad's football career ended when he left home in 1957 to attend Southwestern Bible College and High School in Oklahoma City. The school had no sports, but that didn't matter to Dad. He was there to become a minister. In the process, he also met a girl named Nancy Price.

She was from a town called Yukon, just outside Oklahoma City. Her family had moved up from Arkansas, where her dad, Roy Eual Price, had been a sharecropper. Roy and his wife had eight kids, and Nancy was the seventh. She was spared the chores her older brothers and sisters had to take care of—pulling cotton, slopping hogs, and milking cows. By the time my dad met her, in the summer of 1959 at a church camp meeting, her father was working the night shift in the warehouse of the *Daily Oklahoman*. He was a big man—six-foot-five—which explains where my size came from. And he didn't put up with any nonsense. He had only a fourth-grade education, but what he lacked in schooling he made up for with wisdom and hard work.

The Price family were Pentecostals, too. My mother's grandfather, Elisha Montgomery Price, had been a circuit-riding preacher at the turn of the century, traveling by horseback from church to church. My mother was raised as religiously as my father, and they both knew by the time they graduated from high school in 1960 that they were going to get married. A year later, they did.

My dad was studying at Bethany Nazarene College by day and working as a dispatcher for the Bethany Police Department near Oklahoma City at night when my brother Dan was born in 1964. My brother Doug came along a year after that, and by the time I arrived, my dad's plans for the pulpit had been pushed aside by the demands of feeding a family of five.

He was working for the Top Value trading stamp company, managing a redemption center, when I was born October 5, 1966, at St. Anthony's Hospital in Oklahoma City. The front page of that morning's newspaper was covered with stories about the rising cost in dollars and troops of America's growing involvement in the war in Vietnam. There was football news, too. The American Football League's statistics, released that day, showed a quarterback named Joe Namath averaging a league-best 259 passing yards a game for a team called the New York Jets.

The doctor who delivered me was a man named Harry Dupree. A few years before—nineteen, to be exact—Dr. Dupree had delivered another baby boy who would grow up to be a pretty good professional athlete. His name was Johnny Bench.

The way my parents tell it, I almost didn't make it out of infancy. From the time I was six months old until I was two, I was in and out of the hospital with what the doctors could only figure was pneumonia. Every time my parents took me in, my mother said she wasn't sure if I'd be coming home. The worst trip was the last, when they found a spot on my lung. The doctors sent me home that afternoon, telling my mother to bring me back in the morning. That night I was extremely ill. I wouldn't eat. I could hardly hold my head up. My mother was holding and rubbing me, praying intensely when my dad got home. She told him what the doctors had said, and Doug overheard them. This little four-year-old guy came out of his room, walked over, kissed me on the forehead, and said, "Jesus will make him better." My mom swears I was up and myself again in fifteen minutes. The lingering pneumonia, the spot on my lung—those things just disappeared.

We were about as middle-class Midwest American as it gets, living in a suburban Oklahoma City neighborhood of two-story houses, big yards, and kids everywhere. Religion was woven into the texture of our everyday home life. Ours was a strong, quiet, comfortable family faith. I remember sitting on my mom's lap in the bathroom—I couldn't have been older than three—all dressed up in a little three-piece suit, a little vest, black patent leather shoes. She was putting Dippity-Do in my hair and combing it while everyone else was piling in the station wagon to go to church.

We went to church Sunday mornings and nights and Wednesday nights as well, but what sticks with me even more than that were our evenings at home. My parents sat on their bed, and all the kids tumbled in or grabbed a seat on the floor to listen to my dad read us a Bible passage or an inspirational story. He'd always select something about somebody making it through a struggle, and he'd usually connect it to something he'd read in the newspaper that day or seen on television. We'd talk about it, then listen to him read to us from the Bible. It's hard to explain how warm that felt.

Dinner was the same way. We'd all hold hands and say a prayer before eating, but there was nothing quiet about the meal itself. You had to fight to get a word in when the Byrds were gathered around the table. On holidays, we'd add special prayers. If it was Father's Day or Mother's Day, we'd have a prayer that would go around the table, each kid telling the Lord why he or she was thankful for Mom or Dad. On Thanksgiving or Christmas, we'd go around the same way, each person giving thanks. Chain prayers, that's what we called them.

Those were the two most important things in our lives, the Bible and our family. There's a verse in Proverbs, and it's one my parents really hung their hat on: "Raise up a child in the way of the Lord and when he is old, he will not depart from it."

Which is not to say we had a house full of angels. Ours was about as wild as a home filled with five kids could get, and no one was wilder than me. That hair my mother combed so carefully in the bathroom would be a mess by the time we pulled up to church. The suit would wind up stained with dirt and grass after I was done playing tackle tag with the other kids after church. Dennis the Menace, my parents called me, and that was putting it mildly. From the age of two, I was wired. Ninety miles an hour with my hair on fire—that was me from morning to night.

Naturally that had some effects on our household. Once I flooded the attic after a buddy and I punched a hole through a roof tile so we could put up a homemade periscope and spy on the neighbors. Later that day a rainstorm hit, and my dad noticed water leaking from a ceiling light fixture. When he climbed up and pulled back the attic opening, he got soaked. And I got spanked.

Then there was the tree I set on fire with a flaming arrow. I got the arrow ready about dusk, wrapping the tip in toilet paper and soaking it with gasoline. It was my buddy Jay Butler who did the aiming. All we wanted to do was see what it would look like flying into the sky. But it wound up thunking into the top of one of our front-yard sycamores. My dad came driving home just in time to see the smoke billowing out of that treetop, with Jay and me frantically aiming a pitiful garden hose at it. That was another good spanking.

And there was the baby skunk I caught after my dad showed us where the mother was raising her babies. He warned us to keep our distance, but I couldn't keep away. And I paid the price. I wound up stripped and naked in the kitchen, my mom scrubbing the skin off me. I didn't get spanked for that one, but I did get an entire bottle of my dad's cologne poured over me. We didn't know about tomato juice at that time, how the acid counteracts that stink, and no one came close to me for a week.

Of course having two older brothers just fed my fire. They used me as a guinea pig for everything. I remember when I was about seven, they took a giant refrigerator box, cut it up, and put together a huge pair of cardboard wings. Somehow they con-

vinced me these things could actually work. So I climbed up on
the wall behind our house, strapped them on my back, dove off
like a bat . . . and went down like a brick.

Luckily, I didn't break anything. But I did spend more than my
share of hours in emergency rooms—so many, in fact, that my
father finally got tired of it. I've got two scars on my chin where
my dad, rather than take me to the hospital for stitches, closed
the wounds with Super Glue. He was a medic in the National
Guard before I was born, but I don't think they taught him that
one. I think that was just ingenuity born of necessity.

I spent my entire boyhood trailing behind my big brothers, just
like a little pup. And they *were* big. As far back as I can remember, Doug's nickname was "Moose." On every baseball team they
joined, Dan would pitch, Doug would be behind the plate, and
they'd dominate the league, making the All-Star team every year. I
wasn't a bad baseball player myself, a pretty good-hitting second
baseman, good enough to make a few of my own All-Star teams.
I'll never forget the year all three of us—Dan, Doug, and I—
started in the same Little League All-Star game. I was nine that
season. Dan was twelve and Doug was eleven. There were Byrds
all over the bases that day.

But the sport we loved best was football. Dad had played a little flag football in college, keeping his hand in the game, and I
remember him coming out in the yard with us when we were little, showing us how to pass and punt. I still remember how high
those punts seemed to go. To a six-year-old, they looked like mis-
siles.

Like just about everyone else in the state, we were big Oklahoma Sooner fans. We had plenty of favorite players, but none
compared to number 24, Joe Washington. Joe was *the* guy. Our
whole family would be around the set on Saturday afternoons
watching the game. When it was done my brothers and I would go
out and play tackle in the yard. But before we did, we'd fight over
who got to wear that crimson and cream number 24 jersey.

My dad and mom didn't want us playing in any actual leagues,
with pads and helmets, until we were older. They thought it
would be too rough. But no league could have been rougher than

those games my brothers and I played out in the yard, tossing the ball in the air and creaming whoever caught it. The other kids in the neighborhood were always coming around our house to join us in whatever game we were playing—our house was a magnet for kids—but when we pulled out the football, they took off. They didn't want anything to do with the Byrd boys when it came to football. We were just too intense.

Dan especially liked to mix it up. A classic first-born, he was always driven, goal-oriented, the one who turned whatever we were doing into a contest. The back yard, the bedroom, it didn't matter where you were, there was something to battle for, something to be won. I'd be headed to the bathroom, Dan would appear at the other end of the hall, the bathroom door midway between us. We'd freeze, face off like two gunfighters, then wait for the other guy to make his move. The loser was last to bed.

If there's anybody on the face of this earth that doesn't like to lose, it's Dan. The three of us would play a simple game of Monopoly, and it would invariably turn into a war. We'd fight, argue, *throw* the money at the other guy. I mean, it's amazing the pieces stayed on the board.

Doug was more laid-back, more a romantic dreamer than Dan, more like the lone cowboy born a hundred years too late, and I know I got some of that from him. We shared a love for the outdoors that Danny never had back then. Doug and I would sit for hours shooting snakes and turtles off ponds. We could spend an entire afternoon that way and wonder where the day went.

Being the middle child, I could face my two brothers and be the runt, or I could turn toward my sisters and be the big brother. I was closer in age to Jeni and Dawn than my brothers were, both for good and for bad. I was to them what my brothers were to me—both their protector and their tormentor. When we played, it was usually my way. They'd be the Indians and I was the cowboy.

My dad switched jobs several times during those years in Oklahoma City, managing a variety store, going back to school for a while with the idea of entering dental school, then working for a fast-photo processing company setting up kiosks in shopping centers and doing some photography work himself. Dad was always a dreamer, hungry for new ideas, the kind of man who was always reading, devouring information. I can't remember any subject we had a question about that my dad didn't readily have an answer for. To this day it amazes me how much he knows about everything from European history to the insurance market. And, like all dreamers, he's always been a sensitive, emotional person, not afraid at all to show his feelings. He got misty-eyed at the drop of a hat. He cried watching TV movies. He tended to be restless, too, always ready to take a risk. Take your shot. If you make it, great. If not, at least you went for it. That's my dad.

And that's how, in the summer of 1975, he went for something that changed all our lives.

That spring, he took a trip with two preachers to a Pentecostal Holiness convention in Columbia, South Carolina, where he was assigned to shoot photographs for a church magazine. He wasn't feeling great about his faith or his dreams at the time. He was thinking about the ministry he'd left behind, about his predental studies, which he'd stopped, about how working and raising five children had pushed aside every other priority in his life. Then, outside Memphis, in a driving rainstorm on a slick stretch of road, the station wagon he was driving was run off the road by another car. It flipped over, completely totaled, just crushed. Miraculously, no one was hurt, but my dad was shaken. He felt like he'd been delivered for a reason. He went on ahead to the convention, and during that week, he met a family called The Musical Taylors. They were puppeteers, staging shows with biblical messages for children.

By the time Dad got back home, he'd decided to do the same thing. Suddenly our house was filled with the sounds of carpentry and sewing, my dad putting together a stage, he and my mom stitching the puppets they designed. Freddy the Frog. Daniel the Lion. Cathy the Caterpillar. There were about a dozen characters, and my dad came up with parts for all of them, inventing skits that illustrated stories from the Scriptures. Day after day Dad developed the show. Around the house, in the car going down the road, whenever an idea hit him, he'd take it and work it into the script.

Our whole family, all seven of us, had a part. My dad was Daniel. Danny was Freddy the Frog, who was a mute since Danny got stage fright and wouldn't make a sound. I didn't have a speaking part; my job was to move the mouths of the characters in time with the songs we had on tape.

Together we were The Happy Day Express. We made our debut that summer at the Northwest Pentecostal Holiness Church of Oklahoma City, and not long after that, my dad gathered everyone around the kitchen table to make an announcement.

We were moving to California.

3

I was nine years old, in the fourth grade. I'd never lived in any house but the one my parents took me home to after I was born. All I knew about California was it was a place on the map, something I studied about in geography class. But now we were going there to live, to stay with Delbert Byrd, my dad's father—Poppa—in a place called Elk Grove, just south of Sacramento.

Poppa Byrd was foreman of a grape vineyard operation by then. He oversaw ten vineyards—thousands and thousands of acres— for a company called Grape Tech. He and his wife, Helen— Nanna—lived on some of that land in a double-wide mobile home, a Fleetwood, bigger than many of the houses in town. When we first got to California, we moved in with them, and it was there that I really began developing my love of the outdoors.

I remember vividly those tens of thousands of rows of vines stretching across rolling slopes. Poppa took me with him every evening, driving up and down them with a .22 rifle, hunting for jackrabbits. Those rabbits could destroy a whole crop, chewing through the vines. Poppa's deterrents were the .22 and a shotgun. That's where I really learned to handle firearms. Poppa took me out along the levees around the reservoirs on the property and let me shoot at the reeds sticking out of the water. I got to be a pretty good shot.

Every weekend, it seemed, my dad took us camping. Up to the Sierras. Into the Redwood Forest. Out along the coast. And I was still as wild as ever, like a colt. One weekend we were camping at a place called Timber Cove, where my dad and brothers could do some scuba diving. I was still too young for that, so Mom and Dad had let me bring a friend along. Late that afternoon, my mom was sitting down by the campsite, watching the tide come in below the steep cliffs that rose from the beach. She noticed a couple of kids off in the distance, climbing on the sheer wall of rock, with the tide rushing in below them. She shook her head and told my dad somebody ought to be keeping a better eye on those children. Then she looked a little harder and realized who those children were.

My buddy and I made it off the rocks the only way we could— by climbing straight up, hand over hand. My parents held their breath the whole way. And yes, I got a good spanking when it was over.

My mom was the unsung hero of my childhood. It's asking a lot to pick up a household and move a family the way we did several times. I respect her for that, for always keeping her humor, for always filling whatever house we lived in with jokes and laughter, for keeping her kids first no matter what. Wherever we went, it always felt like home, with good food on the table and plenty of warmth in the air, and that was largely because my mom made sure those things were there.

Living that summer on the vineyards gave me a chance to know my dad's parents in a way I never would if we had stayed in Oklahoma. I can still see Nanna wearing her soft pastels, painting the tiny ceramic figures that lined her living room shelves. I can still smell her perfume. I remember sitting and talking to her for hours, about nothing, the way a nine-year-old boy and his grandmother can do.

After three months on the vineyards, we moved into a classic California stucco home in a nice middle-class neighborhood in Sacramento, where my dad did the same work he had left in Oklahoma City, leasing and building photo kiosks. But now The Happy Day Express was almost a full-time job as well.

What we had done with the show in Oklahoma City was just a warm-up. Now we were taking it on the road, going anywhere anyone invited us, to churches of every denomination in towns throughout central California. We even went to public schools—Dad just toned down the biblical theme a bit. It was a kick, all of us piling in our station wagon—a Chevy Country Sedan, with that wood paneling down the side—and driving as far as three hundred miles. Typically we arrived on a Friday night, so my dad could meet with the church workers and set up what we needed. We stayed the night at someone's house, usually the minister's. Then Saturday we put on a small public performance outdoors, in someone's yard or lot. We passed out free snow cones to the kids in the neighborhood and asked them all to bring their families to church the next day. Then came Sunday, and we arrived for the service, five blonde kids tumbling out of the station wagon. People had to love that sight. No sooner was the show over than we pulled out the football and started clobbering each other out on the church grass.

That was really an idyllic time for me, as happy in its own way as my first nine years in Oklahoma had been. But the year I entered junior high school, everything changed. It was as if a curtain dropped on our lives in California, at least as far as my brothers and I were concerned. And it all had to do with race.

I'd never been around anything like racial tension before. I didn't even know what racial prejudice was. We were raised to believe that everybody was the same, that we are all human beings created by the same God and sharing the same hopes and dreams and feelings, no matter the color of our skin. I'd had plenty of black classmates in elementary school back in Oklahoma City and there in Sacramento, and race had never been an issue.

But now, almost overnight, it was. The school I stepped into to begin junior high, a place called Fern Bacon, was just crackling with tensions among three groups, Chicanos, blacks, and whites. I had no idea where it all had started, but almost every kid in the school was part of one of these factions and despised the other two. I do know there were actual physical separations in the neighborhoods, one street separating the area where the Chicano families lived from the area where the whites lived, another separating the black neighborhood from the Chicanos. If you happened to be walking just a couple of blocks from your own house and wandered across one of those streets, you were in danger of a pretty good thumping.

My seventh-grade year, the trouble had really turned serious. There were square-offs in the lunchroom, big commotions where half the teachers in the school would have to run down to break things up before a riot began.

One afternoon a fight that had almost started at lunchtime was carried across the highway after school, a big group of white kids facing off against a group of black kids. The police showed up and broke it up, and everyone began heading home. Which is how my brothers and I got swept up in this stuff.

We were walking home from school that afternoon when a couple of black guys who had been part of that confrontation over near the highway came riding by on bikes. One of them kicked my brother Dan as they pedaled past. Dan ignored it, as did Doug.

But these guys wouldn't let it go. They turned around, came back, and began taunting me, maybe because I was the littlest. Even then my brothers held back from reacting. But when one of the guys reached out and punched me in the face, that did it. There was no more holding back. Dan and Doug beat this guy and his friend very soundly, to say the least.

Within hours, word of what happened spread through these guys' neighborhood. They claimed my brothers jumped them. My parents were so worried they kept us home from school the next day, which turned out to be a wise move. The school was on red alert. They had locker searches, knives were found and confiscated—it even made the news.

That's when my parents decided they'd had enough of Sacramento, that this just wasn't a great place to raise kids. In a matter of weeks, we had moved back to Elk Grove, into a huge five-bedroom, Spanish-style house in one of the nicest neighborhoods in town.

Two doors down was the Elk Grove high school basketball coach, a man named Dan Risley. He always had a lot of players coming by to visit, including a huge guy who had been a big star at Elk Grove before going on to college at the University of San Francisco. This guy had just signed a contract with the New York Knicks, and I could see why. He'd drive up in this little gray Colt—I think it was his girlfriend's—and when he climbed out, he just kept climbing *out*. I'd never seen a person so tall in my life.

His name was Bill Cartwright, the same Bill Cartwright who starts at center for the Chicago Bulls. It's hard to believe he's still out there on the court, a world champion running with Michael Jordan. It seems a lifetime ago that we'd wander over to Coach Risley's house to see if his sons could come out to play and Bill Cartwright would answer the door as if he lived there, which basically he did. We were just a bunch of neighborhood kids, but he was always friendly with us, always took a few minutes to shoot the breeze.

But it wasn't Bill Cartwright that I remember most about that year in Elk Grove. It was something far more important and much more personal, an experience that set the course of my life as much as football, my marriage, and fatherhood.

It happened the summer before I turned fourteen. I was at a youth church camp up in the mountains, the kind of place I went every summer, with plenty of outdoor activities and plenty of prayer.

Prayer has always meant a lot to me, in a very personal, internal way. My way of worship is very quiet, and it's certainly not limited to church. I pray all the time—driving to work, sitting out on a coyote stand. Just getting up in the morning, I thank the Lord for the things He's given me, for the things He's given all of us. I don't have to get down on my knees to pray. I don't even have to shut my eyes. I have always felt like I can converse with God anywhere, and I do.

But until that summer I had not felt the Lord speaking back to me. Like my father, I had grown up seeing the adults around me in church receiving messages, speaking in tongues. I remember being about six or seven when I first heard a woman talking in a language I couldn't understand, and I wondered why she was doing it. My mom and dad explained it to me, and I realized how emotional prayer and receiving the Holy Spirit can be. I saw it plenty of times during my childhood, and there was nothing disturbing about it at all. It was normal. In fact, it was pleasant, to see that someone could be moved like that.

But I had never been moved that way. I had no reason to expect anything extraordinary to happen when we gathered one evening that summer at the church in the center of camp. It was a giant log cabin, and there were about seventy-five of us, mostly teenagers. We came together every night that way, to worship as a group. As always there was an altar call, an invitation to come down to the front and pray.

I'd gone down and prayed like that plenty of times, but this time something felt different. Something had shifted inside me. I'd always felt connected to God when I prayed, but I had never truly taken the Lord into my heart and fully given myself to Him. Maybe I'd been too young. But now it was time for commitment. It wasn't something I thought so much as I felt, deep inside. I just *knew* it was time to give myself to Christ, to culminate what my parents and church had been teaching me my entire life. I had been fortunate in the way my parents had raised me, but I understood now that I could not make it to heaven on their coattails. I had to make this decision on my own. I was accountable for my own salvation.

No voice came to me. No vision. This was a *choice*. It's something you just decide, from the bottom of your soul. You have to *want* that gift to receive it. It's a very spiritual thing, something you really feel. That night, for the first time, I felt it.

There were other kids around me feeling it, too. Pretty much everyone had come down. Some of them were crying and praising the Lord. There was a lot of emotion sweeping through, lots of sobbing and tears of joy.

I wasn't doing any of that, but I was praying in a way I never had before. I just continued praying, softly, to myself, and at some point I realized I was praying in a language that was *not* English. I had never doubted the validity of this experience in others, but now it was happening to *me*. I was swept with this incredible feeling of joy, of having this undeniable gift given to me from the Holy Spirit.

That night changed my life forever. I was filled with a mixture of joy and compassion, as strong as any emotion I had ever felt. When I came home at the end of that week, I knew I had been through a passage, that something had shifted inside me, that I was growing up now not just in years but in terms of my relationship with Christ—and with myself.

It was not long after that that we were rocked by a death in the family. We'd already lost my grandpa, Roy Price, the winter before. He'd come home one evening from his job at the newspaper, driving his pickup through horrible weather, sliding on the ice and snow covering the roads. He came in and told Granny he was going out after supper to put chains on the tires. He had his favorite meal that night—red beans, potatoes, and gravy. He told Granny he'd never felt so good. She remembers him saying those exact words. Then he went out to change those tires, and he never came back. After a half hour, Granny threw on her coat and went out to check on him. He was lying there in the snow, dead of cardiac arrest. He was sixty-seven years old.

That news hit our family hard. And it seemed like we were barely recovered when death hit us again. This time, it was Nanna. And we were all there when it happened.

It was a Sunday evening, and we were in church. We were big enough to sit apart from Mom and Dad by then, and I remember being in the back row. My mom and Poppa and Nanna were in the front, and Dad, who was the children's pastor, was conducting the service.

It was a testimonial service, with everyone invited to stand and share their feelings. Nanna had just come through a series of surgeries but was doing well, and that's exactly what she stood up to talk about. She turned to my mom and said, "You know, the Lord has *healed* me." Then she turned to my dad.

"Danny," she said, "the Lord *has* healed me one hundred percent tonight, completely and totally."

She had hardly sat down before my Poppa stood up. I don't

recall any commotion at all, just my Poppa calmly announcing, "We need to pray for Helen."

Nanna had slumped over, seized with a cerebral hemorrhage.

Someone went to call an ambulance. People were praying. But she never regained consciousness. Two days later she died.

And that was it. Our life in California had somehow seemed to lose focus. My parents decided it was time to go back where we came from, and so, in the spring of 1981, near the end of my freshman year of high school, we packed up our RV and headed back to Oklahoma, to a place called Mustang.

TAKING FLIGHT

4

Mustang is a small, quiet town. Most of the ten thousand people who lived there when we arrived were connected in one way or another with cattle ranching or farming, mostly wheat and corn. It was the kind of place where the center of social life, for the kids at least, was the Dairy Queen or the Sonic, complete with carhops. There was no traffic light in town, just a four-way stop at the intersection of Mustang Road and Oklahoma Highway 152, which ran through the center of town, two lanes going east and west.

For businesses, you had Briscoe's LP gas, Snyder's IGA grocery, and Del Rancho, home of the Del Rancho steak sandwich, the only sit-down restaurant in town besides Dairy Queen. But what Mustang lacked in commerce, it made up for in churches— twenty-one, according to the count I made when we first got there. Literally one on every corner. Ours was the Mustang Assembly of God.

Granny and Papa Price had moved out to Mustang while we were in California. When Papa Price died, they were living on a piece of land about six miles outside town, and that's where we parked our RV when we arrived from Elk Grove, right between Granny's toolshed and her trailer. Uncle Tony, Aunt Rita, and

Dwayne had a house there, just across the yard from Granny's, so we were far from alone.

When I think of Granny, I think of mornings, of hot homemade biscuits and what we called chocolate gravy. She'd make this hot chocolate sauce and pour it over those biscuits, and it was awesome. I know it sounds like a nutritional nightmare, but it was the best thing I'd ever tasted.

Granny was as different from Nanna as night is from day. While Nanna wore perfume and soft pastels, with a presence as delicate as a silk scarf, Granny wore country colors, maroons and greens. She was a laugher and a joker, and she never wore perfume.

We stayed with Granny through that spring, Dan and Doug and I living in the RV while my parents and sisters stayed with Granny in her trailer. To me it was a lark, like camping out, but I know it wasn't easy for my mom. One week she was living in a beautiful five-bedroom, three-bathroom house, and the next she was in a trailer. But my mom's faith has always been just as strong as my dad's, and as hard as things got—and things would get harder— they were in this together. We all were.

We hadn't been there a week before Charlie Carpenter, Mustang High's head football coach, got a call from one of the school's counselors, a man named Terry Spencer.

"Hey, coach," he said, "I've got these three new kids that just moved in from California, and two of them, you can't believe how huge they are. The third one, well, I don't think he'll make it."

I was about six feet tall, maybe 145 pounds. Not exactly a striking physical specimen. Dan was six-foot-three, 220, and Doug was six-foot-two, about 205. Big Byrd and Middle Byrd, they called them. I was Little Byrd.

The first time I ever wore a football helmet was that spring. That was all the equipment we wore—no pads, no hitting. Just light drills. I had good hands, I was pretty fast, so they put me down at flanker and outside linebacker. That's where I'd be when they *really* began playing football, at preseason practice in August.

Meanwhile, I had a summer to get settled into Mustang. We moved at the end of that spring into a neighborhood called The

Branches, about four blocks from the center of town, walking distance to the school. The house was a nice, solid, three-bedroom place, but Mom was still terrified at even the sound of the word "tornado." Every time a storm came up, she'd throw everybody in the car and head for the hole at Granny's house. We'd hit that cellar as many as fifteen times a season, spring and fall.

Mustang is only two miles wide, from north to south, and six miles long, from east to west. You're never far from open country, and that's where I spent most of my time that summer, out in the sage and buffalo grass, calling coyotes and catching water moccasins. Or rather, making sure they didn't catch me. It's not exactly a science. The first step in catching a water moccasin is being unfortunate enough to come across one. Then you just pound it with a stick. There was a guy at church who made leather goods, and he paid ten dollars for a good-sized snake skin. I sold him about a half-dozen that summer and used most of the money to buy my first shotgun, which gave me even more reason to spend time out in the wild.

I also got quickly acclimated to the social rhythms and cliques of the kids in town, which were similar to those you see in communities all across America. There were the Heads, the Preps, and the Jocks, of course. But then you had a group that was endemically Oklahoman: the Ropers, or Cowboys, the guys who kept a big slug of chewing tobacco in their cheek and a can of Skoal in their back pocket, who wore cowboy boots and cowboy shirts and blue jeans with colorful woven belts and big buckles. These were the true country kids, usually in the FFA (Future Farmers of America) or VOAG (Vocational Agriculture) classes.

It wasn't long before I had friends in all those groups. I was the jock who had a lot of cowboy friends and hung out and visited with the heads as well. Marijuana was the only drug around. I'd tried it out in California, when we were living in Sacramento, and decided it wasn't for me. Back then I wanted to be cool, so I joined some of the older kids who were smoking it out on the neighborhood sidewalks or in between houses. Grown-ups would go by and think we were just smoking a cigarette, the way kids do. Then some of us, including my brothers, would play a game called tackle hide-and-seek, thumping the tar out of each other. That's all pot did to me, it just fanned that fire inside and made the thumping I got in tag easier to take.

Let me emphasize that in no way am I condoning the use of any kind of drugs. Drugs are a problem in our society, a serious problem. But a person would be naive to think a kid's not possibly going to try that stuff, that he might not experiment. The problem with a lot of the kids I knew who smoked pot back then was that they had parents who weren't involved with them at all. They had no direction, no real sense of connection to their lives at home, so they were filling the vacuum with this stuff. What could be just an experiment became something they got absorbed in, something they gave themselves over to entirely. We had a word for the kids who went that far, who became totally unmotivated, who never played sports, who never did anything but get high. We called them burnouts. And I was seeing them in sixth grade.

By the time we moved to Mustang, pot was far behind me, as was the need to be cool. There was no peer pressure among the kids I knew to do drugs, absolutely none. There was beer, lots of beer, but you could take it or leave it. Most kids took it. That was the common denominator in Mustang. The Preps drank beer, the Heads drank beer, the Ropers drank beer—*everybody* drank beer. Well, almost everybody. Somebody picked up a six-pack, then you drove around looking for whoever was having a party, and as often as not, you wound up in a parking lot. I remember spending plenty of Friday nights sitting in the parking lot of the Ben Franklin store in Dan's pickup truck.

Again, there were kids who occasionally overdid it and got smashed. You had to load them up, throw them in the car or truck, and take them home. They just didn't know when to quit. But for the most part, we were just a bunch of kids getting a little tipsy and laughing at each other.

The point is, I was a Christian, but I was a regular kid, too. I tried pot. I drank beer. But those things could never overshadow the strength I drew from my family and my faith, and they couldn't compare to the high I found that first fall in Mustang, a high that never faded from then on, no matter how many times I pulled on a helmet—the high I got from football.

Which is not to say it came easy. I learned right away that nothing comes easy in this game. The preseason two-a-days at Mustang were as tough as any I would ever go through in all my years of football. For two weeks we were out there in the broiling Oklahoma sun, the grass just cut, our skin hot and itching as we did hours and hours of monkey rolls, calisthenics, and wind sprints in the morning and again in the afternoon. I'd never been through anything like it. At one point I turned to Dan and said, "Man, I don't want to *do* this." He and Doug were in my face in a heartbeat.

"Excuse me?" they said. "If you quit now, we're gonna kick your butt."

And they would have, badly. My brothers wouldn't let anyone else lay a hand on me, but they were allowed to beat the stuffing out of me at will.

So I endured. And a whole world was opened up to me, a world I hadn't really understood until then, the world of Friday nights in the fall in Oklahoma.

There are still places in America where high school football remains close to a religion, where malls and MTV and the pace of modern life haven't pushed aside the magic of a bright green, freshly striped football field shining under the glare of the stadium lights, where the entire town turns out to see its boys take the field, where kids are proud to wear their high school football jersey down the streets and where that jersey brings smiles and slaps on the back, congratulations on last week's game, and questions about this week's. There are plenty of towns like this in Texas and Pennsylvania and Ohio. But no place has more of them than Oklahoma. And none of them is crazier about football than Mustang.

The big bad Broncos. They fielded their first football team in 1968, back when there were only sixty-two kids in the graduating class. That number had grown to 150 when I arrived, and we were playing in the 3-A division, the state's next-to-largest classification. Choctaw, Chickasha, El Reno, Ada, Guthrie, Broken Bow,

Tahlequah, Noble, Stillwater ... these were the schools we played. And Yukon. The Yukon Millers. One town away, they were our archrivals. Garth Brooks played quarterback for Yukon the year before I moved to Mustang. Not many people knew he could sing back then, but everyone knew he had a good arm. And he wasn't a bad free safety, either.

Mustang had a terrific program going by then. They qualified for the state play-offs just about every season, and they'd been to the state finals the year before. Coach Carpenter had established quite a tradition, and my brothers stepped right into it. Dan was a senior, a tight end, and a good one. He split time with another guy, and Doug played varsity too, mostly on goal-line stands.

I was on the jayvees, playing on Monday nights in front of crowds not quite like the ones my brothers saw. But that didn't matter to me. I was hooked on this game. Sitting the bench for most of that fall didn't matter either. I knew sooner or later I'd get my chance, and finally, almost at the end of the season, I did.

We were playing Choctaw, we were way ahead, and they sent me in to help mop up. I remember the grass had turned from green to brown. It no longer had the supple feel of summer. Now it crunched underfoot. But it still felt like magic running out there under those lights.

The first play was a running play to the other side of the field. I pursued, the guy cut back, and I tackled him. I'm not sure who was hitting who. All I know is my mouthpiece came flying out and snot bubbles blew out of my nose. That's what happens if you get hit real hard and unexpectedly: All the air is pushed out of your lungs in a sharp burst and snot comes flying out with it. Anyone who's ever made or taken a hit like that knows what I'm talking about.

I'd never felt anything like it before, that impact, that strong, jarring sensation, that momentary bit of limbo as you're floating through the air before you hit the ground. I remember the guys picking me up and slapping me on the back. That was the first hit of my life, the first real tackle in a real football game.

And it felt fantastic.

From that moment on, football totally consumed my life. I ate, drank, and slept the game. The essence was that it was combat, that one-on-one, man-to-man competition, clean and direct. I was responsible for beating the guy facing me. Pure and simple. It was me against him. No maybes, no gray areas. Either he whups me or I whup him.

There's no question where that taste for combat came from. All those years I followed behind my brothers, they never did *anything* half-speed. When we played football, it was always tackle. Not once did we play touch. When we played baseball, it was never slow-pitch. I remember asking Doug one time to toss me a pitch underhand. I was six years old. He looked at me like I had to be kidding and threw it all the harder for asking.

The glamour of the game was another thing that intoxicated me. It was one thing playing with my brothers and other kids in the yard, but this was something else. Shoulder pads, thigh pads, knee pads, a helmet, pants, and a jersey—now I was dressed up like a soldier. There was something undeniably glorious about that.

Then there was the element of competition. I had the drive to win inside me, and it didn't come from my parents. It came from my brothers. We weren't driven, we drove ourselves. And it was a healthy drive. I see that same drive on outdoor basketball courts in the inner city. I see it in kids who don't have Nintendo, a swimming pool, all the neat stuff that makes life pleasant. There's nothing wrong with having these things, but I'm not sure the kids who have them feel this same competitiveness, maybe because they don't *have* to compete.

But any sport could have fed my need to compete. The thing about football that appealed to me most of all was its physicality. I was never a bully, never a guy getting in fights because I needed or wanted to. I'm not saying I never got into a fight, but it was rare, and it was always over something, always a matter of principle.

No, there was something deeper inside me that was drawn to the physical aspect of this game, and it wasn't any need for a release from anger or pain or poverty. I didn't feel any of those things. It wasn't a need to release so much as a need to *consume*, to just *devour* what was in front of me as well as inside me.

This was a very visceral feeling, and I felt it almost as strongly when I watched someone else make a hit as I did when I made one myself. I just *loved* great hits. I hate to say it, but I even loved to see defensive guys on the other team make a great hit on one of *our* guys. When that happened, I'd look at one of my defensive teammates, and we'd both be thinking the same thing: "Wow, that was a solid lick."

I knew if hitting was going to be my game, I had to get stronger. So I got a job that summer, along with my brother Doug, laying pipe on some of the farms in the area, connecting water sources to oil wells. We turned it into a contest, pulling these twenty-foot sections of aluminum pipe off the back of a moving truck and connecting them quickly enough to keep up with our boss, who was driving. Each piece weighed about forty-five pounds, and by the end of the summer, we were laying them down at a rate of about two or three a minute—and that includes connecting them.

When my junior year began, I was in the best shape of my life. And I'd grown. I was six-two now, about 165, still playing jayvees, but I was a starter, at flanker and linebacker. I was doing great on offense, catching a lot of passes, scoring touchdowns. To this day I believe I could have been a pretty good tight end in the NFL. I've always had good hands. But then again, every defensive end thinks he has good hands.

Defense was where I lived and breathed. Scoring touchdowns was great, but this game is about hitting, and on offense you're more likely to be *taking* the licks. You're the guy getting hit. On defense, you're the one searching people out, delivering the blows. You can hit pretty much anybody, anytime, anywhere. I loved that. It was just fun, big fun. And the thing was, you could do the same thing in practice. The atmosphere wasn't the same as a game, but everything else was. I loved practice. Practice was just as much fun for me as the games themselves, until I got in the NFL. You can't *hit* people in practice there. I understand it, of course. Careers wouldn't last long if everybody was getting hit every day. But as far as I was concerned, I'd have loved it if we were allowed to hit there as well. Pads or no pads, game or practice, I always wanted to play. That's what it was to me, *playing!*

What I looked like out on that field my junior season at Mustang was a big, unleashed kid at play. And like a kid, I had a lot to learn. I was all over the field, running like a wild man, but it was frustrating because too often I wasn't getting in on the hit. I'd be just a little late, and that's because I didn't know enough about the game yet to be in the right place at the right time.

Still, the coaches loved what they saw. I remember the jayvee coach, Walter Ryan, taking me aside that season and saying, "You know, you got a great motor, a *great* motor. You pursue so damn good. Just keep at it. The tackles will come."

It's funny he used those words, because years later, when I arrived as a rookie with the Jets, that was one of Jet head coach Joe Walton's favorite phrases, and he used it to describe me. "He's got a great motor," he said, "and that's something you just can't teach."

By the end of my junior season, I was suiting up with the varsity as well, as a backup linebacker, and when the season was done, I was thinking seriously about my future, not just on the football field but after high school. My dad had made a big move that year, making a deal with a partner who had plans to develop fifty acres south of Mustang into a housing subdivision. The deal was my dad could have ten acres in return for building the homes. So at the end of my junior year, we moved back into the countryside, onto this raw piece of Oklahoma.

My dad's plan was to get the development's houses going, then put up a dream house on our ten-acre plot. He sank everything he had into the deal, so for a while we had to do without. We moved onto the property that spring with a trailer and an old school bus refitted as a mobile home, and we lived like homesteaders, like the settlers from a century before. My mom and dad and Jeni and Dawn stayed in the trailer while my brothers and I lived in the bus. It had a refrigerator and plenty of lights, as did the trailer. It had air conditioning, too. The only thing it didn't have was running water. My dad had drilled a well at the site where our house would eventually be built, about seventy-five yards up a hill from the bus and trailer, and every day we'd make a couple of trips up that hill, dipping the water with a six-gallon bucket and carrying it back for cooking and drinking and bathing.

I never felt bothered by how we were living. I never felt poor, never felt ashamed. Then again, Angela reminded me that we were dating six months before I could bring myself to show her where I lived, so I guess I might have been a little sensitive on that score. Bobby Proctor, the University of Oklahoma secondary coach who recruited me my senior season, told my high school coach after I'd made it to the NFL that he thought he'd seen some pretty harsh living conditions in the inner cities he often visited but that he had never seen anything like the place I lived. Still, to me this was as much a home as the nice houses we'd had in Oklahoma City and in Sacramento. We were a family, we had each other, we had our faith, and that was enough.

But I knew I wouldn't be living there much longer. Soon it would be time to be on my own. And it was pretty clear that my parents couldn't afford to send me to college, not at that point in their lives. If I wanted a way out that was a way up, it was going to have to be through a football scholarship, and the only way I was going to win a scholarship was to make myself into more of a player than I already was. Leading a jayvee team in tackling and receiving was not going to be nearly enough. I needed to get even stronger, even bigger, and I had only one summer and one more season to do it.

Which is how I wound up with the pole.

I had heard a story somewhere about a football player who built up his body by going one-on-one against a billy goat. Day after day he bashed and butted this goat, literally locking horns with this animal to toughen himself up. We didn't have any goats, but the dirt yard outside our family's trailer was nice and flat, a perfect place to put a pole in the ground.

I found a four-by-four green oak post, about six feet long, sunk it about three feet deep and began a routine that became my evening ritual that entire summer. By day I lived in the school's weight room, where Coach Carpenter had just put in a new set of free weights. Then, each night, as the sun was setting and the air was cooling off, I'd go out to that post and settle into a good, solid three-point stance, digging my cleats into the bare earth beneath my feet. Then I'd fire out and slam that wood with my hands or my forearms, using the form and techniques my coaches had taught me. Over and over I hit that post, until the sweat was pouring off me. I'd hit it until my hands actually bled through the calluses that had already formed. Then I'd hit it some more. I'd keep going until tears were streaming out of my eyes. That's when I knew it was time to stop, when the pain and exhaustion turned into tears. Only then would I finally drop to the dirt and call it a day. The next night, I'd be back to do it all over again.

I had a dream by then. I told my parents and friends I was going to go to college on a football scholarship. Privately, I believed I was going to play professional football, too, although I had nothing to base that belief on but bare faith and determination. I shared that dream with no one. My friends gave me a hard enough time just for talking about playing college ball. I had a buddy, Rich Stukie, who cracked up every time I mentioned it.

"*Look* at you," he'd say. "You haven't even played varsity ball yet, and you're talking about *college?* Man, you're *crazy.*"

Well, I played varsity ball that next season. I *definitely* played varsity ball.

5

They say I came out of nowhere my senior season at Mustang, and in a way that was true. I had played hardly any varsity football at all. I had never started a game. There had been no newspaper stories written about me, no headlines, no films or scouting reports filed in coaches' offices at other schools. Other schools didn't even know I existed. So when I started making waves that fall of 1983, people were stunned, even people in Mustang. They were asking themselves, "Is this the same kid?"

But I wasn't surprised. I knew I had put in more time than anybody else. If somebody was going to beat me, he was going to have to have worked harder than I had, and I didn't think that was possible. I knew how much I could give, how deep I could reach. I'd answered all those questions myself that summer.

I was six-four now, 205, and it didn't take long for other teams to begin noticing me. Pretty soon I no longer had just one man to beat. It was always two, then three. I remember having to beat first of all the tight end, then the tackle, then there'd be a running back in there, too, and I'd have to go through them all.

Noble, Guthrie, Western Heights, El Reno, Yukon—we mowed through the early part of our season with fans packing our stadium for the home games. Not bad for a high school program.

We were 5-0 before we lost our first game, to Carl Albert. They ran one play to my side at the start of the game, and I dropped their quarterback, Jamie Weatherspoon, for a six-yard loss. I didn't see another play to my side the entire game. They ran it the other way all night, and we ended up losing, 14-3.

Our only other regular season loss that year was to Chickasha, in the tenth game. They beat us 28-14, largely because of a running back named Donnie Maloney. He wound up going to the University of Oklahoma, where Barry Switzer called him RT, for "raw talent." Donnie later transferred to the University of Tulsa, where we were teammates. He was still a tremendous player, but he never had the kind of career they hoped he'd have. One reason was he was the kind of runner who liked to dance a lot, to improvise, and that didn't fit into the blocking system we had at Tulsa. Ours was more of a high-powered passing attack. But the night he played against me at Mustang, Donnie danced his best—to the tune of 176 yards.

We finished 8-2 that regular season, good enough to get into the state play-offs, where we faced a school from Tulsa called Bishop Kelley in the first round. If any one game epitomized my senior year, that was the one.

Bishop Kelley had won the state championship the year before, and we weren't supposed to have a chance. Early in the first quarter they ran an option to my side, their strength against ours. The quarterback kept it, and I nailed him—along with the fullback, all in one blow. They had to help the quarterback to the sidelines; he was done for the night. The very next play, they ran the option again, to my side again, with the new quarterback keeping it again. And I took out the whole backfield again, putting *that* quarterback out of the game. Charlie Carpenter told me he'd never seen anything like it in his life. They had to go with their third-stringer the rest of the way, and we won 30-6.

When the game was done, Tom Stockton, the Bishop Kelley coach, came over to Coach Carpenter and said, "*Who* is number sixty-eight?" Coach Carpenter told him, and the next morning Stockton drove over to the University of Tulsa football department, where his good friend John Cooper was the head coach. Cooper wasn't in, so Stockton left a note on his door.

"GO TO MUSTANG," it read. "RECRUIT DENNIS BYRD. ONE TOUGH S.O.B."

The next week we beat Tahlequah 12-3, which put us into the semifinal game against Broken Bow the day after Thanksgiving. I had no doubt we were going to win that game. They had a tremendous running back named Vernell Ramsey. He'd gained close to 3,500 yards in three seasons, an incredible number. I really relished taking him on. But I never got the chance. Their coach, Tom Condict, had seen film of the Bishop Kelley game. He tried two plays to my side in the first quarter. The first lost five yards. The second lost three. And that was it. The rest of the night, they ran the ball to the other side. It drove me nuts. Darren Warren, our other defensive end, did the best he could. Darren's nickname was "Spindly Legs." His heart was bigger than his body, and his biggest strength was he could drink more beer than anybody on the team. Unfortunately, Vernell wasn't impressed.

Broken Bow beat us 28-23, and that was it. I was crushed. We all were. We were sure we were going to win the state championship, and now it was over. There's nothing like the feeling in a locker room at the end of a senior season. For most of my teammates, this was the last football game they'd ever play. There were a lot of tears that night. It was hard to let go.

I was devastated too, but I knew by then that my football career was just beginning. I'd set a state record that season with thirty-nine sacks, an average of three a game. It's still hard for me to believe that number. Now it was me they were calling Big Byrd, and the college coaches were starting to come around.

Every year about seven or eight players from Mustang got scholarships to play college football, mostly to junior college, NAIA and smaller NCAA schools in Oklahoma, places like Southwestern State in Weatherford and Northwestern State in Alva. Only one player in the school's history had ever been recruited to play Division I football, and that was an offensive tackle named Riley Goodin, who made All-State in 1975 and went on to play at Oklahoma State.

I hadn't thought specifically of where I wanted to play college ball. I would have been happy going anywhere. Just the thought of being able to go to college, *any* college, and to keep playing this game was enough. I remember after our second game of the season, against Guthrie, my best friend, David Oliver, and I and a couple of other guys on the team went driving out to this field where we often went to kick back and do our Socrates thing. These guys were all juniors, I was the only senior, and I'd had a really good game that night.

I remember sitting back on the hood of David's yellow and white Chevy pickup, under a big starry September sky, and David turning to me and saying, "Hey, D. Maybe you'll go and play big-time college."

I'd never actually pictured it. He was talking about the world I'd watched on TV when I was a kid, the world of the Sooners and the Cowboys and the Razorbacks, of Saturday afternoons with seventy thousand or more people in the stands. I couldn't *let* myself actually imagine it.

"Aw, David, you're crazy," I said. "That only happens in the movies. That only happens to someone else."

But by the end of that season, it was happening to me. I wasn't exactly swamped with recruiters, but I'd gotten letters during the year from Texas A&M and Missouri, as well as from a lot of smaller schools. Tulsa and Oklahoma State both sent coaches to see me as soon as the play-offs were done—Bill Young from Tulsa and Paul Jett from OSU. I arranged to visit both schools in late January, just before the February signing deadline. I also made a date to visit SWOSU—Southwestern Oklahoma State—along with one of my teammates, Lance Hutson, an outside linebacker. You're allowed a limit of three campus visits, and those were my three.

I've got to admit I was disappointed that I hadn't heard from Oklahoma. Every kid who grew up playing football in this state dreamed of playing for Barry Switzer, just the way kids who play basketball in Indiana dream of playing for Bobby Knight. They'd *settle* for Oklahoma State or Tulsa, but their dream was Oklahoma. My dad drove me down to Norman one weekend that December, just to see the football field, and I was blown away. I'd never stood in a stadium that size. It seats seventy-eight thousand. You get out there in the middle of that field and you feel so incredibly small.

And you're looking up at that sea of seats and you realize every one of them is filled on Saturday afternoons—it was overwhelming.

But as far as I knew, OU didn't know I existed, which was strange, since the father of one of our players, a running back named Jeff Jones, was Mike Jones, the Sooners' receivers coach. He came to a lot of games to see his son play, but I never heard from him or anyone else on Barry Switzer's staff—until after the All-State teams were announced at Christmas. I was named to all those teams, and the day after they were announced, Coach Jones came bursting into Charlie Carpenter's office, agitated and out of breath. Switzer had seen the papers too, and he'd called Jones in to explain how come this kid from Mustang was on all these All-State teams but wasn't on their recruiting list.

All Coach Jones could do was tell the truth. He'd only paid attention to the games when Mustang's offense was on the field and his son was playing. He spent the rest of the time visiting with his friends and relatives.

That's all Switzer had to hear. "You get your butt to Mustang," he said, "and you look at some film on this boy."

Coach Jones looked at about five minutes of film there in Coach Carpenter's office. Then he said, "My God, we're recruiting three kids out of Texas that aren't as good as this kid."

The next day, Merv Johnson, the offensive line coach at OU, came up to see Charlie. Jones had taken some film back to Norman, and Johnson had taken a look. "Dennis Byrd is a ten-footer," he told Coach Carpenter. "You watch ten foot of film, and you know he's a player."

The next day, Bobby Proctor came to see me. The Oklahoma City region was part of his recruiting area. He told me how badly Oklahoma wanted to have me and asked if we could set up a weekend for me to come down and visit. I would have died to have gone down to Norman, but I'd already committed to the other three schools and I wasn't about to go back on my word. It killed me to say no, but I had no choice.

So Lance Hutson and I drove to Weatherford in late January. It was way out in *Boga Cheetah*, out with the rattlesnakes and buf-

falo grass, a great place to be *from*, as the joke goes. But I actually liked that. What I didn't like were the facilities. Our high
school weight room was nicer than theirs. And the players I saw
weren't as big as I thought they should be. It just didn't feel right.
Lance and I went to a movie that night, and that was about it.
When I called home just before leaving to drive back, my parents
told me Bobby Proctor had left a message. Clearly Oklahoma
didn't consider themselves out of this hunt.

The next weekend I went to Tulsa, and they treated me and my
parents like royalty. Tulsa really wanted me. Maybe it was feeling
the pressure from OU but they surely rolled out the red carpet.
My mom and dad drove me up and the school put them up in a
hotel. A couple of coaches took them to dinner that night while I
went out to a steak house with two players, Doug Richardson and
Wendell Wood. Doug was a linebacker and Wendell was a defensive lineman. They wound up turning the meal into a contest, to
see how many steaks you could put down. My brothers would
have been proud—I think I ate six. But Wendell beat that by two.
Eight steaks. This guy was about 280 pounds, just an eating
machine.

The next day they took me to see the field, Skelly Stadium. It
wasn't anything like Norman, but it was still impressive. Forty
thousand blue and gold seats surrounding a new artificial turf
field.

Their facilities were great, but what set Tulsa apart from the
other schools in the state was its academic reputation. Tulsa is
known throughout the Southwest for the quality of its classes. It's
a private school, pricier than any in the region, but you get what
you pay for.

I liked what I saw that weekend. My folks had been treated
great, and so had I. I felt real good about Tulsa. But I still had one
more trip to make, to Oklahoma State.

Jimmy Johnson was getting set to leave OSU for the head
coaching spot at Miami, but no one knew that yet. I certainly
didn't. Paul Jett had things set for me to fly out to Stillwater, and I
was pumped. Even the flight was something to look forward to.
I'd ridden in a jet once in my life, in California, but I'd never been

in a small plane like the one that was supposed to take me to OSU that weekend.

I never made the flight. I was all set to leave when Coach Jett called me late Thursday night to say the trip was off. His explanation was that Jimmy Johnson and he had decided I couldn't cut it academically at Oklahoma State. My credentials were good enough for Tulsa, so it was hard to believe they weren't good enough for OSU.

The next morning, Bobby Proctor was on the phone, and that afternoon, after school, he came out to Mustang and picked me up in a large Town Car. I climbed in and he put his radar detector on the dashboard. I don't think I'd ever seen a radar detector. Then we jumped on the highway and took off.

Forty-five minutes later we were in Norman. Coach Proctor dropped me off at the athletic guest bungalows, a complex of little brick huts, each one complete with a kitchen, dining room, and living room. He told me to make myself at home, that my roommate for the weekend, another recruit, should be arriving soon.

He did, and I'd never seen anyone so huge in my life. His name was Bill Roden, from Cleburne, Texas. Nineteen years old, six-five, 265 pounds, and a cowboy all the way. His clothes were starched so stiff he could take them off and lean them up against his bed. You could cut yourself on the crease he had in his jeans. And he wore a big white Stetson.

I felt small. Here I was, this great big defensive end eating up the world at Mustang High, and here's this high school guy who looks like he's a *man*.

We went out to a movie that night with our host, an offensive tackle named Jody Britt. He was bigger than Roden by about ten pounds. After that Bill and I went to shoot pool at a little arcade on campus. As we were leaving, a Camaro shot past and almost hit us. Bill kicked it with his boot. Suddenly the driver slammed on his brakes and backed up. Out jumped two guys. They took one look at Bill and they both came barreling straight toward *me*.

I'd only been in two fights in my life, and both times it was when someone pushed me too far and I had no choice. Each time

I'd followed some advice my brother Dan had given me when I
was little. If you're going to fight somebody, he told me, if it's a
given, if you're resolved . . . then *take the first shot*.

So I did. As soon as the first guy got within range, I let him have
it, *smack*, right on the conk, right in the nose. He went down like
someone pulled a plug. The other guy backed off, shrugged, and
helped his buddy to the car.

Roden was impressed. All he could talk about the rest of the
night was how I dropped that guy with one shot.

The next day they brought all the recruits together in the press
box of Memorial Stadium, where we had lunch. Barry Switzer
gave a speech. Then, as we were heading down to watch an OU
highlight film, Switzer came up beside me and introduced himself.
He knew my name.

"You had a great game against Bishop Kelley," he said.

I thanked him. My knees felt like rubber.

Then he reached out and grabbed my wrist.

"You got big bones," he said. "I think we can put some weight
on you."

I couldn't believe Barry Switzer had touched me. I couldn't
believe he knew who I was. I could hardly keep my mind on the
highlight film, and when it was done, he invited us each individually into his office. When my turn came, I walked in for the most
intimidating one-on-one I've ever had, before or since, on or off
the football field.

There were trophies everywhere, photographs covering the
walls, everything red and white. It was dazzling. It was *meant* to
be dazzling.

Switzer took out a wooden box and opened it. It was lined with
velvet and full of rings. Big Eight championship rings. National
championship rings. Bowl rings.

"Would you like to have one of these?" he asked. He didn't
wait for an answer. "Come to school here," he said, "and you'll
win one."

Then he leaned back and said, "We want you to play football
here. Whatever vehicle it takes to get you to come to school here,
we'll provide it."

He never offered me an outright scholarship. His language was vague. I didn't know exactly *what* he was offering me. I left Norman that afternoon overwhelmed and uncertain. I later found out they'd already offered their limit of scholarships for that season before they heard about me. What they later said they were hoping was that I would commit to come there, and that by the fall someone would have backed out of one of the scholarships, freeing it up for me.

But all I knew was Oklahoma had promised me nothing, while Tulsa was committed. The next day, Monday, I called Bill Young and told him I was in.

The funny thing is later that week one of Oklahoma's kids told them he was going someplace else. They immediately called Charlie Carpenter to see if I'd commit to OU. He passed the message on to me. I would have killed to be a Sooner. But I wouldn't break my word.

I was going to Tulsa.

6

By the time I signed my letter of intent to attend Tulsa, I had begun dating Angela Hales. Until my senior year, I had never had a steady girlfriend. I was too interested in football to date much, and during the season, I didn't date at all. That's just the way it was. Being with your buddies, that's what football was about. You knew the girls would come along sooner or later, so there was no hurry.

At the end of my senior season at Mustang I went out with one girl for a couple of months, then we broke up just about the time I really began noticing Angela. We'd seen each other in church for a couple of years—church had never stopped being a big part of my life. I still went Sundays and Wednesdays, and Angela and her family were always there. Her dad, David, was an engineer for AT&T, and her mom, Betty, worked as a secretary for the superintendent of schools. She had one younger brother, Chris. They lived over in Yukon, in a subdivision about ten miles away, but Angela went to Mustang High.

She was a year younger than me. I'd watched her sing many times, in the church youth choir and with the school's musical groups. She had a beautiful voice, good enough to be selected for solos. She also had a boyfriend. But that changed just after Christmas, and pretty soon we began spending time with each other at church, just talking, just trying to get to know each other.

She was tall and blonde, she was skinny and she had braces, but she was the most beautiful thing I'd ever seen. One Sunday I turned to my mother and said, "Someday, Mom, I'm gonna marry her."

The feeling was not exactly mutual, not in the beginning. I didn't own a car, and I didn't have what you would call a wardrobe. When we started dating, my parents or one of my brothers would drop me off at her house and we'd go out in *her* car, a little baby blue Mercury. That, or we'd double-date with David Oliver and his date, and David would drive.

I didn't have a lot of money. My dad was working for a television station in Oklahoma City as a carpenter and art director, but just about everything he and my mom had was still sunk into that ten acres, so we were living paycheck to paycheck. Sometimes my parents gave me a few dollars to take Angela out, squeezing the money from the weekly budget.

As often as not, Angela and I would spend our evenings together watching TV at her house or going out to dinner with her parents. The fact that I was a big football star meant nothing to Angela. She wasn't interested in the sport. She never went to games. She didn't even know I was on the team when she first met me, and she didn't care. Church and choir, that was the focus of her life outside school.

One Wednesday night I had finally gotten up enough nerve to ask Angela to join me for a Coke at the local pizza parlor where all the kids hung out after church. I asked for her phone number, and within a couple of weeks we were dating.

Even then, Angela wasn't sure about me. She told her mom I just wasn't her type. But something drew us together, and by the end of the school year, it was pretty serious. We'd double-date with David, go out to eat or to a movie, then drive David's truck to a place called Lake Overhoulser, which all the kids called Lake Hold Her Closer.

Over the summer I spent most of my time with Angela and working out, getting ready to go to Tulsa. Sunday afternoons I still joined Doug and Danny and a bunch of the guys for tackle foot-

ball over at the high school field, the same as we'd been doing forever. No pads, full contact, no holding back. We'd knock the *soup*
out of each other. There were plenty of bloody noses, lumps and
bumps and bruises, but never anything serious. Still, my dad was
horrified. He could see my college career ending before it began,
with a knee blowout in a pickup game. But that didn't stop me
from playing. Even during my career at Tulsa, I'd still come home
on weekends and play crushing sandlot tackle games with the
guys, all the way through my senior year. By then I was an All-
American, sure, but that didn't matter. I *loved* this game.

In August, just before my freshman year began, the top graduated seniors in the state came to Tulsa to play in the annual Oklahoma Coaches Association High School All-Star game. Now I
learned what Skelly Stadium looked like with people in it. And
that's where I got my first look at Troy Aikman.

Troy was from Henryetta High School, a little town southwest
of Tulsa. The Henryetta Fighting Chicks. People knew who he
was. If you're headed to Oklahoma as a scholarship quarterback,
people know who you are.

Troy was on the East team that day, and I was on the West. I
sacked him once, early in the game, then went to the sidelines
with what I thought was a severely sprained foot. I had them tape
it up, said, "Hey, this happens only once in a lifetime," and went
right back out. It wasn't until after the game that I found out I'd
been playing on a broken bone.

I had a few tackles that afternoon, got in a couple of good licks,
but nothing to grab any headlines. We wound up losing 21-20
when Lydell Carr of Enid, who went on to make a name for himself as a fullback at Oklahoma, was stopped on a two-point con-
version at the end of the game.

All the guys you play with in a game like that you follow closely
thereafter. You read the newspapers. You look for names. I
remember reading all about Troy becoming a starter for Barry
Switzer his second year, then breaking his foot, being replaced by
Jamelle Holieway, and transferring to UCLA. I never dreamed
Troy would go on and win the Super Bowl, which shows how you
never can really know. Who would have thought *I'd* get as far as I

did, that six years later Troy and I would be on the same football field again, this time in the National Football League, and that I'd be sacking him again?

When the All-Star weekend was done, I came home and began packing. I also bought Angela a "promise" ring. I'd meant what I said when I told my mom this was the girl for me. Angela was equally committed. She and her mom began keeping a hope chest, filling it with the things we'd need once we were married. Meanwhile, I boarded a bus with my suitemate-to-be, a strong safety and wide receiver named Steve Hill, and headed for college.

Now I was a Golden Hurricane. It's not exactly a nickname that strikes fear into people's hearts. Everyone knows who the Miami Hurricanes are. But mention a Golden Hurricane to someone outside the state of Oklahoma, and they think you're talking about a drink in a bar. We were always kind of embarrassed about that.

But there was nothing embarrassing about the football program at Tulsa. It's always had the challenge of being in the shadow of Oklahoma and Oklahoma State, but two years before I got there, the Hurricane went 10 and 1 and were ranked seventeenth in the nation. They didn't go to a bowl game that year, which says a lot about the problem they've got with respect. People in Tulsa were really disgusted about that. In fact, the team had had six straight winning seasons when I arrived and for the last four of those years, they had the best record in the state—thirty-three wins and eleven losses. The Sooners were switching from the wishbone offense to the I-formation to accommodate Marcus Dupree, and a lot of people were calling for Barry Switzer's job. As for Oklahoma State, they were playing good football, as always. But during that time span, neither of those schools won as many games as Tulsa.

This was college football at its best. That year's schedule had us going up against eventual national champion Brigham Young, with their Heisman Trophy candidate, quarterback Robbie Bosco. And Arkansas. And Oklahoma State. The next year we'd have Houston, Texas A&M, and Florida State. Then, Miami and Oklahoma and Florida.

These were the big boys, the best talent in the country, the teams with the players who became superstars. Some already

were. But not me. Definitely not me. Here the game was played at
an entirely different level than Mustang. I'd been a monster in
high school, capable of running over and through people. Here I
was just another body, and a relatively light one at that. I was six-
four, 215 pounds when I arrived, and the first day of practice they
actually tried me at strong safety. That's how small I was. I wound
up at outside linebacker, where I spent the next few weeks doing
what I loved most—roaming the field like a madman and hitting
anything that moved. Just before the season started, Coach
Cooper called me in and said I was good enough to play some
that year but that he'd like to redshirt me so they could have me
for four full seasons.

That's a hard thing to take, even if you understand it's in the
best interests of everyone, the team and yourself. Spending a season simply practicing and never actually suiting up is tough. I
didn't like the idea that I'd be spending my Saturdays watching
my teammates play while I stood on the sidelines, but I understood that true freshmen rarely start anywhere. I knew I had to
be patient, that there would be lumps I had to take before I'd get
my turn. I was seventeen years old, playing against guys who
were twenty-one and twenty-two, guys who physically had me
outdeveloped. So my challenge was to work as hard as I could
and do some developing myself.

I *loved* practice. Whether it was Wednesday afternoon on the
scrimmage field or Saturday afternoon in front of forty thousand
fans or Sunday afternoon with my brothers, it was all the same to
me. Hey, I was playing *football*.

I was on the meat squad, playing the role of whichever opponent we were meeting that week, and I turned it into a game. I
took magic markers and tape, drew the logo of the team we were
playing that Saturday, colored it in, and put it on my helmet.
When the whistle blew, I went at it. The older guys had never seen
anyone play with that kind of fire in practice, and they didn't
know how to take it at first. They got pissed because I played so
hard, *hit* so hard.

My model as a player then, and he remained my model until the
day he died, was Lyle Alzado. I loved the way he played. Totally
unrelenting. Never quitting. Never giving up. Never stop coming.

Never stop charging. I remember my senior year in high school watching him in the play-offs when he was with the Raiders and seeing him tear this guy's helmet off and throw it at him. That was a classic. I *loved* that. Guys were flat-out afraid of Lyle because he was so tenacious. He once said, "Quite frankly, I don't think there's a man alive who can kick my ass." That's not how I would put it, but the sentiment is the same, that feeling of utter boldness, of putting it all out there.

That's the attitude I brought to practice every day, which didn't make a lot of friends among my offensive teammates. I had a buddy named Rodney Young, my suitemate, who was three years older than me. He was running to the sidelines one afternoon, and I pelted him. He went skidding across the turf and slammed into the wall. He came up livid, but the coaches loved it. They'd move me around and put me in the position of the opponent's strongest player, because they knew I was going all out, just having a ball.

Actually, it was only the defensive coaches who were crazy about me. The offensive coaches didn't like me any better than their players did. One day I was put at cornerback, and Eric Borders, one of our wide receivers, came across the middle. The ball was thrown high, and I just *slicked* him, really gave him a shot. Mark Logan, our receiver coach, came sprinting up to me, his jugular vein bulging. "If you hit one of my players like that again," he screamed, "you'll be running Alpines until the sun goes down."

Alpines were what we called the sprints we had to run up and down the north end-zone bleachers. That section of seats was ultra-high, ultra-steep, and whenever you got in trouble, that's where they sent you, to run up and down those steps. The offensive coaches made sure I did my share that season.

Every weekend, Angela, her parents, and her brother drove up. When the season was done, I went home every weekend, usually with Eddie Epps, who had been my teammate in the state All-Star game. Eddie was from Midwest City High School, the Bombers. He was a cornerback, which is what he played at Tulsa as well. Every Friday we climbed into his green Monte Carlo and he drove me to his house, about twenty miles east of Mustang. Angela picked me up there, and we spent Saturday together, usually at her house. By this point I had become close to Angela's family. We went to church together Sunday, and she dropped me back at Eddie's in the afternoon. That's how it went every weekend for two and a half years.

Steve Hill and Eddie Epps are both black. So is Crawford "Fish" Ford, who was another of my roommates at Tulsa. With race relations being such a crucial issue in our country today, I think it's important to mention this. I had black coaches, teammates, and roommates throughout my football career. My closest companion in professional football, the man who became dearer to me than any friend in this world, is black. Several of the nurses and orderlies who became an intimate part of my life when I wound up living in a hospital are black. So is the physical therapist who taught me the ways of a whole new world. It would have been easy after the experience I had in Sacramento, when those black kids attacked me, to have hard feelings, to be hateful and resentful toward an entire race. But my faith and football made that impossible—my faith because of its insistence that we are all equal in the eyes of God, and football because of the intimacy and brotherhood it nurtures. Nothing can bring a group of individuals closer together than to see one another bleed and sweat, laugh and cry, win and lose. Once you've been through war with a man, race becomes a trivial thing. They had a saying in Vietnam, where black and white U.S. troops fought together for the first time as fully integrated units: Same mud, same blood. That's how it is with football, too. I don't think it's a coincidence that the two segments of our society that seem to be healthiest in terms of race relations are the military and sports.

We went 6-5 my first year at Tulsa, which turned out to be John Cooper's last. I really enjoyed Coach Cooper. He was straightforward, he told you how it was, and he didn't pull any punches. He'd give out battlefield promotions right on the field. If he didn't like something he saw, he'd yank a guy, put the backup in, and say, "*You're* the starter now." The best person played for Coop, no two ways about it.

It was Arizona State that lured Coach Cooper away, offering him their head coaching position. He took it, and he took some of his assistants with him, including the coach who had recruited me, Bill Young. Coach Young told me, subtly, with a lot of hemming and hawing and hinting, that I was welcome to come with them, to transfer to Tempe. But there was no way. By then, Tulsa was where I belonged.

So now I had a new coach, Don Morton. He came from North Dakota State, where he'd won a Division II national championship. I was excited but a little wary as well. I was starting all over again, proving myself to a new coach. I'd spent all that time showing John Cooper that I could start, proving it in practice day after day. But no one watches old practice film. Game film is what a new coach has to start with when he's assessing what he's got, and I didn't play in any games under Coop. Whatever Don Morton saw of me, he'd have to see in person. So once again, I had to be patient and believe my chance would come.

I started out the season on special teams—the kickoff team, the kickoff return team, the punt team, the punt return team. It seemed like I never came off the field, which was great. Being in on every play I could, staying on the field all day, that's what it was all about. I got to start every game no matter which team took the kickoff.

Which is not to say my eagerness wasn't equaled by anxiety. There's nothing like the nervousness that sweeps through you, the adrenaline rush that invades your body just before a kickoff. You know you can get blasted from anywhere, from any direction. Anyone who's ever played on a kickoff team knows the kind of butterflies I'm talking about.

My first college game was at home against Texas Tech. It was so scary going out there to run defensive plays. All I could see was what was directly in front of me—I was seized with tunnel vision, as if I had blinders on. I had no peripheral vision whatsoever. And that's dangerous. This is a game where peripheral vision is everything, where your sense of everything happening around you is crucial, where you're constantly soaking in and processing a flood of information, of visual cues: signals from the sidelines; keys from their players about what they're going to do; your strong linebacker barking out his calls while the quarterback's calling *his* signals; the defense changing and shifting. When you're young like that, there's so much information you *can't* absorb. You're dizzy trying to put everything together, your head is swimming from this cataclysmic overload. You're just about to snap from pressure, and then the ball's hiked, and then it all breaks loose. And all you've got to go on are your instincts.

That's the way it was in the beginning, and thank goodness my instincts were sharp enough to keep me from being burned.

By the fifth game of the season, I'd done well enough that Coach Morton gave me my first start. It was on my birthday, October 5, and it was against the school that had chilled on me my senior season, Oklahoma State. Their star at that time was Thurman Thomas, "Squirmin' Thurman." Thurman was already a superstar, of course. He had *always* been a superstar. I might have come out of nowhere, but everyone knew when Thurman was coming. The first play of the afternoon, I actually nailed him for a two-yard loss. But I didn't see a lot of him the rest of the day, except from behind. I've still got a nice newspaper photo from that game of me chasing after Thurman as he shot up the sidelines, on his way to a fifty-four-yard first-quarter touchdown run. Thurman finished with 157 yards that afternoon—not bad, considering he only played the first half.

We wound up 6-5 that year, and I finished with the same number of tackles as my jersey number—forty-eight. I'd put on fifteen pounds and established myself as a starter at outside linebacker, which made it a little surprising when Mike Daly, our defensive coordinator, took me aside in the spring and told me they were going to move me to defensive end. Still, I relished the change. I enjoyed playing linebacker, dropping off to cover the flat, but there was nothing I'd rather do than rush the passer, and that's what defensive end was all about.

When my sophomore season began, I was in my element, bigger and stronger than ever (I was up to 245 pounds), smarter after a season of experience, and playing in the place that would become my home for the rest of my career—the defensive line. I also had a reputation as a guy with a pretty reckless style of play. One columnist wrote that I played football "the way the bulls run through the streets of Pamplona."

We had a good season my sophomore year—the best, in fact, of all my years as a Hurricane. We went 7-4, including a win that is still considered probably the biggest in Tulsa football history.

It came in our third game of the year, against those Cowpokes of OSU. The largest crowd ever to see a game in Skelly Stadium arrived that Saturday night wondering how badly Thurman and company would run us over. The first play of the game went just as the year before, with me nailing Thurman for a loss. We were already fired up, and that hit just stoked the flames. Years later Thurman still remembered some of the licks he took that game. We held him to eighty-eight yards, one of the lowest totals of his college career, and we had a 27-23 win. They still talk about it in Tulsa.

By the end of the year, I was really coming into my own. We played Wichita State, and in one series I sacked their quarterback, Brian McDonald, twice for twenty-five yards in losses, then knocked him out of the game as he let go of a pass on the third down.

Two weeks later we played top-ranked Miami at the Orange Bowl. We lost 23-10, but I sacked Vinny Testaverde twice and fell on a fumble to set up a field goal. That made the score 10-3, but Vinny came right back with a bomb to Brian Blades that just finished us off.

We thought we had a shot at a bowl game that year, but it didn't happen. Which was just as well, because by then Angela and I had made plans to marry. We said our vows five days before Christmas 1986, at the Mustang Assembly of God Church, with our minister, Jim McNabb, presiding. After our honeymoon in Dallas, we came back home to be with our families for the holidays. Then we both drove to Tulsa—in Angela's Camaro, of course. She went to work in the office of an insurance company, and I went back to classes.

Far from making life as a college student more complicated, being married made it simpler for me. Instead of spending my evenings goofing around with the guys in the dorm, generally wasting time, I was home now every night, with a wife who, among other things, made me study.

Home at first was a small three-room apartment with green shag carpeting, just behind the athletic dorms. Angela's parents furnished it for us and helped us get settled. It became a second home to half my teammates, but no one spent more time there than a couple of guys named Gus Spanos and Dan Tarabrella. They were two high school kids from Pennsylvania when I first met them during a recruiting weekend. Gus was a short, pudgy defensive lineman from Pittsburgh, and Danny was a defensive tackle from a town called Elizabeth—two partners in crime eager to see what the real Wild West was like. I was assigned to show them around that weekend, and all they kept asking was, "Where are the *cowboys?* Where are the *Indians?* Where's the *cactus?*" They were dead serious. They thought Sitting Bull was still riding around out here.

Gus and Dan both wound up coming to Tulsa on scholarships, and they became more than teammates to me. They were like little brothers. Their dorm room wasn't forty yards from our place, and every night they'd walk across the quad, knock on our door, walk on in, and begin eating whatever they could get their hands on. If we had just had dinner, Gus and Dan would finish it for us. If Ange set out some candy, they'd scarf that down in a matter of seconds. I thought I had a pretty good appetite, but these guys were vacuum cleaners. They both grew into very good football players, Dan on the defensive line and Gus as the quintessential strong guard—he was about six-two, 275 by the time he graduated. And I think their raids on our refrigerator should get some of that credit.

By no means was I the only married player on the Tulsa football team. About a dozen of our players had wives. I'll bet we had more marriages on our team than any college in the country—the only records Tulsa was setting at the time. About six of the team's couples lived in the college-owned duplexes where Ange and I moved just before my junior year.

Eddie and Rhonda Epps. Richard and Lisa Sambrano. Mike and Renee Rosson. Steve and Rachelle Kropp. Weekends we'd get together for a cookout in the back yard or a game of Pictionary or a trip to the dollar movie in town with dinner afterward, usually at Taco Bueno. That's all we could afford. Even then, we couldn't have gotten by without some help from Angela's parents.

Most weeknights Ange and I spent with our next-door neighbors, Gil and Margie Crowhurst. They were an older couple, in their sixties, and they pretty much adopted me and Ange. Every night, it seemed, we were over at Gil and Margie's place, playing pitch, our favorite card game.

We didn't own a thing, but this was one of the happiest periods of our life, full of simple pleasures, of long conversations with good friends. As for my faith, it only deepened. I had never stopped going to church, never stopped reading the Bible—but now, with Ange beside me all the time, our faith became even more important. No more carousing with my friends. No more drinking beer—I stopped that entirely.

As things turned out that fall, I needed all the faith I could gather. That season of 1987 was the most torturous—and testing—of my college career.

Once again, for the third time in my four years at Tulsa, we had a new coach. Don Morton took the head job at Wisconsin, and in came George Henshaw, a hard-hitting, free-cursing, southern-drawl-talking fire-eater from the University of Alabama, where he had been the offensive coordinator under Ray Perkins. Nobody was about to trust him. Maybe that was unfair to George, but we'd already been burned by two coaches taking off, and now here comes this guy walking tall, talking tall, letting everyone know in no uncertain terms this was *his* team.

That spring, everything was live, meaning practices were run at full speed with full-out hitting. I was one of the few players who *liked* that, and I wound up getting hurt. I blew out my left knee for the first time—tore the medial collateral ligament and the medial meniscus. And I wasn't alone. We had over twenty major surgeries that spring, almost all for knees and shoulders. Henshaw was trying to evaluate his talent on the field, and he lost half of it. I could see now why coaches don't do this all the time. You get forty-five nuts like me out there, and things can get out of control.

I'll give George Henshaw credit for trying, even if I don't agree with his methods. But no matter how hard you try, one spring and two weeks of two-a-days is too short a time to get any system in place. I don't care *who* the head coach is, that first year you're going to take some major lumps.

And we did, beginning with the opener at Oklahoma State. Thurman was back again, but this game turned into a coming-out party for one of the guys riding the pine behind him, a kid named Barry Sanders. That's how loaded OSU was in the backfield— Barry Sanders was relegated to the special teams. So what did he do with the opening kickoff but bring it back 100 yards for a touchdown. Hello, Barry Sanders.

He almost took a punt back all the way, too. Thurman finished with his usual numbers—three touchdowns, 164 yards—and the final score was 38-29, OSU.

The next week we went to Gainesville, where Florida had Kerwin Bell at quarterback and a freshman running back we'd heard a lot about: Emmitt Smith. We were all wondering if he was the real deal. It didn't take long to find out. Emmitt zipped sixty-six yards for a score in the second quarter and by the time the smoke cleared the Gators had stomped us 52-0.

Then we went to Fayetteville to meet the team I hated most— Arkansas. I can't explain why, but everything about the Razorbacks rubbed me the wrong way, from their fans to their players to their nickname. Maybe it's because they beat us every year I was at Tulsa. They did it to us again that weekend, 30-15.

Finally we came home for our first game in Skelly Stadium, and it was one the whole state had been looking forward to: Oklahoma. It had been forty-five years since the Sooners last played in Tulsa. More than 47,000 people squeezed into Skelly—six thousand more than there were seats—to see us play our third top-ranked opponent in four years.

What they saw was a nightmare—ours.

Oklahoma scored nine touchdowns and a field goal. We scored nothing. Jamelle Holieway took the afternoon off early, and his replacement, Charles Thompson, ran for three touchdowns and 105 yards—on *eight* carries. Lydell Carr, my teammate from the high school All-State game, didn't have a bad afternoon either. He had a sweet little thirty-five-yard dash in the second quarter that made the halftime score 31-0. They ended up shellacking us 65-zip.

It's humiliating to lose by scores like that. It hurts. But I believe that's the kind of thing that tempers you as a person, that teaches you to see what you've really got inside you. All that losing did was make my resolve even stronger. The way I felt was that we had sixty minutes of football to play every Saturday, and if we were down by sixty points and it was only the beginning of the third quarter, we still owed somebody thirty more minutes. I couldn't imagine not giving everything I had every second I was on that field. No matter what the score, no matter whether it was the first play of the game or the last, I always took it personally. I considered each play a game in itself, and I got very upset if I ever saw anybody beside me giving up even a little bit.

I wasn't the kind of guy who would holler at anybody. They knew. When it's the fourth quarter and you're behind, *way* behind, and you're a defensive lineman making a tackle downfield, beating a defensive back to the ball, and you come up off the bottom of that pile because you got there first, you don't have to say a whole lot. You've challenged the other guys. You've said, "Hey. Look. There's still a game going on. There's still a reason to play hard." There were a few guys on our team who kept pushing like that. I didn't corner the market on this attitude, not by any means.

But then we had guys who, when they saw the game was out of hand, would rather be sitting on the bench waving at their girlfriends in the stands. Every team has some of those, and there's nothing you can say to them to make any difference. If you've got to slap a guy around to get him going, if you've got to plead with him to play football, who wants him around anyway?

We were awful that year. We lost to Central Michigan, a team we'd crushed 42-6 the year before. They beat us 41-18, and that Monday we had a practice I'll never forget. Black Monday, we called it. Instead of our regular workout, all we did were tackling drills and beat-'em-up drills: bull in the ring, king of the board, one-on-one head-bashing all day long. Henshaw was livid, and I could understand why.

We finished 3-8 that season, and the following March, George

Henshaw resigned to take a job with the Denver Broncos as their offensive line coach. So now here I was, looking at my fourth coach in five years. I couldn't believe it. And I decided to do something about it.

Henshaw announced his retirement in the morning. By lunchtime I had called all the seniors together, talked with them, and asked what they thought. We all agreed we'd like to have Dave Rader, Henshaw's assistant and the team's quarterback coach, stay on as head coach. Dave had played for Tulsa in the late seventies, he had the respect of everyone on the team, and, most important, he was a communicator, someone who was in touch with the players, and with whom they felt comfortable.

Once the guys made it clear they wanted Coach Rader, I went to see the president of the university, J. Paschal Twyman. What did I have to lose? I knew the university would be launching a search for a new head coach, and I thought we deserved to have him know how we felt. We'd been through a lot as a team.

President Twyman saw me, and he really listened. That night, less than twelve hours after Henshaw's resignation was announced, the university had another announcement to make: Dave Rader was Tulsa's new head football coach.

We didn't expect any miracles my senior season, and we didn't get them. The university understood this was the new coach's first year, and they were ready to be patient. Rader rewarded their patience with loyalty. He's still at Tulsa, and he's taken them to two bowl games since I left: the Holiday Bowl and the Independence Bowl.

We went 4-7 that fall of 1988. The school was promoting me as an All-American candidate, and I didn't let them down. I opened up with twenty tackles and two sacks in our first game, a win over Kansas State. Strange thing about that game was K-State's right offensive guard. I don't know who he was, but he lined up for the first play and started talking trash to me, telling me that, in his words, I "sucked."

I didn't know where this guy was coming from. You just don't see a lot of trash-talking among linemen. It's different with defensive backs. They're a mouthy lot. They and the receivers are way out there in the wide-open field, pointing at each other, talking their nice games, threatening and counter-threatening, and in the end they might come in contact with each other—*really* make contact—maybe three or four times in an entire afternoon.

But defensive and offensive linemen, they're hands-on every play, fighting it out with every snap. You don't have to *talk* about what you're going to do to somebody. You just *do* it. Seventy plays a game gives you plenty of opportunity to make a statement.

That's what made this guy so odd. He certainly didn't help himself. The first play I crushed him, shoved him all the way into the backfield. The back actually ran into him and fell down, and that's pretty much the way the rest of the day went. I whaled on this guy for four quarters.

It was games like that one against Kansas State that eventually caught the attention of the NFL scouts. There are always one or two players the scouts come to see, and while they're looking at those guys, they notice the other players on the field. Whenever they're breaking down film, they see eleven guys out there. If you're doing something that stands out, they're not going to miss it. That's how you get into these guys' notebooks in the first place. Over the course of a career at a school like Tulsa, you get plenty of opportunity to show the pros what you can do.

The scouts had begun talking to me during my junior year. A scout from Green Bay came by at the end of the season and left me a belt buckle. My dad has it now. And I got letters from a lot of teams. The Cowboys. The Falcons. I've still got the envelopes in a scrapbook.

As soon as my senior year ended, things kicked into high gear. The scouts came down and began running me through drills in early December. For the next two months I worked out probably three days a week, running drills for more teams than I can remember.

The club that showed the most interest was the Jets. At one time or another, they sent seven different coaches and scouts to see me: the defensive coordinator, the defensive line coach, the defensive secondary coach, they all came down and ran me through workouts.

Minnesota was high on me, too. I had a really nice workout for them, running the shuttle drill, running the cones—they even had me running passing routes. When I was done, the Vikings guy told me to keep working hard and I'd be playing somewhere in the NFL for sure.

"You're gonna get paid a lot of money," he said.

"Oh Lord," I told him, "I'd play this game for nothing."

"*Shhh!*" he snapped. "Don't let anybody hear you say that, or that's just what they'll try and give you."

I didn't have to worry. By that time, I already had an agent. The search had begun the day after our last game, November 26, against Colorado State. I suddenly got a deluge of phone calls. I'd gotten some letters during the season but that was about it. Your marquee college players are getting letters and phone calls their freshman and sophomore years, but I began my senior season at Tulsa still a relatively obscure player at a school with a program going through hard times. By the last game, however, the agents were coming out of the woodwork and suddenly here came the invitations.

The first one I accepted was from a man named Vic Vines. Vic was a really good guy, very sincere, and he had a great plan. He had come and visited Ange and me, and he made it clear how important financial planning was after you'd gotten your money. That was his priority, and that appealed to me. Vic worked as a recruiter for an agent in Texas, and he arranged for us to fly down to meet this man at his home in Dallas.

It went very nicely at first. We had a pleasant dinner at a good restaurant. But I was far past the point of having my head turned by a nice evening out. I'd been through it with the college recruiters. I understood that this was all a prelude to the pitch, a setup for the real reason we had all gathered together this evening.

Sure enough, he had us out to his house, with its own horse track and stables. That's where he had his office, out at the stables. And that's where the visit turned sour.

Vic was a Christian. I could see that. His faith was genuine, but he didn't dwell on it or try to use it as a bond between us. The agent was a different story. We weren't in his office long before he told us he wanted us to pray together, to pray about this decision Angela and I would be making. So we held hands, all four of us, and he prayed for what must have been twenty-five minutes.

I never want to judge a person's Christianity, but I felt that this man was full of baloney. What he did was just so insincere. And it was an insult to something I take very seriously. Angela and I have always based all our financial decisions, all the important decisions in our life, on prayer. Prayer is a precious thing to us. It's a time to meditate, to sit still and talk to the Lord. To use it as an instrument to make a deal was just wrong. We left Dallas still in search of an agent.

My next trip was to Orlando. I had a wonderful time there, totally different from Dallas. The man I met was named Robert Fraley, who represents, among others, Orel Hershiser, who was the hottest thing going at the time. Mr. Fraley was sincere and straightforward. He gave me a good, honest handshake, and he looked me right in the eye whenever he was telling me something. He put on the ritz, but in a very professional way. His secretary picked me up at the airport in a nice big Mercedes. He had very impressive offices, but they weren't ostentatious. I left suitably impressed, but in the end we decided to go with a man I had met at the end of the season, an attorney from Baltimore named Rick Schaeffer.

Our offensive line coach, Mark Thomas, had introduced us after the Temple game. He and Rick were friends, Rick had represented several players Mark had coached at Murray State and at Duke, and Mark felt he'd be a good man to represent me.

On the face of it we had nothing in common, a big blonde Christian from Oklahoma and a short, dark Jewish lawyer from Baltimore. But Rick Schaeffer had everything I was looking for in an agent, namely smarts, a direct approach, and a sense of humanity that was missing from most of the agents I'd seen.

Rick was only in his late thirties, but he'd been around. He'd started out in sports work in Washington, D.C., where he helped handle some of the basketball and tennis contracts of players represented by the group that would become known as ProServ. While there, he had worked with Moses Malone, John Lucas, and Bobby Jones, as well as Arthur Ashe, Harold Solomon, and Brian Gottfried. He then spent three years as a lawyer with the NFL Players Association, where he worked on everything from injury grievances to contract negotiations for players like Bob Hayes, John Riggins, and Bert Jones.

As soon as my season was over, Rick came down to Tulsa and visited *us*. He didn't fly us anywhere. He met Angela and me at our own place, on our own terms, really. Rick rubbed elbows with some huge people, but that's not what mattered to us. What impressed us most was how much he knew about the front office part of football. Everybody else knew how to wine and dine you, but Rick Schaeffer clearly knew the business. We sat for two hours in his hotel room in Tulsa, drinking Cokes and listening to him explain everything from the historic macroeconomics of professional sports to the component parts of a contract to his personal philosophy of negotiation.

Rick also talked about the injury grievance work he had done while with the NFLPA. He talked about the fact that the length of the average NFL career was 3.8 years. I remember him saying, "Every football player's career hangs on something as thin as a medial collateral ligament," and talking about the importance of preparing for life after football *before* that football life has ended.

At the end of the conversation, Rick talked about the type of person he represented. He said he wouldn't come near a client who, when invited to go over to a children's hospital to visit some kids, would ask, "How much are they paying?" It was hard for me to believe anyone would respond like that, but Rick said it wasn't rare.

We liked this man. After praying together, Angela and I decided to tell him we'd like him to represent me.

I'd been named second-team All-American in December. Later that month, Christmas week, Angela and I went down to Montgomery, where I was invited to play in the Blue-Gray game.

The thing that struck me from the moment we arrived was how there seemed to be more agents there than players. It was a meat market, a frenzy of agents trying to pick up ballplayers. We'd have dinner with some other guys, and everyone would be asking one another the same question. "So who tried to pick you up today?"

It was the same with the East-West Shrine game out in Palo Alto, California, in January. These guys were hanging in the hotel lobby, wooing every loose ballplayer they could lay their hands on. Even if you *had* an agent, they'd try to steal you away, putting down the guy you had, telling you he was a small fish and explaining why you should come with them.

As for the football itself, I had a blast at both games, and I made a lot of good friends, including a guy from the University of Virginia named Jeff Lageman. I had never heard of him before. He was a tall, long-haired outside linebacker, the biggest OLB I'd ever seen in my life, six-five, 250. And he was real quiet. He didn't talk to a whole lot of people. But he could flat-out play the game of football. He had one interception and six tackles in the Blue-Gray game, and he came back with a sack and eight tackles in Palo Alto. They say those games don't mean anything, but I guarantee you performances like that don't hurt when draft day arrives. They didn't hurt Jeff.

I had a good game myself in Montgomery—two tackles for losses, a sack, and I blocked a field goal late in the game with us ahead 21-20. That was the final score.

I didn't have a great game in Palo Alto, finishing with one sack, but I met some more players I'd never forget, including an offensive tackle from Washington State who was the biggest thing I'd ever seen on two feet. I mean, he was stinking huge. His name was Mike Utley. He was just a big, fun guy. Loud, but in an appealing way. Full of life. Angela liked him as much as I did. She took our snapshot together outside a ballroom before dinner one night that week.

When we left Palo Alto, I knew I'd be seeing Mike Utley again. I figured I'd be seeing a lot of these guys again, since most of us were bound for the NFL. The only question was where we'd wind up.

By the time of the draft in April, I knew I was probably going to one of two teams, the Jets or the Vikings. I had a good idea of what the Jets had in mind for me. Ralph Hawkins, the team's defensive coordinator, came down and took me and Ange to dinner in March and told me there was this kid they wanted to select first, a linebacker at the University of Virginia. I couldn't believe it. I told Ralph I knew Jeff. He then said the Jets wanted to take me second, because they could see the two of us working well together, Jeff rushing on one play with me dropping off, or vice versa. It all sounded good to me . . . if it turned out that way.

Which was a big "if." Various football publications were project-
ing me as a fourth- or fifth-round pick. I thought I'd go higher than
that, but I couldn't be sure how high. Or to whom.

Draft day Ange and I joined a crowd of friends and family at my
parents' house in Mustang. They had moved off that land by then.
The development deal had fallen apart while I was away at college, and they'd lost just about everything they had. But my dad
had finally been able to turn things around. He had a job selling
insurance now, and he and my mom and sisters were living in a
nice subdivision, two miles straight north from where we'd had
the bus and trailer.

Like dozens of seniors around the country, I had a crowd
around me, watching the TV, waiting for the selections to start.
My dad had leased a satellite dish for the year—we were pretty
certain I'd be playing somewhere, so he'd need it in the fall.

Still, I was extremely nervous. What if things didn't go the way
the Jets said they would? What if I wound up someplace else?
The Rams had told me they might be trying to get me at the end
of the first round. The Vikings were trying to trade up to beat out
the Jets early in the second. I didn't know what was going to happen.

When the Jets' first pick came up—the fourteenth pick overall—and they took Jeff, I figured, okay, so far so good. Neither the
Rams nor the Vikings made a move. The first round ended, and it
went into the second. Finally it was the Jets' turn, their pick for
the second round, the forty-second overall selection of the 1989
NFL draft . . . Dennis Byrd.

That was it. I was a New York Jet.

The house went nuts. My dad and my brothers rushed out to a
nearby sporting goods store and bought every Jets cap they had,
three.

No sooner had the Jets made the pick than Mel Kiper, an ESPN
analyst, came on with Chris Berman and questioned the choice.
Actually, he questioned both Jets choices. He said Jeff Lageman
was a "reach." Then when they picked me, he said Dennis Byrd
was *also* a reach. Two reaches, two big mistakes.

I wasn't bothered. My entire career people had been telling me
I wasn't big enough or I wasn't fast enough or I wasn't strong

enough. There are always doubters, always somebody who wants to see you fail. I'd learned a long time before not to depend on what other people think, not to believe what they tell you you can and cannot do.

And so I made a special trip back to my family's old place. It was a classic April afternoon, clear and bright. And quiet. The place was deserted.

Angela was with me, and she sat in the car, tears in her eyes, while I got out and walked over to the pole. Weeds were grown up around it now, it was weathered and gray, but it was still there.

I had always told myself that if I ever made it, if I ever got to the point where I was leaving Oklahoma behind, leaving my roots, I'd take some of those roots with me, something I could always have, something I could actually hold onto and touch, something to constantly remind me of where I came from.

I had brought a can with me. Nothing fancy, just an old Folger's coffee can. I bent down and filled it with dirt, the same dirt I'd sweated and bled into back when I wasn't sure what I'd become, when all I had was a vague dream.

Now that dream had come true. I was going to play professional football. I was going to live in New York City, farther from Mustang than mere miles could measure.

And I was bringing some of that soil with me.

A JET

7

It was two weeks after the draft that I was on a plane to mini-camp. I spent the flight talking with the couple sitting beside me. During the course of the conversation the woman asked me if I was going to New York to attend college. I told her no, I was going to play professional football. We moved on to other subjects, but as we were leaving she turned to me and said, "You know, you must not be a very good football player. You're far too nice."

That hurt.

I'll never forget taking a cab that afternoon to the Jets complex at Hofstra University. I'd never been in a cab in my life. I didn't even know how to find one after I got off the plane. And I'd *heard* about New York cab drivers, so when I finally flagged one down, climbed in, and asked the driver to take me to the Jets camp in Hempstead, I was wondering how he was going to take advantage of me. Instead, he asked me how O'Brien was going to do this year. I said, "Who's O'Brien?"

I'd heard of Ken O'Brien, but I didn't know he was the Jets quarterback.

In fact, basically all I knew about the Jets was what they had on the defensive side of the ball, particularly on the defensive line. I knew they'd lost a lot of punch since the peak of their "Sack Exchange" days in the early eighties, when Mark Gastineau and Joe Klecko had made their marks as two of the league's best pass rushers. The fact that five of the Jets' first six picks in the draft, including me, were linebackers or defensive linemen spoke volumes about where they considered themselves weakest.

Those other four picks were there when I arrived: Marvin Washington, a defensive end out of Idaho; Ron Stallworth, another DE out of Auburn; Joe Mott, a linebacker from Iowa; and my roommate for the next six weeks, Jeff Lageman.

You couldn't have found two more different people on the face of the earth than Jeff and me. He was single, drove a Harley-Davidson, pulled his hair back in a ponytail, wore dark T-shirts and torn jeans, would just as soon go without socks, liked listening to The Who or the Rolling Stones, and hated small talk. Early on he picked up the nickname "Spook" for his habit of slipping away from crowds, especially in the locker room, and for his moodiness, especially in the morning.

Then there was me, married, clean-cut, with that midwestern politeness, calling everyone "Sir"—even reporters—eager and outgoing, talking to anybody, anytime. My musical tastes ran in the direction of REO Speedwagon and Boston, and I always, but *always*, wore socks.

I called Angela every night those first couple of weeks, to make sure she was okay. We'd never been apart like this before. Jeff would just lie on his bed and shake his head at me in amazement. To him I seemed about as young and naive as they come.

Jeff and I butted heads in the beginning, but there were some essential things we had in common, including a love of the outdoors. Jeff enjoyed hunting and fishing as much as I did. But more than that, there were aspects I could see of this man's character that drew me to him right away. He was an incredibly hard worker, which I respected in anyone. We were very similar in the way we played football. And Jeff was unbelievably loyal, which he would prove over and over during the coming years, especially after I was hurt. And, though he was a tough nut for strangers to crack, once you got to know him, Jeff was an amazingly sensitive guy, especially around kids. He'd hate to hear this, but it's true. There was nobody on the team who had as soft a heart as Jeff—off the football field.

There was no such thing as a soft heart on it, especially not in camp. We all knew we were there to fight for our football lives, and I knew exactly who I had to beat out for a job on this team. The Jets' roster of veteran defensive ends was anchored by three exceptional athletes, Paul Frase, Marty Lyons, and Willard McDowell. Frase had been a rookie the year before, stepping into Gastineau's starting position when Mark retired midway through the year. If I was going to start, I was going to have to move him.

I realized the challenge I was facing, and I approached it with the same attitude I'd had when I first arrived at Tulsa. These guys were older than me; they had a big edge in terms of sheer savvy. They weren't necessarily bigger, faster, or stronger, but they were *wiser*. And everyone there, rookies and veterans alike, was a tremendous athlete. Each one had been his college's best football player. They were *all* All-Stars. I was wary, but that didn't mean I was afraid. Far from it. I was fully confident I could play the game at this level, that I could stand up to the best out there, and I knew that confidence would be tested from the beginning.

It was, the very first day the veterans arrived. We were running a pass rushing drill, and the guy blocking me, a third-year tackle named Jeff Criswell, kept shoving me after I'd gotten past him. Basically, I was beating him and he didn't like it. Finally I said enough is enough. My brother Danny's advice about taking the first shot was as sound on the football field as off. I gave Criswell a punch under the chin, and we went at it.

There's definitely bad blood with a fight like that, and you see a lot of it in the preseason. But it's *competitive* bad blood, and it doesn't usually carry off the field. More often than not, you'll go to dinner together that night and everything's forgotten. It was that way with Criswell—we wound up hanging out together as a matter of fact. He took to calling me "Denny," which drove me nuts.

The coaches apparently liked what they saw of me. Wally Chambers, our defensive line coach, talked me up to the reporters from the beginning. He said I had "super quickness, super use of the hands, and super overall awareness of how to play the game." Just as important, he said, "Byrd's the kind of guy who's not going to take no bullcrap from anybody."

The minicamp lasted only a week; then the veterans left. The rookies stayed five weeks longer, working with weights and playbooks. By the time those six weeks were done, Joe Walton had anointed me with his favorite phrase—I had "a good motor."

But I hadn't hit anyone yet. No one had. That wouldn't come until training camp began at the end of July, which is when I'd find out exactly where I, and everyone else on the team, stood. You never really know about a football player until the pads are on. I couldn't wait to lace them up.

But before then, there was the matter of signing a contract.

Between the end of my senior season and the day of the draft, Rick Schaeffer and I had had dozens of late-night telephone conversations, talking about everything from hunting to religion to the latest movie we'd seen. Beyond cementing a friendship, this was a necessity to prepare for what lay ahead of us. When you take on an NFL team in a contract negotiation, you're taking on some of the most powerful men in the country. There is nothing like the pressure of an experience like that to test the relationship between an athlete and his agent. You've got to have an incredible level of trust and confidence in each other to endure.

Rick had begun talking with the Jets in the days immediately following the draft. He'd had several conversations with Jim Royer, the Jets' personnel director. By the time of minicamp, they had exchanged contract proposals.

By the beginning of July, they were talking almost daily. Generally speaking, few players sign a contract until just before camp begins. Then you suddenly have a spate of signings. The reason is simple: Typically, the earlier you sign, the less you get. Each player builds off the last guy's deal.

Rick hadn't counted on there being a problem with my negotiation. In fact, he'd scheduled his vacation during the first week of Jets camp. And that's where he found himself, up in Maine, still hammering out my contract as training camp opened. And I was in Mustang, chewing on my nails.

Rick understood my anxiety, but he also was committed to getting the maximum fair deal he could from the Jets, as we'd agreed. He didn't feel the Jets were offering all they could—and should. He compared what the Jets were putting on the table with what other second-rounders around the league were getting and with what the Jets were paying other players, and he thought they weren't making their best offer.

I trusted Rick's judgment totally. Still, as my holdout lengthened, I was starting to sweat. Rick and I talked two or three times a day on the phone as he reassured me that we were making the right moves.

Meanwhile I kept working out, picking up the paper each day and looking for any mention of the Jets. There was nothing, of course. Not in Oklahoma City.

I was nervous. I didn't like not being up there in New York. I knew this was something I had to do financially, in terms of business, but I also knew I was a rookie, that I needed that week of camp, that this was precious time I was missing. Naturally, I was also worried what the coaches would think of me, and what the other players would think.

As it turned out, I didn't have to worry about what anyone thought. The players and coaches understood. This is a profession. You're paid to play, and negotiating your salary is part of the job.

Finally, on Monday, July twenty-fourth, three days after training camp had begun—it felt like a month to me—Rick called to say we had a deal: a three-year contract for $1.2 million, with a fourth option year and a $250,000 signing bonus.

I was on the next flight to New York, which left at seven Tuesday morning. My alarm was set for five. I arrived at Hofstra just after lunch, and within five minutes I'd changed out of my street clothes and was on the field. I literally hit the ground running— running forty-yard dashes.

As far as the reporters were concerned, I was the news of the day. Lageman had been holding out as well, and he still hadn't signed, so for the time being, I was the top draft pick in camp. I got a lot of questions about how my new teammates were treating my arrival, where I thought I'd fit in with the team, how I felt being the supposed savior of the Jets' pass rushing game.

But most of all I got a lot of questions about my hair.

Ever since high school, I'd gotten my hair cut by one of Ange's friends, Rhonda Jemaladine. The day before I came to camp, I brought her a photo of the Jets logo and had her shave it into both sides of my head. I don't know how to explain it other than to say that this was just part of a wild streak that hops in every once in a while and decides to catch a ride with Dennis Byrd. I'd worn an earring once in college, the summer before my junior year. Just a little diamond stud. My dad wasn't too fond of it, so it came out rather quickly. But Ange loved it. She thought it showed a little individuality. Then again, that's the rub with the trend monster. You try something like an earring or a ponytail, something you think shows a little uniqueness, then you look up and everyone's got one. So much for standing out.

I never tried to stand out in the world beyond football. I never have sought attention off the field. But on it, that's where my wild side could have its day, and my energy and enthusiasm and excitement could be unleashed. There was nothing brash about my haircut. It simply said, "Hey, this is *fun*. The kid's excited to *be* here."

The press had a field day with my hair, and they played up the "Okie" theme, too, portraying me as the small-town kid from the prairie plopped in the middle of the metropolis. "Huck Finn in a helmet," one writer called me. I didn't mind at all. That was just part of the fun.

Football had always stayed fun to me, whether it was high school, college, or the pros, whether it was out on the sandlot on a Sunday afternoon or in the middle of Giants Stadium with sixty thousand people watching. I think it was kind of refreshing for the press to have a guy like me show up in New York. Instead of the get-drunk-and-beat-people-up-in-bars type of guy, they were getting a guy who liked to laugh and goof off, who played pranks on his teammates, tossed balls around with kids on the sidelines, and was just basically a big kid himself.

I was easygoing as far as interviews went, and I know the reporters liked that. One thing they all wanted to know was how I felt about filling the shoes of Mark Gastineau, who, oddly enough,

had been a second-round pick out of Oklahoma himself, exactly
ten years before me—he'd played his college ball at East Central
Oklahoma.

I was flattered to be compared to a player of Mark's ability. He
was a great football player. No one has ever equaled the twenty-
two sacks Mark got for the Jets since the league began keeping
official statistics in 1984. Only when I got to New York did I begin
hearing all the negative things about his personality, about his private life. And I didn't think that was entirely fair, everyone focusing on his bad points rather than on the fact that this man was a
great football player, a tremendous pass rusher. I suppose you
earn the criticism as well as the praise by the way you live your
life off the field as well as on it.

I did know that despite some surface similarities, I was no
Mark Gastineau. We shared that same churning energy that's the
mark of any defensive lineman. We both unleashed it, too, after
making a good play. But my way of letting it out was to simply
exult, to leap and let loose my joy, to punch the air, howl, and
share my pure pleasure with my teammates and the crowd. A
move like Mark's signature "sack dance," performed over the
body of a quarterback he'd just crushed, wasn't my style. I definitely did my share of dancing on the football field, but opponents
never minded it and my teammates loved it. They can tell the difference between genuine emotion and grandstanding. Only once
in my career was my emotion on the field ever taken for anything
but an honest, healthy release of the fire that's burned inside ever
since I was a boy.

That was in our first rookie scrimmage against the Washington
Redskins, four days after I arrived in training camp. We drove
down to Lehigh, Pennsylvania, for the game. I remember every
detail of the day, how I dressed, how Joe Patten taped my ankles,
how I then took a magic marker and drew the ichthus symbol—
the outline of a fish with an eye inside it, the symbol of Christianity, of Christians as fishers of men—on the outside of each ankle.
In Oklahoma, everyone knew I was a Christian. Now I was in a
place where people didn't necessarily know, and this was a way
of telling them. It's something I did before every game of my professional career, and it began that morning in Lehigh.

I began another ritual that morning as well. Not long after the draft, after we knew I'd be going to New York, my dad took me with him on one of his trips to sell insurance. Those trips took him all over the state, into the tiniest towns in Oklahoma, and on this particular one, we wound up stopping at a small Indian trading post in the northeast corner of the state. Among the hand-made goods lining the shelves was a small leather sack, a pouch decorated with buckskin fringe and tiny metal bells and etched with the beaded outline of a thunderbird. My dad noticed me admiring it, and a few days later he gave it to me as a gift.

I filled it with some of the dirt from my can and brought it with me to minicamp in May. My teammates constantly asked me, "What's with the bag?" They wanted to know what kind of voodoo I was working. I'd just tell them it was a memory bag. "It's where I've been," I'd say. "It's who I *am.*" I didn't tell anyone what was in it. In later years I told a few close friends, but most of the guys never knew.

A memory bag is exactly what it was. I added a lock of Ange's hair to it the day before I left for training camp. I put a tooth from a buffalo skull in there, too. And a feather. And a little clip of hair from our dog, Roxie. When Ashtin was born, I put a clip of her hair in there, too.

There was no special magic to it, unless you believe in the magic of memory, in the power of the past.

I do.

That day in Lehigh, just before we took the field, I sat by myself, squeezed that bag tightly in my hands, and meditated on my life. I thought about the things I'd been through, about the people I loved. And I prayed. I prayed that I'd play to the best of my ability, that no one would get really hurt, that the Lord would take care of each one of us and allow us to fulfill ourselves in whatever way He saw fit.

Then I untied the sack, sprinkled some of the soil into my palm, and hung the pouch in my locker. As we ran out onto the field, I opened my hand and let the dirt fall onto that Pennsylvania grass.

It's a ritual I would repeat on every NFL field I ever played on. Anaheim. Seattle. Indianapolis. Cleveland. Chicago. Tampa. Phil-adelphia. Pittsburgh. Foxboro. Miami. Denver. New Orleans. San

Diego. Cincinnati. Buffalo. Houston. Detroit. Artificial turf or natural grass, every one of those stadiums has some Oklahoma soil
in it.

As does the field in Lehigh. They called it a controlled scrimmage that day, but it was war out there. Guys were fighting for a
job, fighting to feed themselves and their families, fighting for one
of the forty-seven spots on the roster. In practice, we'd been fighting one another. Now, for the first time, we were teammates, fighting someone else.

I was pumped. And when, early on, I got through for a good hit
on one of their quarterbacks—I don't remember who it was—I
came up hollering, letting out a war whoop they could've heard
back in Tulsa. Our guys were psyched. They loved it.

When I went to the sidelines, Marty Lyons took me aside.
"Great play," he said, "but go easy on the war chants and stuff.
You don't want to get a bad reputation."

Marty hadn't berated me by any means, but the next morning it
was all over the newspapers, how I was this wild kid, out of control. I thought it was funny how it got blown out of proportion, as
if New York, or its newspapers at least, *needed* another Mark
Gastineau.

The next day they got more ammunition. We had an offensive
tackle in camp named Steve Collier, who was by far the largest
football player I ever saw. He had come to minicamp as a free
agent from Green Bay and weighed in at 380 pounds, making him
the biggest New York Jet in history, maybe in NFL history, period.
I was six-five, 270, and I felt like a dwarf. They said Collier had
lost thirty pounds by training camp, but this guy still looked as big
as a house.

And he moved like one. I whiffed him three straight times in
pass rush drills, and things went rapidly downhill in terms of my
relationship with big Steve. He began grabbing me, just blatantly
snatching me so I couldn't get by. We moved on to running drills,
and he was just *tackling* me. I had to put a stop to this. You let a
guy get away with that stuff, and it never stops. I told him, "Don't
do that again. You do *not* want to do that again."

Well, of course he did. He held me the next play, and I gave him
a shot with both hands under his mask—a "face massage" is what

Curt Singer called it. Curt was one of our offensive tackles, a huge redhead and a scrapper. He'd fight you at the drop of a hat. He'd fight *anybody* at the drop of a hat. His favorite move was to shove a hand under a guy's mask, grab the face with his fingers, dig them in, and *grind*.

A face massage. That's what I gave Collier. Somehow I then flipped him on the ground and was on top of him, just going to town, letting him have it until we were finally pulled apart.

I knew the fight wasn't over, and I was right. Offensive linemen stick together just the way defensive linemen do. The next play I was double-teamed, with the tackle and the tight end. I took them on the way we're taught, striking the tackle—what we call the "post man"—and leaning into the "chipper," the tight end. The idea is to bring them both down and create a pile, to plug the hole.

I did my job, which put me in a perfect position for Collier to just pin me. The best I could do was get my feet under him and kick at his stomach. He wound up with gashes where I'd raked him with my cleats.

And I wound up with more ink in the newspapers. My team-mates had a lot of fun with it, too, after Collier was cut the next morning. He got that wake-up call that no one wants. You want your own alarm to wake you up, not a knock on the door. That knock always comes early, about six in the morning, and it's a coach telling you to turn in your playbook and pack your stuff. "An apple and a road map," that's what we call it. That's what you get when it's time to hit the road.

Collier got that knock, and now the joke around camp was "Don't screw with number two." Number two. That was me, the second-round draft pick.

There was some definite tension among Marvin Washington, Ron Stallworth, and myself. The same things that tied us together—that we were all rookies and that we played the same position—kept us apart until the final cuts were made. We were all after the same job. And after I went down with a hip flexor in our second preseason game, against Philadelphia, and had to sit out ten days, I began to get a little worried about that job. Ron came on strong, earning the starting spot at our position, right end. I was moved behind Marty

Lyons on the left side, and that's when the veteran decided to have some big fun at the expense of the rookie from Oklahoma.

They called it Bridgeport-scam.

Marty Lyons is the quintessential prankster, a big, strong guy from Alabama with a head that looks like it's been chiseled from stone. Buffalo Head, that's what we called him. He'd been in the league ten years, and he knew all the ropes, including a gag they'd tried on a couple of rookies in the past. But no one, he later told me, ever bit on it the way I did.

A couple of days after I went out with that injury, Marty began mentioning something about the Jets having a "farm team" in Bridgeport, Connecticut. He told me how tough it was that I'd gotten hurt and how the club might have to send me down there for a while to protect me, how they didn't want to cut me and how this was a way of keeping from losing me to another team.

The Jets had actually had a minor league team in Bridgeport back in the sixties, but that relationship had long been finished. I didn't know any of that. All I knew was our assistant equipment manager, Bill Hampton, Jr., came up one day and casually went over the bus schedule to Bridgeport with me. Our public relations assistant, Brooks Thomas, showed up with a bogus Bridgeport Jets information sheet, including names of all the players and coaches and up-to-date statistics. Marty even got a reporter to interview me about the possibility of being sent to Bridgeport.

All along, I was like, "Right, Marty." I didn't believe it. I'd never once heard of a professional football farm team anywhere. They don't exist.

But then again . . .

This thing kept going and growing, and as little as I knew about the East Coast, well, in the back of my mind I began thinking, "Man, what if this is true?"

Finally, the day of our final preseason game, Marty let me know it had all been a hoax, a big joke. I celebrated by going out and getting two sacks and a fumble we returned for a touchdown. One of those sacks was for a safety that ended the game against the Chiefs in overtime—the only time in NFL history that an overtime game has ended on a safety.

When they announced the final roster, I was on it, along with
six other defensive linemen: Marty, Marvin, Ron, Paul Frase, Gerald Nichols, and Scott Mersereau. This was my family now, a
group of men I would get to know better than anyone in my life
besides my wife and my own parents, brothers, and sisters. I
began the season where I'd begun with Tulsa, on the kickoff and
punt teams, with the first kickoff of my regular season career
coming in Giants Stadium against the New England Patriots. The
feeling was the same as I'd had in college, a mixture of exhilara-
tion and dread. I don't know anyone who's ever been on a kickoff
team who's not been either absolutely horrified or a complete
lunatic. The best are a mixture of both.

Over the first few games I split time on the line with Ron, playing behind Paul at left end. They used Ron mostly in run situations and brought me in against the pass, which, according to
Marty, was the place to be to launch a career.

"If you can pass rush in this league," he told me, "you don't
have to be able to do *anything* else, and you'll stick."

A sack is the milestone by which a defensive lineman is judged.
It means you've beaten not only the guy you're rushing against
but the quarterback. To me, a sack has always been the ultimate
high in football. It's hard to describe that feeling, when you've got
a quarterback in your hands, when you take him down and the
crowd goes crazy and your teammates mob you. It's just like a
score. Touchdowns, sacks, long interception returns—these are
the things people come to see. Just like the home run in baseball.
That's what a sack is, the defensive lineman's home run.

I came close in Cleveland, in our second game of the season. I
bashed Bernie Kosar three times, just after he threw the ball. I
came up blank the next two weeks, against the Dolphins and the
Colts. Then, finally, I got the first sack of my career against Jay
Schroeder and the Raiders, and it couldn't have come at a better
time—Monday night.

There really is something special about a Monday night game.
That's when the pomp comes out and the spotlight is on. Every
other player in the league is tuned in, which means, among other
things, that Monday night is where you pick up a lot of your Pro
Bowl votes.

Monday nights are special for fans, too. To this day, people come up to me and say, "Oh, man, I seen that hit you put on Schroeder on Monday night." As if it happened last week.

I kept giving my all, still coming off the bench, and we kept losing game after game. After the eleventh game, a loss to Indianapolis, we were 2-9 and Joe Walton called all the rookies into his office and just hammered us. He said we weren't pulling our weight. We were the future of this football team, he said, and we weren't doing our job.

The problem, as I saw it, was we couldn't do our job with the defense Joe was using. He had a 3-4 set in place, a defense that calls for size and strength, not speed and athleticism. In a 3-4, you've got a big nose guard and two great big tackles who basically sit in there fighting and throwing aside the guys in front of them so the linebackers can come in and make the tackles.

But Ron and Marvin and I, we were 4-3 type guys. We were slashers, quick guys, with games geared more to finesse, to movement and attacking the gaps. By this point we were asking ourselves why we were drafted into this defense we could hardly run. It was frustrating.

Joe Walton was under a lot of pressure that year, and he just did not seem to be a man who handled pressure well. As things got worse, he began falling apart, cutting players and bringing players in, cutting players and bringing players in. You don't win like that.

It actually got to the point where he was cutting and then bringing in the same player. We had a tight end named Greg Warner, who was a good friend of mine. His wife, Nancy, was a good friend of Ange's. We were sitting in a team meeting, listening to Joe give a speech, and Jim Royer came in and told Greg he needed to talk to him. They left, and Greg didn't return. They cut him.

Then, a few weeks later, they cut somebody else and suddenly Greg Warner was back. That's no way to build a team.

I have difficulty talking anyone down, and personally, Joe Walton was a very good man. He sent us all Christmas cards, and he even wrote me personal letters, which I really appreciated. But the way he handled our team that year was a nightmare. Toward the end of the season, the fans were calling for his head. We'd take the field and it sounded like the whole stadium was chanting, *Joe must go! Joe must go!* I wondered what I had gotten into.

But while the season was deteriorating, individually I was getting more playing time, and I made the best of it. I started against San Diego and wound up with my first game ball, after sacking Billy Joe Toliver twice and sharing a third. I got two more sacks the next week against Bubby Brister and the Steelers, playing against Tunch Ilkin, an All-Pro tackle. Going into the last game against Buffalo, I had seven sacks, one short of the Jets rookie record, held by Joe Klecko. I was very aware of that record, and I badly wanted to beat it, or at least tie it.

I got only one real shot at Jim Kelly that day, and I just plain missed him. So I wound up one shy of the record. Still, only two rookies in the league—Derrick Thomas with the Chiefs and Burt Grossman with the Chargers—had more sacks than me. One football publication named me to its All-Rookie team that year, but it hardly took the sting off what wound up an awful season for the Jets. We finished 4-12, the worst record in the AFC. Only two teams in the entire NFL had a poorer record than ours that year, and one of them was Troy Aikman's Dallas Cowboys. It's still hard to believe they went 1-15 that year and three seasons later Troy has a Super Bowl ring.

But then it's hard to believe how my life changed in those three years as well.

had been through a lot of shifting in my life, lots of transition, but none more than in 1990. And all the changes that year were for the better. In many ways, this was probably the best year of my life.

It began with Angela and me finding our first home, the first and only house we've ever owned. We had spent my rookie season renting a place in the New York area, as we would do throughout my career—my first two seasons, we stayed in Garden City, Long Island, and the last two in a neighborhood called Point Lookout, also on Long Island. We knew we wanted to live the off-season in the Tulsa area, but we had had no time in the swirl of the previous summer—from the draft to minicamp to the contract struggle to training camp—to hunt for a house. Now we had time. And now Angela was two months pregnant, due in July.

We left New York for Tulsa as soon as that first season ended in December, assuming we'd start house-hunting on the city's south side, where most of the residential development was. I hadn't even considered looking north, where there's basically nothing but open country. Then one afternoon I ran into an old teammate from Tulsa, our long snapper, Scott Goodsell. Scott and I had lunch together, and he began telling me about this place where he'd grown up, a little town called Owasso, about twenty miles north of Tulsa. He said there was a lake near there where he'd done a lot of fishing, a nice, secluded spot, and he'd heard they were doing some building around it. The next thing I knew, we were in Scott's car headed toward Owasso.

This was January, the dead of winter. As the Tulsa skyline receded behind us, this began to look like a waste of a good afternoon. The sea of prairie grass we were driving by was brown, the trees bare. This was the same sort of rolling ranchland I'd hunted on all my life. Great for calling coyotes or tracking turkeys, but it didn't look like the place to find our dream home.

Then we came over a small rise, and suddenly we were in Eden.

Thick stands of oak and sycamores rose around us as we drove into a quiet dell. I could see small creeks and streams flowing through granite outcroppings. A waterfall spilled out of the lake Scott had told me about, and the lake itself looked like a mirror, shimmering in the winter sunlight.

A month from that afternoon, Ange and I were looking down on that lake through our back bedroom window as we unpacked our boxes.

We'd found our home.

That was in February, the same month the Jets named the eighth head coach in the club's history. His name was Bruce Coslet. All I knew of him was he'd been the offensive coordinator of the Cincinnati Bengals, the same team he'd played for as a tight end back in the seventies. I knew that, and I knew he was young, only forty-two.

So here I was again, starting over with my *sixth* coach in seven seasons. I was beginning to lose track now, and I was starting to lose trust. I felt like an orphan who keeps getting passed from foster home to foster home. Pretty soon you start closing yourself off. Why get close to somebody when you know he's going to be gone in a year? It's not in my nature to be aloof, but by the time Bruce Coslet arrived, I was learning how—at least with the coaches.

As it turned out, Bruce had come to stay. He brought everything we needed to turn things around. From his personal style to the system he put in place on the field, he was a breath of fresh air.

Joe Walton was not what you would call a player's coach. He kept his distance most of the time. He'd visit with some of the older guys, the ten-year guys, but as for the rest of us, he basically stayed away.

Bruce was different. He was the kind of guy who was comfortable hanging out with the players, talking with us, even goofing off. It was the same with the assistants he brought in—Pete Carroll, our new defensive coordinator, and Greg Robinson, our defensive line coach; Monte Kiffin, our linebacker coach, and Larry Beightol, the offensive line coach. I could sense a whole new atmosphere on this team. It looked like football might be *fun* again.

My teammates knew how much fun I liked to have off the football field as well as on it. The Bridgeport gag Marty Lyons had played on me my first year wasn't the only prank pulled that season. I've always been pretty handy myself with a locker room stunt, and I got Mike Faulkiner, our secondary coach that year, with a pretty good one. Mike had a beat-up piece of an automobile he liked to drive in the city because he said it didn't matter who ran into him. One morning I brought in a smoke bomb. A *serious* smoke bomb, a military-issue landing zone marker that throws out a tremendous amount of smoke—forty thousand cubic feet. We rigged it with tape and string to ignite when the string was yanked. Then we climbed under Mike's car, taped the bomb to his tailpipe and tied the string to a fence. Sure enough, Mike climbed in after practice, fired her up, took off, and the next thing he knew smoke was just boiling out not just from under his car but *into* it. He slammed on the brakes and leaped out.

A woman was walking past, and Mike screamed, "Get *back*, lady! It's gonna *blow!*"

The amazing thing is Pete Carroll had precisely the same reaction when I pulled the same thing on him that second season.

We were having fun again, but that's not to say we weren't all dead serious about changing the direction of our football team. Bruce was earnest about the system he had created and professional about the way he pursued putting it in place. He told us how fortunate he was to have played and coached under some of the most knowledgeable minds in this game: Bill Walsh, Sam Wyche, Paul Brown, Forrest Gregg and Lindy Infante. Bright football minds. But more than their knowledge, Bruce said, the most important thing he took away from each of these men was the understanding of how essential *consistency* is to creating a successful football program.

"I'm going to be consistent with you when you're winning football games," he told us, "and I'm going to be consistent with you when you're losing."

That promise got tested, and that's where Bruce Coslet won my trust. He was true to his word. He didn't bail out, and believe me, when you start losing a few games in a city like New York, it's tough not to fold. Bruce didn't do that, and it began to pay off almost immediately.

So now I had a new home, a new coach, and that summer I became a new father, which was by far the most incredible thing I'd ever experienced. Angela gave birth to Ashtin Elizabeth Byrd on July 11, two and a half weeks before the due date. Angela prayed Ashtin would be born before I had to leave for training camp, and her prayer was answered. Still, it was hard leaving after only two weeks with our new baby, and when I got to camp, yet another change awaited me: a new position.

Pete Carroll had coached at Minnesota before joining the Jets. With the Vikings, he'd built a mobile, attacking, speed-oriented 4-3 defense anchored by a tackle in the middle who more or less "floated" from side to side, keying off the other team's guards. Carroll called this position the Eagle tackle. It was the key to his entire defensive scheme, and it required a player who was a blend of linebacker and defensive end, who had the size and the athleticism to roam the line, find the gaps, and burst through to close on the quarterback. At Minnesota, that player had been Keith Millard, who flourished under Carroll's system, becoming an All-Pro and the league's Defensive Player of the Year. The season before, Millard had led the league with eighteen sacks.

Now Carroll had brought his system to New York, and the player he was relying on to make it work was me.

I was elated. I had started the final five games the season before, and now I was going to be out there from the beginning, playing the kind of position I was born for. I wasn't the fastest guy in the league—I was no Chris Doleman, Millard's teammate at Minnesota. I didn't have the quickness of a Bruce Smith or the strength of a Reggie White. But I had *enough* quickness, *enough* speed, and *enough* size for this position. I was a hybrid, a blend, and that's exactly what the Eagle required.

Greg Robinson summed it up pretty succinctly early that training camp.

"We're just gonna put you in the middle," he said, "turn you loose, and let you kick some butt."

Sounded good to me.

The hardest thing about training camp that year was being away from my new baby, wondering what she was doing, what I was missing. Finally, after six weeks, Angela and Ashtin arrived, and I was stunned by how much she had already grown.

Just before we broke camp, I had yet another change laid on me: a new roommate.

Paul Frase had been my roommate the year before, and I almost didn't survive. He snored so loudly, it was like trying to sleep in a cave with a bear. I literally could not sleep. I'd wake up the day of a game with bloodshot eyes, after maybe a total of an hour and a half of real rest. I loved Paul, but I finally had to find a new roommate. If I hadn't, I would have dropped dead from sheer exhaustion.

Marvin had roomed with Ron Stallworth that year, and they were tight. So we were both surprised when Bruce put me with Marvin for the 1990 season. For a while, it didn't look like it was going to work.

Marvin was even more different from me than Lageman. He was black; I was white. He was a Texan; I was an Oklahoman, which anyone can tell you is not a match made in heaven. Marvin grew up on the streets of Dallas—he likes to say he's from concrete and I'm from grass. When I'd talk about hunting to Marvin— this was before he was married—he'd shake his head and say, "You're hunting the wrong kind of foxes."

Marvin was the flatlander who'd gone to the high country, playing his college ball in Idaho. We were both religious, but while I was a Christian, intent on getting together with others and sharing our faith, Marvin's was more private, more personal. We talked a lot about this, about his aversion to what he called "organized religion." He said he had his own relationship with Christ, and I respected that. I never tried forcing the way I worshiped on Marvin. I never tried forcing it on anyone.

Our first two months together, Marvin was hardly ever in our room. He spent most of his time down the hall with Ron. But as time passed, we started talking more and more. The last game of that season, we traveled to Tampa Bay, and somehow that weekend marked a real turning point for Marvin and me. I remember we sat out on the balcony of our hotel room, overlooking the bay, and we just really opened up. We must have been out there three hours. When we came back for camp at the start of the next season, we picked up where we left off, staying up late at night, having long philosophical discussions about everything from religion to race.

Marvin really educated me about what it is to be black in America; he really opened my mind. I'd always had a healthy attitude about racial issues, but there was so much I didn't know, so much I couldn't know, simply because I was white. Marvin helped me understand many things. I asked him question after question about Malcolm X, about Dr. Martin Luther King, people I really knew very little about. Marvin pointed out that there were a lot of people in the *black* community who really knew very little about these men, but that more and more, people were learning. He helped me realize how hungry we all are for our own history, blacks and whites alike, and how we can see the problems we have today more clearly if we understand more about our past.

Somewhere along the line, and I can't say just when—it wasn't a conscious decision, it was just something natural that evolved over time—Marvin and I began telling each other "I love you" just before going to sleep. It was just a simple heartfelt statement of the bond between two men. We weren't embarrassed or ashamed to share that feeling aloud.

Which is not to say we weren't on each other's case all the time, especially in the film room. If I did something wrong or if I really got planted, Marvin would make sure nobody in the room missed it. Of course I'd return the favor. Once he just got drilled. Totally knocked on his can. "Roached," as we call it, where you wind up lying on your back with your feet in the air. From the back of the room, I went, "*Ding! Ding! Ding!*" and the whole place started howling. I wasn't about to let a moment like that slip past without giving Marvin the barb.

We all drew closer that season—Marvin, Mersereau, Marty, Jeff, and the rest of the guys on defense. The whole team was clearly coming together. We weren't going to turn things around overnight, but we were starting to win almost as often as we lost, which was a vast improvement over the year before. And I was beginning to make a name for myself on the field.

It always puzzled a lot of people that I could be such a Clark Kent outside the football stadium and such a crazy man in it. It puzzled them, too, that I could claim to be a Christian and yet play such a violent position in such a violent game.

My answer to begin with is you've got to be careful when you use the term "violence." People use it too loosely in connection with football. They use it in the same way they talk about someone beating somebody up on the street. A distinction has to be made in terms of motivation. In most instances of societal violence, someone is out to *hurt* someone else. That's not the motivation on a football field. It's combat out there, it's explosive, and often brutal. But it's not personal, it's not about hatred and it's not about hurting someone. People *do* get hurt, but that's not the intent. The intent is to defeat your opponent, to hit him harder and play him better than he does you.

As for being a Christian, the Bible speaks openly and frankly about competition in a healthy manner, about running the race in the manner in which you will win. That's the way I played football. I usually played clean. And I had no problem knowing where the line was drawn between the aggressiveness you needed to have on the football field and the danger of that same aggression being carried out onto the streets.

I realize the sports pages occasionally look like a crime blotter, with the names of professional athletes beside the description of their arrest. But again, just as I've learned you can't judge a race of people by the actions of an individual, in the same way I don't think it's fair to generalize about professional athletes on the basis of the behavior of a few. I've read some commentators who warn that football players today are such fine-tuned, highly trained machines programmed for destruction that it's hard for them to turn *off* that aggression once they cross the sidelines. I think that notion is ludicrous, although I think it *was* true back when the use of steroids was much more unregulated and prevalent than it is today.

I know, because I was one of the players who used them.

It was the summer before my sophomore year in college, a brief time, six weeks, six very difficult weeks. The reason I tried them was simply the competition. I wanted to be bigger. I wanted to be stronger. It seemed like everybody at the time was taking steroids, and they were easy to get ahold of. If you had the money and could afford to do it, good for you. That was the prevailing attitude.

There was no enforcement to speak of. There were no NCAA tests. Coaches were fully aware of it. They didn't overtly encourage it, but they didn't discourage it either. They knew players were taking this stuff, but I never heard a coach say, "Don't. These things are bad for you."

I got bigger. I put on about fifteen pounds. And I got stronger. I was able to work harder in the gym, which is what steroids do. But it didn't take long for me to realize this stuff was poison.

I was wise enough to keep notes from the beginning, to keep a diary of what happened to me, not just physically but in other ways as well. I was extremely worried about side effects, and I quickly saw what these things did to my emotions, to my personality. I'm usually an up, happy guy. But now I was getting out of bed feeling bad. I was moody, testy, snapping at everybody, not a nice guy to be around at all. One day Angela said to me, "You know, you're *real* unpleasant. What's wrong with you?"

But she knew. It was the steroids.

Finally I stopped. I did get bigger and I had gotten stronger, but it wasn't worth it. And there's no telling what would have happened to me if I'd continued. The guys around me kept taking it, but that didn't bother me. I just worked harder in the weight room, because I knew what I was competing against now.

The thing to keep in mind is steroids don't make a guy a super football player. They simply help him work harder in the weight room. They help him get stronger, but he still has to get out there and *play*. Steroids have nothing to do with skill. They've got nothing to do with savvy or athleticism. And they've got nothing to do with desire. Those things come from inside. They don't come from the weight room. Physical strength is just one aspect of playing this game, one of many. Football is in your mind and heart just as much as it's in your body.

In the NFL today, steroids are almost nonexistent. The testing is incessant. One year I was tested nine times. There's no way you can use those drugs in the league today. Even masking agents are prohibited. Getting caught using a masking agent is the same as getting caught using steroids. There are penalties for both. The only steroid-type drug you can use and get away with it is HGH—human growth hormones—and the cost of those is something like twenty thousand dollars per cycle. A cycle is about eight weeks. That's what Lyle Alzado was taking when he was trying to make a comeback. We may never know what price Lyle ultimately paid. I'm just glad I knew better and put an end to it as quickly as I did.

Everybody's always looking for an edge in the NFL—in *any* professional sport, for that matter—but the guys who get it are the ones who are best prepared, mentally as well as physically. I was always among the first to arrive at the stadium on game day, hours before the kickoff. I would find a place off by myself, settle in, and play the entire game in my mind. Mental imaging is what they call it, and it was as crucial to me as all the hours spent on the practice field, in the film room, or with the weights.

I'd *see* the man I'd be playing against that day. I'd picture his flaws over and over, whether it was a bad step he had, whether he couldn't kick out of his stance well to pass block, or, conversely, whether he kicked out too *much* and left the inside open. Most important of all, I'd think about how good he was with his hands. Was he a lunger? A puncher? Or a catcher?

A lunger is a guy who's too aggressive. What you do is charge him quick, get right in his face, then, when he punches at you, you slip the punch, like a boxer. His aggression forces him totally out of position.

A puncher is almost always a veteran. He's been through the battles. He *knows* a guy's going to try to slip him, so he sits back and waits and waits until the last possible instant, then, when you get right up to him, *BOOM*, he just knocks the fire out of you. Not with his whole body. That would make him lose his balance, like a lunger. No, he just hits you with his fists, with short, compact, well-aimed blows. These guys are usually the best bench-pressers on the team. They've got that arm and chest strength, and they know how to *use* it, unlike the big raw massive guy who can lift a ton of weights and who goes out there and just tries to overpower you. I *love* playing against those great big guys, because they try to use all that strength in a way that's inappropriate for football. Raw strength is great when you're lying on your back for the bench-press, but it can get you in trouble when you're pass blocking. The best punchers are the guys who know how to use that strength, guys like Tunch Ilkin of the Steelers. He's the best puncher I ever played against.

Now, a catcher is a guy who's not coached very well, who just sits back and waits for people to run into him. He's the easiest kind to beat. No technique at all. He just absorbs you, like a mullet, a fish.

Beyond picturing what type of blocker the man across from me is, I also pictured the angles I was going to get that afternoon. Pass rushing is pure geometry. It's all about angles. You've constantly got three points to work with: the positions of yourself, the offensive lineman, and the quarterback. From the moment you line up, you're gauging where those points are going to be, then figuring out how to optimize the angle and distance between them. The factors affecting those points shift with each play: What down and distance is it? How many steps does the QB drop? Is he a five-step dropper or does he take seven? What point is it in the game? What's the score? How much time is left? Where on the field are you?

Of course the offensive linemen are computing at the same

time you are; they're figuring their own angles based on what they expect you to do. So it becomes a chess game between you and the guy across from you, with him reading and reacting to everything you show him, from the angle of your body, to where you line up, to how you charge him, to where you lined up the play before, even to where you're *looking*, where you're pointing your head.

That's the geometry. Then there's technique, the arsenal of attack skills that every pass rusher in the league is intimately familiar with:

- First there's the most basic move, the BULL RUSH, where you simply run straight through your guy to get to the quarterback. This is a classic move in a short drop situation, when the quarterback is only taking three or five steps. The best bull rusher in the business, hands down, is Reggie White. He could bull rush Kong into the Pacific.

- Another basic move is the RIP. This is where you dip your shoulder and explode up underneath the man, knocking him aside as you move past. The best ripper in the game, without a doubt, is Howie Long. This is a sharp, explosive move, and Howie's an explosive guy.

- Then there's the CLUB. You get an offensive lineman's weight going one way, by faking one direction, then, when he shifts, you bring your forearm over the top and club him in the direction he's shifting. Eric Dorsey of the Giants is one of the most brutal clubbers in the league. He wields his forearm like a war club. And Charles Mann of the Redskins, he's got a fearsome club. It hurts just thinking about it.

- The SWIM is a move used by the more athletic guys in the league. You rush right at the lineman, hoping he'll react with either a punch or a lunge. When he does, you raise your arm, bring it up just like a swimming stroke, hope his momentum has carried him under the arm, then come down with it and sweep him aside as you move past. The best swimmer I've ever seen is Bruce Smith. He's got that move down.

- Another athletic move is the SPIN. What you do here is drive the corner of a guy, then, as he pushes back, once he's committed his weight, you spin off in a kind of pirouette, twirling and shooting past him to the quarterback. Whenever I used this one, they called it the Tulsa Twist. The best spinner in the game used to be Mark Gastineau. He was unbelievable. Now Bruce Smith and Lawrence Taylor have put their names on this one.

• The PUSH/PULL is a two-step move. First you bull rush a guy, pushing into him with both arms. Then when he pushes back, you pull him past you. Keith Millard and our own nose guard, Gerald Nichols, are both awfully good at this.

• Then there's the SHAKE-AND-BAKE, a move much like a running back might use to fake out a tackler in the open field. You come right at the lineman, feint one way—the shake—then shoot past him the other—the bake. This is purely an athletic move. The league is full of guys who can just leave you dangling like a fool with the shake-and-bake. LT is one of them, of course. And Derrick Thomas of the Chiefs.

• Finally there's my personal favorite, the CHOP-SWIM. I invented this one—hey, I had to put my name on *something*. First you draw a punch from the lineman. Then you knock the punch aside with a downward chop and continue around with the same arm into an up-and-over swim. That's an awesome move when it works. Guys around the league knew it was my specialty and they prepared for it. Tunch Ilkin was coached to defend the move when we played Pittsburgh.

I'd hate to be an offensive lineman. Clubbed and ripped and chopped and spun all afternoon. That would be awful. You're taking a lot more than you're dishing out when you're on the offensive line. I really respect those guys.

Of all the offensive linemen I've played against I have the highest regard for Jim Ritcher, the left guard for the Bills. He's not much bigger than a pound of soap after a hard day's wash, but every time he came out on that field, he brought his lunch, and he was there all day. A very tenacious guy.

Not all the guys in the NFL are like that. There are some guys who are really good football players for about ten plays a game. The other sixty they take it easy. The great ones are the ones who

go all out every single down—guys like Jim Ritcher and his teammate Kent Hull, and Bruce Armstrong of the Patriots and Keith
Sims and Harry Galbreath of the Dolphins.

Which is not to say they're the cleanest players in the league.
Galbreath's nickname is "Dirty Harry." He's one of those guys, if
you're near him in a pile, he's going to get a lick in. As far as I'm
concerned, that's all right. That's just part of the game. There's
always something like that going on in a pileup. Everybody's not
just lying there waiting to get up. I don't hold something like that
against Harry. I'd just give it back to him.

Of course the goal of everything you do as a pass rusher is to get
to the quarterback. He's the ultimate target. There are some QB's
I've sacked more than others, but none more than Dan Marino. They
say Jeff Wright, the nose tackle for the Bills, sacked Marino more
than anyone in the league, but I'd dispute that. I think I sacked Dan
more times than any defensive lineman during my four seasons with
the Jets. I can think of six times I brought Danny down.

Not that it's easy. The Dolphins are always a tough team to play
because they have such a quick rhythm passing attack and Dan
can get rid of the ball so suddenly. It's very frustrating. Whatever
you do, even if you beat a guy clean, Danny is so quick, he'll simply dump the ball off. That's a tribute to his savvy and sharpness.
He knows the game so well, he knows precisely where his safety
valves are.

Still, I've gotten some of my best licks on him.

Now the hardest guy to sack in a purely physical sense is Ran-
dall Cunningham. I missed him more times than I missed anybody
else. He's got that speed, of course, and his tremendous vision
makes it almost impossible to get to him.

I missed Jim Kelly a lot, too, for some reason. Slow-footed Jim.
I don't know why, but time and again I'd have a hold on him and
somehow he'd slip away. I had him once in the end zone, and we
would have won the game if I'd gotten that safety, but he got
away. I still don't know how he got loose, but he did. Some guys
just have that knack.

As for sheer toughness, I never saw anyone like Jeff Kemp, who
filled in for Dave Krieg when we played the Seahawks my third
season. Kemp took a ton of shots that day just after letting go of

the ball. I hit him hard at least eight times. Eight times, and every one was a real blow, the kind of lick you always imagine. I hit him with everything I had, driving through him and planting him into the ground. Each time, he'd lie there a minute, compose his thoughts, then spring back up. I couldn't believe it. I was thinking, "Stay down, guy. Just stay *down*. You don't have to take this beating." But he'd just dust off his little body and hustle right back to the huddle. It was amazing. He earned my respect in that one game as the toughest quarterback I've ever played against. Ever.

I got to know a lot of quarterbacks in the 1990 season. The Eagle tackle position freed me up to do what I did best, which was basically roam the line and attack. I wound up with thirteen sacks that season, third among the league's linemen (behind Bruce Smith's nineteen and Reggie White's fifteen), and the most by a Jet since—who else?—Mark Gastineau had thirteen and a half in 1985. I came on strong at the end of the year, getting the bulk of those sacks in the last half of the season. That was the pattern throughout my pro career, coming on hard at the end. I think it has a lot to do with conditioning and never letting up. I was always a good fourth-quarter player, too. When other guys were winding down, that's when I was at my best, coming on strong.

I might have actually had a shot at the Pro Bowl that year. Unfortunately the voting is done in early December, with four games still to go. That hurts a strong finisher like me. I'd be lying if I said I didn't want badly to go to the Pro Bowl. But I already had what meant the most to me, and that was the respect of my teammates and the guys I played against.

We wound up 6-10 that season, but we knew we were going places now. We were incredibly young—twenty-three players on that team had no more than one year of NFL experience. It was clear that we were a club with a fast-approaching future. The rebuilding job Bruce Coslet had begun did not go unnoticed—he was named the league's Rookie Coach of the Year by one football magazine.

Angela and I really felt at home in New York by then. Our neighbors in Garden City and later in Point Lookout came to mean as much to us as our friends back home in Tulsa. We made some wonderful friends, people like the Muellers—Geisela and

Gerhardt—who lived a couple of houses down from us in Garden City. They had four boys, and those guys were like little brothers to me: Eric, Glenn, and the twins, Scott and Jens. I first met them when I looked outside after a snowfall and these kids were out there shoveling our sidewalk. The Mueller boys. I taught Scott how to drive, as a matter of fact—and I'm lucky to still be around.

Angela and I got to know our way around the city itself, to appreciate the variety of pleasures it has to offer. Of course that's not hard when you're a New York Jet. Doors are opened for you that aren't opened to everyone. People lead you to the best table in the restaurant, the best seats in the theater. It's a hard thing to get adjusted to if you're not comfortable being treated that way, and I'm not. The only place I ever sought to be anything special was on the football field. Off it I've never wanted to be anything but a normal person, just like everyone else. There were few things I looked forward to more during each football season than the twenty-one-hour drive back to Oklahoma when it was over. I always made that drive straight through, with Roxie, our chow, for companionship.

Still, New York was my second home, and I tried hard to get to know it. One of the most unforgettable experiences of my life was riding with some members of the New York City Police Department. My teammate Joe Mott set it up, through some friends he had on the force. They offered to let me go with them on their beat in a section of East New York, a burned-out hole of a place. I leaped at the invitation. I figured this would be a great opportunity to really see what the drugs and the poverty were like in this city. I had no idea what I was in for.

The first thing they did was put me in a flak jacket. When I climbed in the patrol car, the officer at the wheel handed me a pistol. I considered myself an expert with the guns I used at home for hunting, shotguns and rifles. But handguns were not my forte.

"This is in case, for some reason, we have to leave the car," he told me. "If you have to use it to protect yourself, don't hesitate."

I couldn't believe I was hearing this. I was wondering what in the world I'd gotten myself into.

It didn't take long to find out. We'd hardly gotten started when a call came over the radio and the next thing I knew we were rocketing down the street, pursuing a guy in a stolen Bronco, right there in the middle of the city.

The guy wound up careening around a corner and slamming into the curb. The Bronco was wrecked, flipped upside down, but the guy scrambled out and tried to run. By then, more police cars had arrived and a couple of officers were able to tackle the guy. I was standing there watching them arrest this man and load him up when a sergeant from one of the other cars looked over, recognized me, and just about went crazy.

"Get him *out* of here *NOW!!!*"

In ten seconds, I'd been whisked back to the patrol car.

"Man," I said, once we were inside, "is he mad at me or something?"

"Nah," the officer said. "He's not mad. He's just protecting you."

"*Protecting* me? From what?"

"Well," he said, "whenever a lot of police gather around like this, and there's a crowd around, a lot of times we get someone sniping at us from the rooftops."

"You're *kidding*," I said.

"No, I'm not. They'll either shoot down from the roofs or they'll stick a handgun out one of those windows and start popping."

Now that's something you just don't hear about in Tulsa.

I saw a lot of things that really opened my eyes and touched my heart in New York. I've always gotten out in the community in my own way, not because anyone asked me to and certainly not because I wanted anyone to know. On the contrary, I'd rather people didn't know. In college I'd often go over to the children's medical center there in Tulsa and spend time with some of the kids. I did that on my own. No one came along with me. No one ever knew I went. This was for the kids, not for anyone else. It's the least a guy can do, to spend a couple of hours with kids like this, just joking with them, picking them up, hugging them, and poking them in the side, just goofing off. That means so much to kids who are sick or sad or both. It means just as much to me.

That's why I responded in a minute when Erik McMillan and Brad Baxter and I were invited to go out and have dinner in Brooklyn one night with a group of kids whose dads were police officers who had been killed or injured in the line of duty. An organization called Survivors of the Shield worked to help some of these kids. I can remember them like it was yesterday. We went out to dinner several times, Mike and Joey, Robbie and Steve, Richie and Danny. That little Robbie really sticks out. He was just a little-bitty kid whose dad had been shot to death trying to wrestle down two drug dealers. So this little guy didn't have a father anymore. That really cut right through me.

So did the story of Jessica Guzman. That was all over the newspapers, how this ten-year-old girl had been missing and no one knew where she was and then she was finally found murdered. It was just so horrible for her family not to know where she was for so long and then to have it turn out that way. It was James Hasty and McMillan who asked me to go with them over to this little girl's school, St. John Vianney, a parochial school in the Bronx, where they were getting a scholarship fund started in her name. I'd already donated a check, but this was a chance to do something more, to show support in a personal way.

I've never been moved the way I was that day. All these little children and their parents were there, just weeping with grief and gratitude. They'd made all these mementoes in honor of Jessica, little placards and signs. Her parents were there, and I felt so helpless when I met them. I remember I hugged them, cried with them, and told them we were going to try to do whatever we could to help.

That was a hard day for me.

There is no way to even conceive how hard it was for them.

9

We came into the 1991 season with something the Jets hadn't had in a while—momentum. Our defense had upped its sack total the year before by ten (from twenty-eight my rookie year to thirty-eight in 1990), and even more was expected from us now. Our line was still basically a young group of kids, growing every game. Jeff had been switched from linebacker to end, and he was just getting untracked. Marvin had played only one year of college ball and was just now really learning the game, but he had unlimited ability. And I wasn't satisfied with the success I'd had in 1990. It meant nothing if our team wasn't winning football games.

The New York press was now comparing our line to the old Sack Exchange, calling us The Byrdmen of the Meadowlands. They were counting on me to be the leader. One columnist wrote, "This is the player who will supplant Lawrence Taylor as New York's most feared pass rusher, maybe even this year." That was going a little far, but I did have high hopes, both for the team and for myself.

What I wound up facing on the field was the same situation I'd seen in high school and college.

I was being double- and triple-teamed now on every play. Tampa Bay, Seattle, Buffalo, Chicago . . . game after game it was the same, two and three guys blocking me—someone sliding

down the line and maybe a running back tossed in for good measure. I was getting the fire beat out of me, taking a pounding.
After nine games I had just two sacks, and the same reporters
who had been comparing me to LT were now writing me off.
"Byrd has pretty much laid an egg this year," was the way one
described it.

I wasn't ecstatic, but I understood what was happening. I knew
all that attention on me meant my teammates were now freer to
step up and deliver. That's what the coaches were telling them
they had to do, and they did. Through those same nine games,
Marvin had six sacks and Jeff had four. Most important, we were
now a winning team. By mid-November, we were 6-5 and aiming
at the play-offs. That's when a tragedy happened in Detroit that
swept through the league like a shock wave.

That's when Mike Utley broke his neck.

It happened November 17. We'd just beaten New England 28-21.
Jeff and Kyle Clifton, one of our linebackers, had stuffed a run at
the goal line on the last play of that game to save it for us. I was in
the locker room getting changed when Bob Reese, our trainer,
came up and told me Utley had hurt himself against the Rams at
the Silverdome. I asked him how serious it was, and Bob said
word was he was paralyzed from his chest down.

I couldn't believe it. When you think of injuries, even debilitat-
ing ones, you think of knees and shoulders. You never imagine a
broken neck. I'd seen one broken neck in my career, and it was
one of the most unsettling experiences of my life.

It happened to a teammate of mine at Tulsa, a safety named
Marcus Anderson. It was my freshman year, and we were playing
Texas Tech. Marcus had just broken up a crossing pattern over
the middle with a good hit to the receiver. They came back with
the same thing on the next play, Marcus came up to hit the guy
again, but this time something went wrong. I can still see Marcus's body the instant after he delivered the hit. It was as if he
were frozen in midair, laid out in a prone, horizontal position a
couple of feet off the ground.

Then he just fell, face-first. He lay there motionless, his neck
broken.

They took Marcus to the hospital, and when he was released,

he was wearing something they called a halo vest. He wasn't paralyzed, but his football career was finished.

Now they were saying it had happened to Mike, only worse. There was doubt that he'd ever walk again. It was almost incomprehensible. And it had happened on the most routine of plays. Nothing fierce about it at all.

We met Detroit a month after Mike went down, so I had a chance to study that play over and over again in our film sessions. It was just a typical pass play. David Rocker of the Rams leaped up to block a pass, Mike lunged at him, missed, and fell to the ground, hitting his head. And that was it. Mike never got up.

My thought, over and over again, was, "Man, he got paralyzed from *that?*" It didn't even look like he'd taken a hit. It looked like he'd just fallen down.

I prayed a lot for Mike that month. The whole league was rocked by what happened to him. And the Lions became a team on a mission, playing on incredible emotion. They tore through us 34-20. They tore through everyone until the Redskins finally stopped them one game short of the Super Bowl, in the NFC championship. That's what Mike meant to the guys who loved him.

Meanwhile, we had our own mission to focus on. We went into the last game of the season head-to-head against Miami for the AFC's last wild card play-off berth. The Dolphins were waiting for us in Joe Robbie Stadium, knowing the winner of the game was in and the loser was out. We added a new wrinkle, slipping me out to left end, and it worked. I had six tackles, along with two and a half sacks of Marino, and we beat the Dolphins 23-20 in overtime for the sweetest win of my professional career. For the first time in five years, the Jets were in the play-offs.

That was the highlight of the season, meeting Warren Moon and the Oilers in the Astrodome, in one of the AFC's two wild card games. Bruce Coslet had been telling us all along that all we needed to do was get our foot in the door, get into the playoffs any way we could, and anything could happen.

We should have won that game. Houston had the best offensive line in football, seasoned and smart. And they had Bruce Matthews. I always put Jim Ritcher at the top of the list of linemen I respected, because he was such a fighter, such a scrapper. But Bruce Matthews was just flat *good*, the best offensive lineman in the game in my book.

Still, the year before I'd beaten him four times. I'd give him my chop-swim and slide around him. But the strange thing was I'd keep falling just as I got a bead on Moon. I couldn't figure out why. All day long, I thought I was catching my toe on the turf. It wasn't until I saw the game films later that I saw what was happening. Matthews was falling, all right, and each time he went down, he reached back with his foot and hooked me, that sly sucker. He wasn't the highest-paid guard in the league for nothing.

This day, our coaches tried yet another wrinkle, geared to Houston's run-and-shoot offense. They slanted me into the teeth of the Oilers' pass protection, inviting a double team and counting on our linebackers to then rush the ends. Good defense, bad execution.

It didn't work. At least, it didn't work well enough. We lost 17-10, and another season was through. We had tasted success now. We couldn't wait for the next one to start.

By then I was more deeply involved in my faith than ever, not only in New York, where our Wednesday night Bible study group had become a foundation of our life, but back home in Oklahoma, where Angela and I were both active in speaking to schools, youth groups, and churches. I'd been coming back to Mustang since I left for college, to our church and to the high school, keeping in touch with the kids there, letting them know what being a Christian had meant to my life. Now I was doing it not just there but across Oklahoma and in some of the surrounding midwestern states.

Angela sang and I spoke to youth groups in homes and churches and under tents all over Oklahoma, Texas, and Colorado. We had always felt a special bond with teenagers and children, and now that I'd become a professional athlete, we were using the opportunities that afforded to be a vessel for God and witness even more. I could see myself maturing, growing up, not just as a football player but as a husband, a father, and a man who cared about his relationship with Christ. More than ever, I was feeling the call to touch other people's lives through that relationship.

And it was that very calling that drew a shadow into my world that summer, a strange fear that's hard to describe, even looking back on it with all that has happened since.

It was a creeping anxiety that something terrible was about to befall me, that my maturing as a Christian would not go untested, that Satan was somehow getting ready to move against me.

I believe Satan is every bit as real in this world as Jesus Christ, and I sensed, as I had never done before, that he wanted to destroy my salvation, that in some way he was going to try to make me deny Christ. I knew how trials like this come, just as they do in the Bible. I knew the stories of Job, of Abraham, of Joseph. My trial, I felt, was going to come through my family, through Angela and Ashtin. I began praying for the Lord's protection over us. I prayed that if in His will some trial was to come for us, I would be strong enough and have the wisdom and courage to get through it.

Never in my life had I had a feeling like this. I had no idea what the trial might be, or *if* it would be. But I was very uneasy that summer. Just before I left for training camp, I called Rick Schaeffer, who was negotiating my second contract with the Jets.

Ever since I was a rookie, Rick had been urging me to buy an insurance policy to cover a career-ending injury. I'd always said no. My attitude toward injuries had been never to dwell on them, never to think about them if I could help it. In a way, a football player *has* to approach the game as if he's invincible, as if there's nothing that can stop him, nothing that can hurt him. Coaches encourage you to think that way, to play that way, with reckless abandon. That's how I had always approached football. You know the possibility of getting hurt is constantly there, but you can't be afraid of it. You can't even think about it, because fear is like a cancer. Once it's inside you, it begins eating at everything around it, growing until it takes over completely. Whenever you think you can get hurt, that's when you *do* get hurt.

I had always turned Rick down when he mentioned the insurance, but that July, I called him up and said let's get it. Rick did the rest. Before training camp was through, I had a policy through Lloyd's of London that would pay $705,000 if I sustained an injury that cut short my football career. The price of the policy was $9,000.

I also had a new contract. Rick and I had considered playing out the option year. Free agency was looming just around the corner, bringing with it skyrocketing salaries. But we didn't know how far around the corner it still was. Another consideration was the fact that teams were shifting away from paying large salaries to rookies based on potential and moving that money toward veterans who had proven they could produce. The Jets considered me one of those veterans. They proved that by offering me a contract that would pay me $550,000 for the 1992 season, $675,000 for the year after, and $825,000 in 1994. Those were close to the numbers Rick and I had targeted, so I signed.

By the time we broke training camp, the fear I had felt that summer had faded. In its place was an anticipation of the season ahead, one I was certain would be the best of my career.

How could it not? All the pieces were in place. Our defensive line was rock solid. Jeff had flourished the year before, leading the team with ten sacks. I'd come on strong at the end again and wound up with seven. Marvin finished third with six.

The success we'd had moving me outside against Miami got the coaches thinking during the off-season. Marvin had shoulder surgery that summer, so they had to do something about left end. It didn't take long for them to decide that's where I'd be. With Jeff at one end and me at the other, they pictured the kind of pinching one-two punch the Vikings had had with Millard and Doleman. One reason Bruce Coslet said he wanted me out there was because I was "a quick-around-the-corner type of guy."

It would be precisely that, a quick-around-the-corner type of move, that would shatter my life. But I didn't know it then. All I knew was how eager I was to get the season started.

I'd arrived in camp with a Mohawk haircut, something to get the guys' juices flowing. Mers said he liked it so much he was thinking of getting one himself. I'd never seen the team so loose, and it showed. We went undefeated in the preseason, winning five games, and our defense was stellar. I even scored my first touchdown as a Jet, a seven-yard interception return against Philadelphia on a ball thrown by my old buddy Jeff Kemp.

There was no reason to be overly worried when we lost our regular season opener in Atlanta, no reason to suspect that when our first-round draft pick, tight end Johnny Mitchell, went out that day with a separated shoulder, it would be the first of what would become a season-long avalanche of injuries. No reason to fear that what we figured to be a dream year was about to turn into a nightmare.

We lost the second game, too, against Pittsburgh. Worse, Jeff blew out his knee hitting Neil O'Donnell, the Steelers' quarterback. The way Jeff laid there holding his leg when that play was done, I knew it was bad. When I got back to the sidelines, I asked Jeff if he was going to be okay. He said they told him he was done for the year. My heart stopped.

They were right. It turned out Jeff had torn his anterior cruciate ligament. Losing him like that was a huge shock to the team. And it was hard for him in so many ways, not the least of which was he was a single guy living alone. His dad and mom and brother came up from Virginia to spend a couple of days with him after his surgery, but when they went back home, he was by himself. I knew how tough it was just getting around with a knee like that. Most single guys don't spend too much time in the kitchen as it is. With a bum knee, I knew Jeff wasn't doing any cooking at all, so Angela and I made him a few meals and I carried them over to him—ham and stuffing one night, some stir-fry another, and his favorite, hot oriental noodles. Jeff loved those noodles.

Marvin stepped into Jeff's spot and did a great job, but you could feel it in the air. The year before we'd had few injuries to speak of, but now our guys suddenly seemed to be dropping like flies. Hamstrings, shoulders, ankles, ribs, knees, feet, groins, backs, fingers, thumbs—before the season was through, twenty-two of our players missed a total of 109 games, including eleven starters.

Including me. I went down in game four, against the Rams in Los Angeles. It was the middle of the second quarter, and I had beaten their right offensive guard, number 71. Jim Everett stepped up, and as I dove at his legs, I stretched out my right arm to reach for him and hit the turf, popping out my shoulder.

Now, for the first time in my career, I had to watch my teammates from the sidelines. I'd never missed a regular season game. Not in high school, not in college. And I had an unsettling feeling about why this had happened.

I've always been extremely superstitious about injuries in that I refuse to talk about them. A couple of days before the Rams game, one of Angela's friends, Chimene Wood, came by to visit us at our home at Point Lookout. Somehow or other she wound up asking me if I ever worried about getting hurt. I told her no, and I added that I preferred not talking about it. Apparently it was too late. That Sunday was when I went down in L.A.

My only consolation that afternoon was hosing the Ram fans on the way to the locker room. Steve Nicholas was walking beside me, holding my right arm aloft, to keep my shoulder raised. We were rounding the back of the end zone, pretty close to the bleachers, and some of these guys in the stands were having a good time giving me a *hard* time. I still had a water bottle in my left hand, and those things squirt pretty well—well enough to give some of those Ram fans a nice bath, which I did. Next thing we knew they were raining beer and empty cups at us, most of which were landing on Steve.

"Dennis," he said, wincing and covering up, "what are you *doing* to me?"

Steve was soaked with beer when we got to the X-ray room, where he and Dr. Hershman had a hard time popping my shoulder back in place. Eventually they wound up standing on the table above me, one at each shoulder, pulling me apart like a wishbone until the shoulder snapped back into its proper position. The thing had hurt plenty when it snapped out, but it was nothing like the pain I felt the moment they snapped it back *in*.

The next four weeks were killers, watching from the sidelines with that separated shoulder as we beat New England for our first win of the year—we got seven sacks in the game, and all I could do was lick my chops—then lost to Indianapolis and Buffalo. One bright spot was we had a bye in there, so I missed just three games instead of four. I was chomping at the bit, spending my energy on pranks since I couldn't spend it on the field. I went for an old standby one afternoon, taking a can of adhesive spray and coating the stool in front of Mers's locker with it. It couldn't have worked more perfectly. When Scott came in after practice, he stripped down to his jock, then took a seat. His reaction was not calm. Suffice to say they had to peel Scott off that stool. Or vice versa.

Paul Frase got married that bye Sunday, and he was pretty nervous. The wedding was scheduled for right after practice, and he was walking on eggshells all day, worried he might get hurt, that *something* would go wrong. He had his entire wedding outfit— tuxedo, shoes—hanging in his locker, ready to go the minute he came off the field. So how could I *not* fill those shoes with shaving cream? Anyway, it was good for Paul. His rage pushed some of that nervousness out of the way.

It actually looked like things might take a turn for the better when I came back for the Miami game at home the first week in November. The Dolphins were 6-1, tied with the Bills for the AFC East lead, but our defense dominated them that day. I had no numbers to speak of, no sacks or tackles, but I was breathing down Marino's neck most of the afternoon. Marvin took Danny down for a safety that day—the first time Marino had ever been sacked for a safety—and no one was happier than I was, except maybe Marvin. It felt fantastic to be back out there, hooting and hollering, cheering the fans on, getting them into the game. I remember thinking to myself, Boy, I hope I never get hurt again.

The next week we went to Denver, where Al Toon, one of the best receivers in the league, a Pro Bowler, went down with a concussion, and we went down 27-16. We came back with a win against Cincinnati at home, then got hammered at New England.

I dragged home that evening about midnight, feeling as low as I could remember. We were 3-8 and we'd just been pounded by the Patriots, who hadn't won a game that season until the week before. When I came through the door, there was Ashtin. She often stayed up late like that on Sundays, waiting for me to get in. I picked her up and carried her over to the sofa. Ange climbed down beside us and we started talking about this whole year, how awful it had been losing Jeff, me hurting my shoulder, the team doing so poorly. Just sitting there like that was wonderful. I felt so good that night, just knowing I had my wife and my little girl, just holding them both in my arms.

I had no way of knowing how ominously the rest of that week would unfold.

It began Monday, when we were breaking down films from the Patriots game. Pat Kelly, one of our special teams players, had made a head-first tackle on a punt return, slamming a guy on the sidelines. Pat got leveled, and he had come up dizzy, groggy. He had to have help getting to his feet. It looked bad, even on film, and Al Roberts, our special teams coach, jumped all over Pat for making a hit with his head like that.

"Son," he said, "I don't *want* to come in here someday and see you paralyzed."

That afternoon, on the way home from practice, I stopped into a toy store to pick up something for Ashtin. I don't know why, but I wound up picking out a doctor's kit. It had everything—a little plastic thermometer, a stethoscope, a little blood pressure wraparound cuff, a syringe, some Band-Aids, and a couple of little fake casts. She and I played with it all the rest of that week. I'd lie on the couch, and she'd come in and doctor Daddy.

That Tuesday night, Erik McMillan was robbed in his own home. He and his girlfriend were held at gunpoint while their house was ransacked. That was such a bizarre, unsettling incident. We were glad no one was hurt, but something strange certainly seemed to be in the air.

The next day, Wednesday, was when Angela verified something we'd discovered the night before with a home pregnancy kit. We were going to have another baby. That was the big topic of discussion as our Bible study group gathered Wednesday evening. Paul and Allison Frase, Cary and Mindi Blanchard, Mark and Jana Boyer, Mike and Polly Haight, Troy and Sarah Johnson, Don and Darci Odegard, and the Jets team minister, George McGovern, and his wife, Cindy, were usually there, but this being Thanksgiving week, it was a smaller group: just the Blanchards, the McGoverns, and us.

We always had very earnest discussions at those gatherings, and that night the Bible passage we looked at was in Acts, in chapter three, where John and Peter are walking into a temple to worship, and as they're entering, they pass a man at the entrance who has been paralyzed since birth. The man asks them for alms, and instead of giving him money, Peter tells him to rise and walk, in the name of Jesus Christ. And he does.

We talked about that story late into the evening. Then I closed with a prayer. "Lord," I said, "give me the opportunity to be a greater witness to my teammates."

The next day was Thanksgiving. Cary and Mindi were with us. We'd gotten real close as couples ever since Cary had joined the team early in the season, after Jason Staurovsky, an ex-teammate of mine at Tulsa, had been let go as our kicker.

Cary had played his college ball at Oklahoma State and he'd grown up in Texas, so we had a lot in common. He and Mindi were also religious. They'd joined our Bible study group soon after they arrived, and Mindi and Angela had become good friends right away. Mindi would spend the night with Angela sometimes when we played away games.

We ate dinner and watched the TV game that day, Dallas against Detroit. Before the kickoff, they did a pregame piece on Mike Utley. Then, there he was, wheeling out beside his teammates on the sidelines. Seeing Mike like that brought up all the feelings I'd had watching the films of his injury the year before. Only now my feelings were compounded, seeing him out there in his wheelchair with the guys he loved. It was all I could do to keep watching. All of us got pretty choked up. And the fact did not escape me that of all the Bible passages we could have selected the night before, we'd picked one about a man who could not walk.

Then came Friday, and another bombshell. Al Toon, who'd been a Jet for eight years and was still at the top of his game, shocked all of us by suddenly announcing he was quitting the game. We got word on the practice field, before the Jets released the news

to the media. The concussion Al had suffered against Denver was
the ninth of his career. The doctors were telling him now that he
faced possible brain damage if it happened again. That was all he
had to hear.

It was easy to see why Bruce Coslet would eventually sum
up the catastrophic chain of events by saying, "There's never been
a season like this in anybody's history . . . just a lousy damn
season."

We were falling apart from injuries and bad breaks. But we still
had five games to play. The code that had been tempered during
the tough times at Tulsa was still at the center of me. We still
owed somebody five games of full-out football. We owed it to ourselves as well. Everyone on the team felt that way. There was no
point looking back. We had Kansas City to think about Sunday.

I'd always played well against the Chiefs' offense. I'd always
gotten a few sacks against them, which was just what I needed
since I hadn't had one yet all year. I had taken to referring to
myself as His Royal Sacklessness, and I couldn't wait to drop that
title.

The night before the game, the team checked into the Marriott
Glenpointe Hotel in Teaneck, New Jersey, where we always stayed
when we played at home. Marvin and I watched a movie on pay
TV—*A League of Their Own*. Then we talked for a while. Marvin
had a book of clichés, and I was reading it aloud, quizzing him on
where these clichés came from. Finally we hit the lights.

"Marvin," I said in the darkness, "I love you."

"I love you, too, Dennis," he answered.

I was up the next morning at 8:15, same as always. Marvin had
already gone downstairs for a cup of coffee. The whole team had
breakfast in the hotel restaurant, then Bruce got up and gave his
thoughts about the game, kind of a *pre*-pregame speech.

The first bus left for the stadium. Some of the guys climbed
aboard, others went back to their rooms to wait for the second
bus. And a few drove over themselves. That's the way I usually
went, catching a ride with Marvin or Mersereau or Louie Aguiar.
That day I took Louie's truck.

Louie had been a rookie free agent the season before, and we took to each other right away. He's a country kind of guy, a cow-boy, pretty big for a punter, about six-two, 200 pounds. He'd played his college ball at Utah State, had grown up in Livermore, California, just outside Sacramento, and had some Aztec Indian in him on his mother's side. He was into the outdoors, he loved rodeos, and he turned me on to Louis L'Amour novels. I felt like we were kindred souls. And Angela loved Louie. He was single, so we'd invite him out to the house all the time, where often as not he'd fix fajitas for us.

Louie tossed me the keys to his truck that morning and went back to bed. There was no need for *him* to get over there three hours early. How much time do you need to get ready to punt?

I got to the stadium shortly after ten. The trainers already had our stuff all laid out, each guy's gear set out at his locker. I put my day bag down and pulled out my memory sack. That was always the first thing I did, a natural reflex I hardly thought about. For the next couple of hours, I'd have that sack in my hands, fiddling with it, rubbing the beads.

I grabbed a copy of "Game Day," the NFL's program for that day in the league, leafed through it, and got a cup of coffee. Hamp—Bill Hampton, Jr., our head equipment guy—had made a pot, as usual. Kyle Clifton always called Hamp's coffee "mud." The mud was especially stiff that morning.

I took the coffee and visited with Scott Mersereau and Paul Frase and some of the other early birds: Jim Sweeney, our center; linebacker Kyle Clifton; Bill Pickel, one of our tackles. You don't usually see the glory-position guys in the locker room that early. No quarterbacks, no running backs. Just the grunts, the hard-hats.

And the trainers. They're always there, bantering with and berating the players. I remember saying, "Oh, this is a rough crowd today," as I went in to get my ankles taped. It was always Joe Patten who taped my ankles.

After Joe was done, I put on my pants and socks and went back so Joe could "spat" my shoes, putting another layer of tape on over the outside of them. Then I stepped over, grabbed a marker, and drew the ichthus on the outside of both ankles.

The second bus hadn't come yet, it was only about 11:00, but already Paul Frase and I were heading out to check the field. You've got five or six different pairs of shoes to choose from every game, depending on the field and the conditions, whether you're playing on grass or turf, whether it's wet or dry, hot or cold.

It was cold that day, in the low forties. Overcast, with a little bit of a breeze. The field was moist to the touch, but not wet enough to worry about. I decided to go with my flats, basketball-type shoes with no cleats, no nubbies.

I grabbed a ball and Paul and I played a little catch, going over the plays, covering the coaching points. We knew we had to stop their running game so we could make them pass. Christian Okoye and Barry Word, they were both tough running backs, Okoye with that monstrous size and strength, Word with his speed.

By 11:30 I was back at my locker, starting to get my mind right. I kept a CD player there, along with a selection of pregame music, mostly heavy metal, something to help get that fire started.

All the guys were there by then, starting to pull the shoulder pads on. One thing all linemen do is cover their pads with carpet tape, which is sticky on both sides, so when the jersey is pulled on it sticks tight. You don't want to give your opponent anything loose to grab onto. In previous seasons, we sprayed silicone all over the outside of the jersey as well, until it was slicker than snot. But the league put a stop to that. Now they were fining you $2,400 if you got caught using silicone, $4,000 for a second offense. Anything after that, you began losing game time.

But carpet tape was still okay. About twenty-five minutes before going out for warm-ups, all the linemen would begin putting on their pads and jerseys, because it took about that long to squeeze into that stuff. You want to cinch those pads as tight as you can, get someone to help you pull those strings as hard as possible. Some guys tie them so tight they can't move their arms. Marty Lyons cinched me up once before a game against Green Bay and actually cut off my circulation. My whole left arm began turning blue. I was wrapped tighter than a Christmas package. And I knew not to ask Marty to help me out anymore.

By the time we were ready to go out, the little guys—the wide receivers and backs—were already gone. The linemen were always the last to leave.

Just before we'd hit the field, we'd all stand in the tunnel and pace, nobody saying a word. Then Larry Beightol would come out. *BOOM*, the doors would explode open, and Bec would huddle us up and give us a little pep talk in that deep, gruff voice of his. He talked like a chubby little drill sergeant.

By the time you get to the pros, you've heard so many pep talks, you might think there's nothing left to listen to. But I found there was always *something* pertinent in what a coach had to say before a game, and I always listened for that. I wasn't looking for something to psyche me up. If you haven't already done that by the time you're about to take the field, it's too late.

Then it was out onto the field for warm-ups. You stretch, break a sweat, but you don't want to get tired. You just want to do enough to get your system going.

Then it's back inside to wait.

I hated that part. I'd waited long enough. I was always ready to go *now*, but it was still thirty minutes to game time.

So I put the earphones back on. Put my memory sack back in my hands. I prayed. I thought.

And then it was time.

"Bring it in!" Bruce called, and everyone came together. I put the sack back on its hook and took a knee along with my teammates. We said the Lord's Prayer in unison. Then a moment of silence. Then a simple sentence from Bruce:

"Let's go get 'em, fellas."

There's nothing like that feeling of sprinting out onto a football field at game time, emerging from the darkness of a stadium tunnel into the light of a Sunday afternoon, the sound of your echoing footsteps and the muted roar of the crowd replaced by the blast of 57,000 fans rocking the air you breathe. If you've got any fire in you at all, it's flaming by then.

We won the toss and received. Three plays, Louie came in to punt, then it was time for our defense.

The Chiefs did what we expected, running Word and Okoye mostly off the guards. We nailed them pretty well that first series, mostly for just one- and two-yard gains. Dave Krieg had to throw the ball, which was what we wanted. But Krieg started out hot, hitting his first four passes, and they came away from that first series with a field goal. They got another at the start of the second quarter, and that's where we were at the half, down 6-0.

I remember Greg Robinson coming up to me and saying the pressure was going good. I was getting by Rich Valerio, the Chiefs' right tackle, a lot. "Just keep it up," Greg told me. "You're gonna get there."

The Chiefs took the second-half kickoff at the west end of the stadium and returned it to their 25. First down Krieg rolled my way and threw a quick sideline pass.

Incomplete.

Second and ten.

They broke their huddle, came to the line, and I *knew* it was a pass by the way Valerio was set. There was the down, too. And the yardage. And their position on the field. Everything said it was going to be a pass.

I remember adjusting outside just a touch. I was counting on Krieg taking a deep drop, seven steps.

On the snap, I came right at Valerio, then chopped him and slid around the outside. There's always a point in the pass rush where you know you've got the guy beat, and I'd reached that point. I'd beaten Valerio cleanly.

I remember coming around the corner, leaning in and lowering my shoulder to keep Valerio from getting back on me. You plant everything low at a point like that, dipping your body and driving with everything you've got, turning the corner at top speed.

I could see Krieg right then, his white jersey filling my field of vision. He was actually above the spot I expected, which was great. That's just how you want it.

But then he stepped up.

Krieg must have seen me, too. Or sensed me. Typically, a quarterback will set up at the back of the pocket and let the offensive tackle ride an outside-rushing defensive end on by. But Krieg, seeing I was bearing down on him so fast, saw that the only way out for him was to step up.

Now it was all physics. My momentum and sheer centrifugal force were slinging me out even as I was straining to lean in. At this point I knew I was not going to be able to tackle Krieg, so I chopped at the football with my right arm as I came past. I remember focusing on that football, bringing my hand down, actually hitting it, and then . . .

In an instant, in the millisecond it takes to bat an eye, something rose in front of me like a wall. A huge green wall, inches from my face, my body hurtling through the air with all its might.

All my years of training, the thousands of tackles I'd made, the way I'd been taught to hit with my head up, to keep that spine bent so it can take a blow, all that meant nothing at that instant. I wasn't making a tackle. My reaction wasn't that of a football player. It was an instinctual reaction, the reaction anyone would have when they're suddenly about to slam into something head-on and they've got a thousandth of a second to respond.

I ducked.

I ducked my head *down* instead of raising it up. I hunched my shoulders, pulling in my head, all in an instant.

I felt a solid thump. And everything slowed down.

Everything fell away.

Then everything stopped.

DESCENT

10

I still had my uniform on, from helmet to shoulder pads to shoes, as the ambulance pulled out from beneath Giants Stadium. My body was lashed down from head to toe. All I could move were my eyes. But I could hear the siren as we lurched into traffic, racing toward Manhattan's Lenox Hill Hospital.

Pepper Burruss was gripping my helmet as Steve Nicholas sliced off my wrist tape and the tape around my shoes and ankles, then slipped off my gloves, shoes, and socks. He cut open my pants and jersey, then sliced open my shoulder pads. He could see I was having trouble breathing. The pads I had cinched so tightly before the game were squeezing in on muscles that could no longer resist them.

I could sense Steve fiddling with my feet. I could feel the pressure of something being laid across my legs.

"I can *feel* that!" I exclaimed. "Is that good? Is that a good sign?"

He didn't answer. Suddenly I could feel us pulling off the road onto the shoulder, coming to a stop. The ambulance had been bouncing too much for Steve to attach the IV lines, so he'd asked the driver to stop a minute. Then we were moving again, the ambulance rocking and bumping as we weaved around the traffic where it was thickest, trying to save every second we could. I could hear the driver commenting how lucky we were that the lanes weren't as crowded as usual for a Sunday afternoon.

Every time I was touched, from an IV line being put into my arm to my uniform being sliced, I made a point that I could feel it. I was trying to convince Steve, trying to convince myself, that everything was going to be all right.

My mind raced to Mike Utley.

"Was Mike able to feel anything?" I asked. "Is this what it was like for Mike?"

No answer. Steve must have really been feeling the adrenaline, because Angela was wearing that fur coat and wasn't even hot, yet Steve was soaked with sweat, just dripping with it as he worked around me while Pepper held my head.

Ange must have told me she loved me a hundred times, over and over and over again. She tried kissing my face but couldn't because of the mask. Pepper cut my chin strap, then tried unscrewing the mask, but the grommets wouldn't budge.

I wasn't thinking about football anymore. For the first time, I asked a question that would become the focal point of my entire life in the months to come.

"Steve," I said, "am I going to be able to walk again?"

His answer was dead honest, one I would hear repeated by every doctor I dealt with.

"Dennis," he said, "I don't know."

I looked toward Angela, who was leaning over me, keeping herself in my field of vision.

"Ange, I don't care about football," I said. "All I want now is to be able to hold you and Ashtin. That's all I care about."

Her eyes were wet with tears as she put her face as close to mine as she could, gripping my left hand and stroking it.

"Don't worry," she said. "*We'll* hold *you.*"

Then we prayed, Pepper and Ange and I.

There were trials ahead of me that I could not imagine, so many moments where my faith and strength would be tested, but none would be more crucial than the prayer we shared inside that ambulance. Because it was then and there that I found the inner core of peace that would see me through everything to come. It was at that moment, en route to the hospital, that I turned everything over to the Lord, that I put it all in His hands.

There's a power to a moment like that that can only really be understood by someone who's experienced it. In a way, it's a total surrender, a serenity that comes from letting go of pain or fear or sorrow and putting it all in the hands of something far stronger than anything we can feel or imagine, putting it in the hands of the Lord. But it's not a simple matter, achieving that serenity, making that surrender. It takes faith. It takes true belief, the kind of acceptance and assurance that's rooted deep in a person's soul, beyond words or even thoughts.

I had that faith. I had that feeling. I had no idea what lay ahead of me, but I knew this was going to be a test, a trial in my life for which I would need God's help and a strong faith. And I believed I had both those things. I had spent my entire life reading the Bible, studying the scriptures, learning about God and Jesus Christ. I understood that the Lord has plans for people and their lives that we sometimes have no way of comprehending. There had been plenty of times in my life when I'd had the opportunity to bail out, to say, "Hey, God, why did you do this? Why did you do that?" But I never had bailed out before. And I wasn't about to now.

Which is not to say that I didn't feel fear at that moment and that I wouldn't continue to feel it again and again in the coming days and weeks. This was going to be tough, no question. Tortuous feelings and emotions were going to be flooding through me for a long time. Questions without answers were going to beat at my brain, frustrating me, filling me with anger at times. But none of those feelings would ever be stronger than my faith in the Lord. Having that foundation, knowing He was going to see me through whatever was to come and that there was a plan, a purpose, for whatever that might be, gave me a strength I knew I would always be able to fall back on.

It wasn't just for myself that I'd need that strength. I knew I'd need it for Angela and Ashtin, and for my teammates, too. The people who loved me needed to see I was strong so they could find that same strength in themselves. In a situation like this, if you start sinking, you don't just go down by yourself—you take a lot of other people down with you.

We were only in that ambulance forty minutes before it pulled up to the emergency room doors of Lenox Hill, on East Seventy-seventh Street. Just before we got there, it occurred to me to ask a question I'd normally ask immediately after a play like the one that had put me here.

"Ange," I said, "did I get the sack?"

Then the doors opened and everything began whirling around me. People passing on the sidewalk stopped and looked as I was lifted out of the ambulance, then rolled through Lenox Hill's emergency room doors. As they pushed me inside, it felt like every hospital movie I'd ever seen, the patient lying on his back, the lights and ceiling tiles flashing by, the gurney being wheeled around one corner, then another, the IV lines connected to the bottles of clear fluid, all swaying above me as we rushed into the emergency room. Ange was taken away and told to wait.

No sooner was I wheeled into a room for X rays than Pepper had a cast cutter in his hands. I remember a nurse asking, "Is this the football player?" An odd question, considering I was still in full uniform, still in my shoulder pads, my green Jets jersey in tatters, my helmet still around my head. I remember the nurse's name. It was Mercedes.

It struck me how jarring this whole scene was, how none of this fit together. Here I was, this professional football player, outfitted like the warrior I had been, wearing the armor that validated me as a man in so many ways, and I was utterly helpless. Paralyzed.

It's hard to explain how much my physicality meant to me, how much it means to any professional athlete. I had a beautiful wife, a beautiful daughter, and another child on the way. Those things were really important to me, but so was my body. I was six-feet-five inches tall. I weighed 270 pounds. I was fast, and I was strong, among the best in the world at the game I loved. My physical size and strength were a big part of what defined me. My body said, "Hey, look. I'm a professional football player. I do *this.*"

I thought about how this defined to me my wife as well, this guy with all these physical attributes. As long as I had known Ange, ever since high school, I had always been this football star, this football hero. Now I wondered how I could validate myself to her without being those things. I wondered how she'd feel about me if the football player was gone, even though I knew it wasn't the football player that had mattered to her in the first place.

Those thoughts would come back later, but now Pepper was turning on the cutter. The whine of that small saw as he lowered it to my helmet to slice off my face mask was incredibly loud, almost excruciating.

There were four grommets attaching the mask to the helmet and Pepper had to cut off each one. Chips and dust flew from the saw and covered my face. Finally, Pepper was able to pull off the mask. Then, very gently, as carefully as if they were handling an egg, Steve and Pepper lifted my head slightly and slid off the helmet. Pepper kept my head suspended as Steve cut off the rest of my jersey and took off my shoulder pads. The rest of my clothing came off, too. Then Steve put a catheter in my penis, not just to drain my bladder but to test for spinal shock, to see how I responded when he did a rectal examination.

By now the IVs were pumping steroids into my veins, to stem the swelling in my spinal cord. There was no telling yet about the extent of damage to that ropy bundle of nerves—whether it had been bruised or even torn to some degree—but it was critical to keep the swelling down as much as possible in these first hours, because swelling can put pressure on the nerves to the point of damaging them permanently.

Steroids cut the swelling, but they also wrack the body with nausea. And I was being pumped full of the stuff. Within fifteen minutes of the first dose I started throwing up. Vomit was just bubbling out of my mouth, running all over Pepper's and Steve's arms and hands. I couldn't turn my head to empty my mouth and I couldn't blow it out because my insides were paralyzed, too. I didn't have the muscle strength to even blow my nose. There was no way I could spit out this vomit.

So Pepper and Steve had to take care of it. Each time I was about to heave, I would tell them, and gently, ever so slightly, they would roll my body to one side and let the vomit run out of my mouth onto their hands and arms.

The X rays they took in the emergency room showed nothing. Then they rushed me to the third floor for a CAT scan—a three-dimensional X ray of the head—and *that's* where they saw it: The fifth cervical vertebra, at the base of my neck, was fractured. Now they could see what they already knew. My neck was broken.

But they needed to see more. They needed to know the extent of the damage, in what ways and how badly I was hurt. They needed to run an MRI scan—magnetic resonance imaging—which is a three-dimensional X ray of the entire body. The MRI machinery was down the block in another building, so I had to be wheeled back into another ambulance. I was groggy now, half drunk from exhaustion and throwing up constantly. People's voices sounded muddy. Everything had that kind of soft glow you feel when you're going under. I saw Angela for a moment. And Pepper above me, Steve beside me, and Mercedes, the nurse, hurrying behind, holding the IV lines.

And then I saw Marvin, leaning over me as we waited in the ER for an ambulance to arrive. The team had been told not to come tonight, to wait, but there was no way Marvin was waiting.

His eyes were so red, he didn't have to say a word. I knew how he felt. He took hold of my hand, walking beside the gurney as they wheeled me along.

"We'll be here, man," he said. "Hang in there. Get through the night. Everything's gonna be okay."

Then they took me down the street. Just getting me up to the MRI room was a struggle. Pepper and Steve and the two ambulance attendants had to tilt and turn me, squeezing up tight stairways and down narrow halls. The building we were weaving through was made for outpatients, not for gurneys—especially not for a gurney carrying a six-foot-five, 270-pound football player.

When we finally reached the room, Pepper backed in first, still holding my head. As they were setting me up, Pepper felt something tugging at his back pants pocket. He felt the same tugging in the front pocket of his shirt. Then he realized what was happening. The magnetic field of the machine was so strong it was pulling the screwdriver he'd used on my helmet out of his back pocket and lifting the scissors they'd used on my uniform out of his shirt.

It was that magnet that would wrap around my body. An MRI test is done by sliding a person into a long narrow tube. It's a claustrophobic experience for anyone, but in my case it was terrifying. First, the tubes are built for average-sized human bodies. Mine barely fit. But worse than that was the fact that Pepper and Steve had to let go of my head. They hadn't let go of me since first putting their hands on my helmet. But now I was leaving them behind as they tucked sandbags on either side of my head and slid me into this cylinder. Alone.

Going into that tube was one of the most horrifying experiences of my life. I was surrounded by a metallic pinging sound as the machinery around me was turned on. But this time the sound wasn't just invading my head. It was wrapping around my entire body, as if I'd been put inside the belly of some robotic creature. My only connection with the world outside was a little microphone through which the technicians could talk to me. That, and I could talk to Steve, who was standing at my feet, holding my toe to let me know he was there.

I was so scared. I knew if I vomited now, there was no one to help me, no way to clear my mouth. I had visions of suffocating, choking to death on my own vomit. Steve was worried about that, too. Each time I felt I was about to puke, I'd call his name. Immediately they'd stop the test, slide me out, and Steve would turn me to the side so I could vomit.

Five times they had to stop the test and pull me out. Five times the whole cycle of fear and terror began again.

Finally the MRI was done. It was seven o'clock, more than four hours since I'd been on the field.

By now a team of doctors had assembled at the hospital. Jim Nicholas, the chairman of the Jets medical staff and director of orthopedics at Lenox Hill, had called ahead from the stadium, alerting the hospital and gathering a team of specialists, who were now all there: Dr. Nicholas; Dr. Stanley Blaugrund, Lenox

Hill's chief of ear, nose, and throat medicine; Dr. Lewis Rothman, the hospital's chief of radiology; and Dr. Martin Camins and Dr. Patrick O'Leary. Camins, a neurosurgeon, and O'Leary, the hospital's chief of spinal surgery, were longtime partners in the operating room as well as out—they'd written two books together on the subject of the cervical spine.

By the time I was rolled back into Lenox Hill's ER, the team was all studying the MRI pictures, not just looking at the break itself and whether bone fragments might be pressing against the cord, but also checking for compression and displacement of the spine and the extent of damage to the disc beneath that fractured vertebra. They were concerned about swelling of the cord itself, too. If they had to operate immediately, before the swelling went down, they'd be running the risk of causing more damage to the nerves. If they could wait for the swelling to subside, the surgery would be safer. The question was, could they afford to wait?

Now I had a whole battery of doctors poking and pinching me, moving my arm, moving my foot, asking me the same questions Bob Reese had asked back on the field. "Can you feel this?" "Can you feel that?"

It was all very confusing, but Pepper and Steve were there, doing their best to keep me calm, to cheer me up. "You're doing fine, buddy," Pepper said, over and over again. I giggled with him once or twice. As terrified as I felt, I was able to giggle. Or maybe that's because I was so terrified.

I was still spitting up, but now it was a greenish yellow bile. I had nothing else left inside me. It was actually pretty amazing to me that I could keep vomiting like that. I had no idea where all this stuff was coming from. And now I was being wheeled into yet another room, for yet another test.

This one was called a CT myelogram. They put a needle into the base of my skull and injected my spinal column with dye, which would help enhance the X rays and give them an even clearer look at how much my cord had swollen.

They needed gravity to pull the dye down into my spine, so I was put on a tilt table and carefully leaned up, still vomiting, with Pepper and Steve still holding my head.

That was at 8:00 P.M. The combination of the medication, the retching, and the sheer number of hours I had spent being put through these tests had completely worn me out by the time I was wheeled up to an eighth-floor intensive care room where Angela was waiting. I was a pretty raggedy sight by then, still filthy from the football game, stinking from the smell of dirt and sweat and vomit.

"I'm right here," Ange said, squeezing my hand. I wanted so badly to squeeze back. But I couldn't.

Marvin was there, too. Along with Paul Frase and Cary and Mindi Blanchard. George McGovern, the team chaplain, was there, too. Paul held my hand as we prayed for the Lord to give us strength, to guide the doctors in their decisions, and to help me heal.

By 9:00 Camins and O'Leary, along with the rest of the team, had decided. The surgery could wait. The swelling would be given time to go down.

Near 11:30, with my friends gone and only Angela and Pepper still with me, I was wheeled out once again, this time into a room filled with beeping equipment and a bank of bright lights overhead. I was lying there studying the hinges on those lights when a technician leaned over and told me what we were waiting for.

"The doctors will be here soon," he said. "They're going to put your halo vest on."

A halo vest.

My mind flashed to Marcus Anderson, my teammate at Tulsa who had broken his neck. I'd watched him live in a halo vest for six months. He had to sleep in a La-Z-Boy chair that whole time. He couldn't lie down in a bed. I could still see him cleaning the screws that came out of his head. Every day he had to clean his screws.

And now they were going to put screws in me. Now they were going to put a halo vest on me. Once more I had to gather the strength to stay calm. Once more I prayed for the Lord to help me.

Both Jim and Steve Nicholas were there, along with a resident surgeon and an anesthesiologist, and Dr. Camins and Dr. O'Leary.

The first thing they did was mark four spots, two on the edges of my forehead and two at the back of my skull. Then the anesthesiologist gave me a shot of xylocane at each of those spots.

Then they simply began screwing.

I remember the metal pins crunching through my skin. Not squeaking. *Crunching*. Each screw was stainless steel, about a quarter-inch in diameter, and they really had to push to get them through the skin and into my skull. They had to push hard, so hard that one of them was on the other side pushing back.

All this pushing and pressure were frightening. I imagined the force it takes to twist a screw into a piece of wood, and I realized these men were using that same force to twist pieces of steel into my *head*. I imagined the bone was separating, splitting open like a piece of pine. I knew that wasn't happening, but that's how it felt. The thought of Frankenstein crossed my mind.

Then it was done, the screws were in, and they pulled out the vest, a plastic shell shaped like the chest armor worn by Roman centurions. The inside was lined with sheep's wool to keep it from abrading my chest.

They put me in that, cinching it down so tightly I wasn't sure I could breathe. Breathing was hard enough already. The doctors were keeping an eye on my breathing, worried I might need a respirator, as so many spinal injury patients do. And now I had this vest adding to that feeling of constriction. That feeling alone was frightening enough, and I had no idea if I'd be wearing it for six weeks, or six months, like Marcus.

Or longer.

Finally they connected four metal rods from the vest to each of the screws, did some tightening, tossed the tools in a little pouch connected to my vest, made a joke about the tool chest I was wearing, and that was it. My head was locked, totally immobile. My field of vision was framed on the sides by two metal bars.

It was 1:00 A.M. when the procedure was done. Now, at last, this day was over. Ange was there as they laid me in bed. It was close to three before I finally fell asleep, haunted by a question that would wake me up in the middle of many nights to come.

Was this really happening to me?

11

When I opened my eyes Monday morning, I was in that semiconscious state everyone knows so well, that half-awake, half-asleep condition where you're straddling the fence between the dream you're drifting out of and the waking world of reality. If the dream has been a good one, all you want to do is turn over and slide back into it; if it's been bad, nothing is more of a relief than to sit up, shake it off, and climb into the comfort of reality, the promise of a new day.

There was no comfort for me that morning, no relief. I wanted so much to wake up and realize this all had been a horrible dream. But I *was* awake, and this was real. Those bars were still there, attached to the steel band circling my skull. My head was pounding with pain. I was in a room filled with hospital sounds, with the beeping of monitors and machines banked beside the bed in which I lay, numb and motionless from my shoulders down.

IV lines were taped to my arms, and there was a tube running out of my nose, a nasogastric tube the doctors had inserted during the procedure the night before, to drain the vomit and bile that was still rising up from my stomach.

Ange was there. She had slept as badly as I had, in an empty room down the hall. Ashtin was okay, she said. Kyle and Lorrie Clifton were taking care of her until Ange's mother could get here. My mom and dad were flying up that day, she told me.

A steady parade of nurses and doctors streamed into the room, checking the machinery, the tubes, taking tests, asking me questions, marking charts, constantly tapping on my toes, my feet, my knees with small probes and hammers.

Among them was a fairly tall man with horn-rim glasses and a pleasant Irish brogue—Dr. O'Leary. He explained what had happened, what they'd done and why, that I'd been stabilized in the halo vest and that they were waiting for the swelling to go down before they operated to repair the damage. The operation, he told me, would be Wednesday.

What he couldn't tell me was what I most wanted to know. Would I be able to walk again? What were my chances? No one would tell me. The answer was always "We don't know . . . " Not "*I* don't know" but "*We* don't know," as if that somehow relieved them of responsibility. I wanted to pin just one person down and say, "Hey, what do *you* think?"

I was desperate for statistics, for odds, for someone to give me a number, a percentage. Percentages had always been such a big part of my life. In football, you're constantly playing the percentages, the tendencies, the odds. What percentage of the time will a particular team pass on a particular down at a certain point on the field with a certain distance to go? I knew how to play the percentages, if I only knew what they were.

But no one could give me them now.

What they did give me, beginning that day and continuing every day throughout the coming months, was an education in the function and physiology of the spinal cord. When I was in college, it had been all I could do some days to drag myself to class. Now I had no choice. I was in class every waking minute, a captive student. Class was coming to me now, and the subject was my body, specifically that two-foot-long bundle of nerve cells and fibers running from my brain into my lower back.

I'd known the rudiments of how the spine works, that it carries messages from the brain to the body's muscles, organs, and skin, as well as relaying messages from the body back to the brain. If the brain is thought of as a powerful computer, the spinal cord can be thought of as the cable, the transmission line that feeds commands from that computer into the body and that feeds information from the body into the computer. When everything's working smoothly, that two-way flow is what allows us to touch, taste, hear, see, speak, feel, and move.

When the spinal cord is injured, the flow is disrupted, and the messages can't get through. The extent of the disruption depends on where and how the cord is damaged. Generally, the higher the point of a spinal cord injury, the greater the extent of paralysis. Injuries in the neck, or cervical area, are usually the most serious, often causing quadriplegia—paralysis in both the arms and the legs.

As I lay there that Monday morning, I was quadriplegic. The only part of my body below my shoulders that I could control were my biceps. With them I could bend my elbows. Other than that, the rest of me from the shoulders down was limp, virtually lifeless. I had sensation in my rectum and penis—I could tell when I was being touched—but I couldn't move a thing. I couldn't tell hot from cold, sharp from blunt. But the fact that I could tell I was being touched at all was a sign that at least some messages were getting through to the nerves, that my spinal cord had not been completely severed.

Dr. O'Leary and Dr. Camins explained that I'd sustained a non-displaced fracture of the fifth cervical vertebra, just above the base of the neck. The term used for what had happened to me was an "explosion fracture." The extraordinary force with which I'd hit Scott had literally exploded that vertebra, breaking it in four places and driving fragments of the bursting bone against the spinal cord. Wednesday's surgery, the doctors explained, would be aimed at removing those fragments, repairing and replacing the bone, and stabilizing the spine.

It wasn't long ago that people in my condition were considered hopeless and left to die, either directly from the injury itself or from infections. Bladder infection is no less lethal today than it was years ago, which was why one of the first things Steve

Nicholas had done when they got me to Lenox Hill was insert a catheter in my penis. That's why I was still wearing a catheter when I awoke that Monday morning.

Another chronic problem among people with damaged spinal cords is decubitis, or bedsores. Normally the brain tells the body to shift when it's been in one position too long. That message can't get through after a spinal cord injury. Sitting or lying in one position too long cuts off blood circulation to the skin at that point, causing skin ulcers, which again can lead to infection. The problem is even worse for spinal cord injury patients because their blood flow itself is weakened, bringing less oxygen to the point on the skin that needs it.

The bed I was in was specially designed to reduce the pressure on my skin. It was called a Clinitron bed, and it operated on the same basic principle as a water bed. It was filled with what felt like sand. Air was constantly pumped through it, providing a cushion that adjusted to the shape and weight of my body. To me, it felt like I was lying in an open refrigerator box. Or a coffin.

But I badly needed that bed. The mere ten hours I had spent on the back board and gurneys before finally being put to bed had given me an ulcer about the size of a half-dollar right on the bony point of my tailbone.

The steroids that were still being pumped into me were something relatively new in the treatment of spinal cord injury patients. It had only been ten years since a national study was begun to determine how safe and effective steroids were in cutting spinal cord swelling. In 1990 doctors discovered that a specific steroid called methylprednisolone, if given in large doses within eight hours of an injury and continued for twenty-four hours, seemed to help patients recover more quickly and more completely from their spinal injuries. It was still too new to tell how well or even *why* it worked. But my doctors were hoping it would work with me—that was why they had been running methylprednisolone through one of those IV lines since I'd arrived at the hospital Sunday afternoon.

Even the surgery that Dr. O'Leary and Dr. Camins had planned for Wednesday was a comparatively new procedure. What they intended to do after cleaning the bone fragments from my spinal cord was something called "plating," which stabilizes the cord with metal plates attached to the vertebrae around the damaged area. The plates not only provide support for the injured spine but make later bone grafts and traction devices unnecessary, and they're supposed to shorten the time a patient has to stay in intensive care.

That's where I was Monday morning, on the building's eighth floor. George McGovern came by that morning to see me and Angela and to pray with us. So did the hospital's chaplain, Ann Williams. She had printed the words to a Bible verse with black marker on a white piece of poster board and hung it from a bar suspended from the ceiling above my bed, a bar normally used to hold IV bags. The words were from Romans 8:18: "For I reckon that the sufferings of this present time are not worthy to be compared with the glory which shall be revealed in us."

I had no idea what was going on in the hallway outside my room, much less in the world outside the hospital. Reading a newspaper was the last thing on my mind. So was looking at television. I knew we'd lost the game to the Chiefs. I think I asked Marvin when I saw him in the emergency room—not that it mattered to him at all. Not that it mattered to any of my teammates after I went down. Not that it mattered to me. There'd be time to turn back to the business of football. What I cared about most right now was how they were feeling. I knew this was an opportunity to be strong for them and to witness to them, to show them the Lord's strength through me. I wanted to know how those guys were holding up. That was the first thing I asked when the coaches—Bruce and Pete and Greg—along with our general manager, Dick Steinberg, came by to see me Monday afternoon. Dick said they'd canceled practice that day and that most of the guys on the team were doing "okay."

Then Jeff walked in.

He looked devastated, as if he'd been crying all day. And he had. He'd been totally shaken ever since he'd talked to me by the cart in the Giants Stadium tunnel. He had been watching the game from up in the press box when Scott and I collided. Jeff had always given me a hard time for making a big deal out of small injuries and for treating serious ones as if they were nothing. When he saw me stay down after that play, he figured I was crying wolf.

But then he saw a replay of the hit on a television monitor. He rushed to an elevator, bad knee and all, and caught up with me in the tunnel.

Now he was here, looking at the dried blood caked around my screw holes, the bars, the vest, the tubes, and the machines. It was pretty overwhelming for him. He took it hard. He couldn't keep the tears from running down his cheeks.

"Don't go soft on me now, Lageman," I said, and that broke the ice. Pretty soon we were both back into the rhythm.

"Geez," he said at one point, "you better not give me any crap or I'm gonna tighten those screws up."

Now that was more like it. Over the coming months, I'd feel the love and support of all my teammates, but none more than Jeff and Marvin. I was going to be seeing a lot of those two guys.

I'd also be seeing a lot of a doctor named Kristjan Ragnarsson. He was the director of the rehabilitation department at Manhattan's Mount Sinai Hospital and a specialist in spinal cord trauma. He'd been reading the *New York Times* and half-watching the game in the den of his home in Westchester County on Sunday afternoon when he saw a replay of my collision with Scott. He could see right away that the mechanics of the impact—my head down, my spine straight—were just like those of the dozens of diving accident victims he'd worked with over the years. He heard no word that afternoon or evening about the extent of my injury, but on his way in the next morning, he heard it on the radio. As soon as he got to his office, he called Dr. O'Leary.

By noon, Ragnarsson was at my bedside, poking and prodding like all the others. He had spent the past two decades specializing in spinal cord injuries. He had helped develop something called the "model system of care," a spinal cord injury treatment program that coordinates care from the site of the injury all the way through treatment and rehabilitation. Mount Sinai was one of thirteen medical centers in the nation designated by the federal government as a "model system." As Ragnarsson checked my condition that morning, he was already looking beyond the surgery to the months of rehabilitation he knew lay ahead of me.

That night my parents arrived, along with Angela's mom. My dad was still in the insurance business, but he and my mom and sisters lived in Louisiana now, where they'd moved the previous summer. It had taken them most of the day to fly up from Baton Rouge, where they'd been on Sunday afternoon, watching the Saints game on TV when their telephone rang. It was Angela, calling to say I'd been hurt. My dad asked if it was my shoulder again. "No," said Angela, talking through tears. "It's serious. They think Dennis broke his neck."

My mom broke down when she heard that. Then, at halftime of the Saints broadcast, they showed the hit and that's when my whole family lost it, Mom and Dad, and my sisters, too.

I thought Mom would fall apart when she saw me in the hospital like this, but she didn't. I found out later she left the room every time she was about to cry, so she could do it where I couldn't see. I remember she left the room a lot.

As for my dad, we talked, and he prayed with me, saying, "Lord, we don't know why these things happen, but we know that all things work for the good of thy will. Give us strength, give us encouragement, don't let us become bitter. Allow us to become a witness through this situation."

That whole day had been a parade of friends, family, doctors, and nurses. Mark and Jana Boyer brought more posters that night, more verses like the one Ann Williams had put up for me. After they left, Angela began taping them where I could see them. She was humming softly to herself. Then suddenly she stopped and walked over to me. She had realized the words to the tune she had been humming. It was a hymn we'd both sung for years in church. The words were from Isaiah, and Angela sang them softly to me now:

"They that wait upon the Lord shall renew their strength; they shall mount up with wings as eagles, they shall run and not grow weary, they shall walk and not faint. Teach me Lord to wait."

We both just began crying together, my head locked in that

brace and my face toward the ceiling, Angela beside me with her hands on my arm.

I was supposed to rest, to sleep, but there was no such thing, not even late at night. The best I could do was to barely slip under, only to wake up every hour or so, completely disoriented, not knowing where I was. Then I'd hear Beres's voice—Beresford Westney, one of the night attendants. He was Jamaican, with a strong, low way of speaking. I'd wake up not knowing where I was, not able to move, absolutely terrified, and Beres would be there to comfort me.

"Dennis," he'd say, in a deep, soothing tone, with a Caribbean lilt. "Dennis, you know, you've got to be strong. You've got to be strong."

I prayed constantly, asking the Lord for the strength I needed, to be a witness to others, to be brave myself. Those late nights, all alone, those were some of the times when I needed that strength the most.

Those were also the times when Mr. Hess would come in, after everyone else had gone. Leon Hess, the owner of the Jets and chairman of the board of the Amerada Hess Corporation. He's seventy-eight years old, one of the most respected owners in the NFL, a man who made his fortune in oil and has put a lot of love and money into the game of professional football. He's owned part of the Jets franchise for the past thirty years. For the past ten, he's been the sole owner. Until now I'd known him the way most of the players did, as the guy who'd come into the locker room and hug the neck of a player here and there and as the man who'd greet us every year at training camp, giving us a welcoming speech, telling us what's expected of a New York Jet.

It was clear to me from the first time I heard him speak that this man was seriously committed to building a successful football program, that this wasn't just a hobby for him. His theme of those speeches was always working for what you want, which is of course how he'd made it. He had pulled himself up from his childhood as a New Jersey immigrant boy to become a magnate in the oil business. He believed in the basics of hard work, and I always agreed with what he said about that. I can think of very few people who are handed something and do well with it. It's usually those who have to do for themselves that do best.

When I'd gotten hurt Sunday afternoon, Mr. Hess hadn't been far behind the ambulance. He was at the hospital through that evening, making sure I'd have everything I needed. When my parents came on Monday, it was Mr. Hess who flew them up and got them a hotel room nearby. He got Angela a room, too, so she could be right with me for the duration. Her mom stayed out at our house in Point Lookout and took care of Ashtin. I hadn't seen Ashtin since kissing her good-bye on Saturday. I didn't know when I'd see her again.

Mr. Hess was crushed by what had happened. Monday he told Rick Schaeffer, "I'm so sorry. If I had known something like this was ever going to happen, I would never have bought the team."

It wasn't enough for Mr. Hess to simply take care of my family. He had to be with me personally as well. He came to see me from the beginning, almost every evening, always shuffling into the room in a very quiet, almost shy way. If there was anyone else there, he'd greet them politely—"How are you, Mrs. Byrd?"—visit for a few minutes, then excuse himself.

But when I was alone, usually late, he'd pull up a chair and settle in for a half-hour, sometimes even more. He's not a large man. He wears thick eyeglasses and has a soft, charming chuckle. It turned out he used to spend a lot of time outdoors, just like me, trout fishing. But he said things had reached the point where he couldn't get around well enough to do that anymore.

He talked to me about how he'd grown up in Asbury Park, how he'd gotten started in business with just a single coal truck, and how when he was about my age, he'd spent Christmas Eve in a hospital after having a wreck in one of his trucks.

He told me about the old Jets, the guys who were playing back when I was born. Joe Namath and Emerson Boozer, Don Maynard and George Sauer. The 1969 Super Bowl Jets. He'd tell a little story about one of them, then he'd let out with that little chuckle of his.

But more than anything else I remember Mr. Hess telling a story about serving in World War II. He was running up a beach in the middle of a battle—I'm not sure if this was Normandy or not—and suddenly the soldier to his left was shot in the head, then the guy to his right was killed by a piece of shrapnel from an exploding bomb. And the point he was making to me was there was no way to explain why a man on each side of him died like that while he was spared. It's beyond our understanding to explain why these things happen, he said.

We didn't talk about religion, but Mr. Hess's message about not knowing when or why something might hit us was one I understood through the power of prayer, through having faith that the Lord had a plan for me, that there was a reason this had happened, that somehow I might be an even better witness for Him now than I had been before. I didn't know His plan. I didn't know *how* I might be that witness, whether it might be from a wheelchair or not. There were so many questions that had no answers. But I understood that that was part of the challenge, part of the test, to accept not knowing and face it with faith.

There is a verse in the Bible that I had gathered strength from many times in my life, and I would turn to it many times more in the coming months. It's in Matthew, where Jesus is in the garden of Gethsemene, deeply distressed by the weakness of Peter and the betrayal of Judas. His soul is torn by the pain closing in around him, and he falls to his knees and prays:

"Oh my Father, if it is possible, let this cup pass from me; nevertheless, not as I will, but as thou wilt."

I went to sleep Monday night thinking of those words.

Tuesday, the doctors gathered Angela and my parents and Rick and explained to them that Dr. Ragnarsson had suggested that beyond the steroids they'd already started and the surgery that was set for the next morning, there was an experimental drug he thought they should consider, a drug called Sygen.

Sygen is aimed at doing something researchers into spinal cord injuries not long ago thought was impossible—rescuing and regenerating damaged nerve cells. It's made from molecules located in the outer membrane layer of central nervous system cells in humans and other mammals.

Here we are, the terrors of the neighborhood — me,
flanked by my brothers Danny and Doug, with our
sister Jeni — in Oklahoma City in the summer of '72.

Some of my best memories are of living in Elk Grove with my grandparents, Poppa and
Nanna. That's me by Poppa's side, as usual, with Doug and Jeni by Nanna.

Here's the nine-year-old
slugger in Sacramento.

The Byrds, circa 1982. Clockwise from
left: Jeni, Danny, Doug, me, Dawn, Mom,
and Dad.

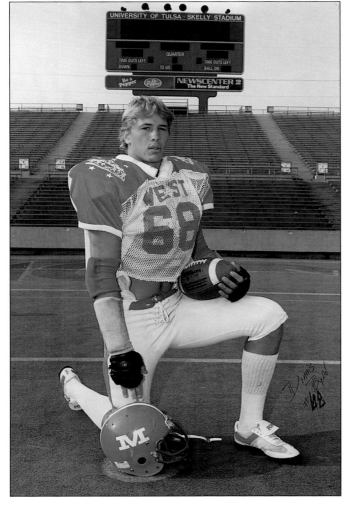

Above: Charlie Carpenter, on the right, was tickled to death when I signed the letter of intent to attend Tulsa, but no one was prouder than my dad, on the left.

I was a starter in the 1984 Oklahoma Coaches Association High School All-State Game, played at Tulsa University's Skelly Stadium. A month later, I began my college career on the same field.

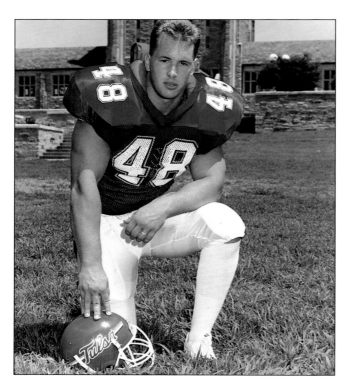

A Golden Hurricane, 1987.
(Courtesy of The
University of Tulsa)

Gus Spanos *(left)* and Danny Tarabrella, my two "little brothers" at Tulsa.

One of the happiest days of my life: December 20, 1986 — the day I married Angela Hales.

Here's my dad, mom, and me on draft day, 1989, wearing the only Jets hats in the town of Mustang.

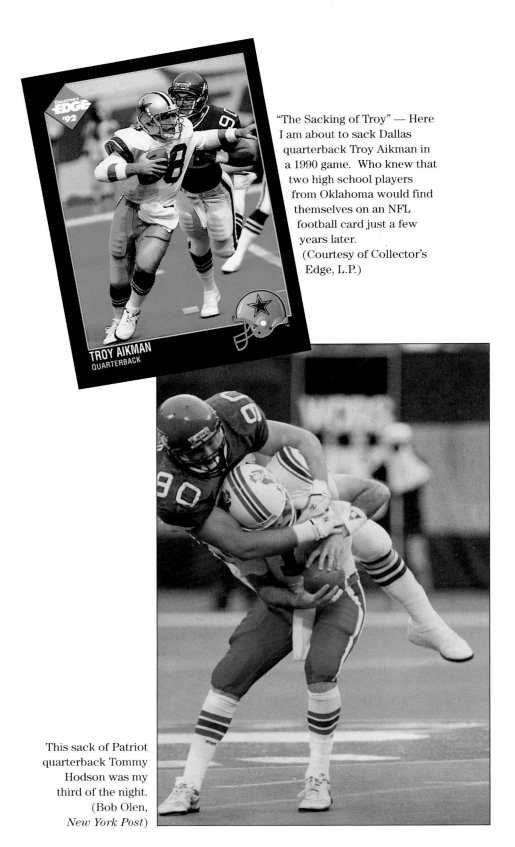

"The Sacking of Troy" — Here I am about to sack Dallas quarterback Troy Aikman in a 1990 game. Who knew that two high school players from Oklahoma would find themselves on an NFL football card just a few years later. (Courtesy of Collector's Edge, L.P.)

TROY AIKMAN
QUARTERBACK

This sack of Patriot quarterback Tommy Hodson was my third of the night. (Bob Olen, *New York Post*)

The 1991 Jets Defensive Line Squad: front row, #97 Marvin Washington, #94 Scott Mersereau, Coach Greg Robinson, #98 Darryl Davis, #71 Bill Pickel; rear row, #96 Mark Gunn, #90 Dennis Byrd, #56 Jeff Lageman, #91 Paul Frase. (Jerry Liebman)

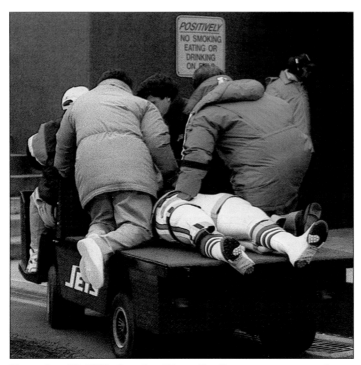

November 29, 1992. Leaving Giants Stadium, on my way to the ambulance and Lenox Hill. (Dan Farrell/*Daily News*)

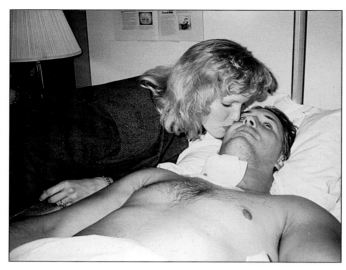

After the halo vest came off, it was easier for Angela to kiss me.

It took three metal plates and nine screws to put my spine back together. (Courtesy of Lenox Hill Hospital)

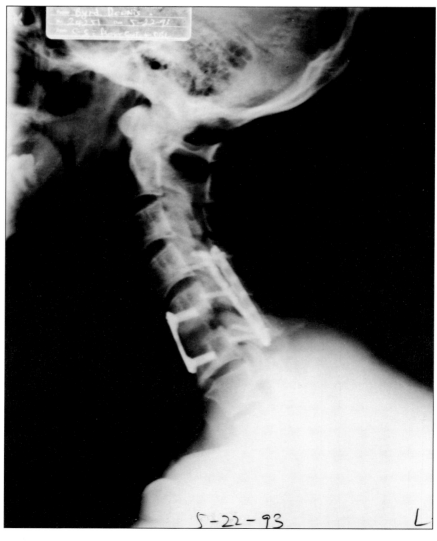

5-22-93   L

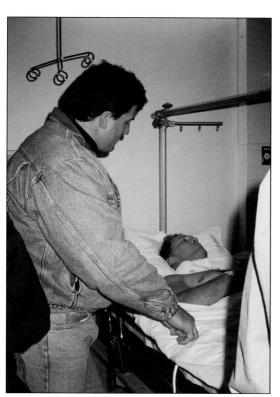

I was as worried about Scott as he was about me.

The entire Jets organization pulled together like a family. Here's Mr. Hess, Cary Blanchard, and Louie Aguiar in my room at Lenox Hill.

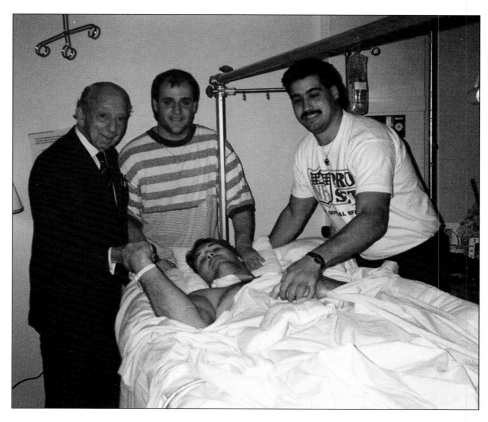

The Jets lifted their no-banner rule for the game against the Colts, the first home game after my injury. Every time I look at this picture, I get choked up. (Dan Farrell/*Daily News*)

I watched from my bed at Mount Sinai as Marvin led a "Get Well" cheer before the Colts game. (Jerry Liebman)

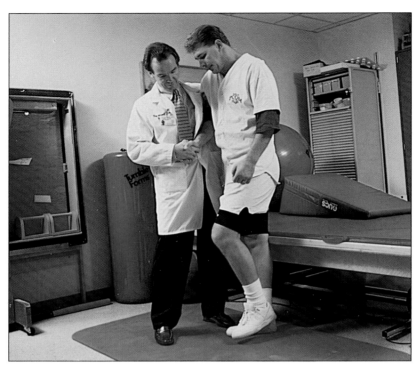

Above: The doctors said it would be two years before I could walk — if I ever walked again. Two months after the injury, I was able to stand and take small steps on my own. Here, Dr. Ragnarsson helps me. *Below*: Joanne Giammetta and Lawrence Harding were the two people who literally got me back on my feet. (Both photographs: Tom Iannuzzi)

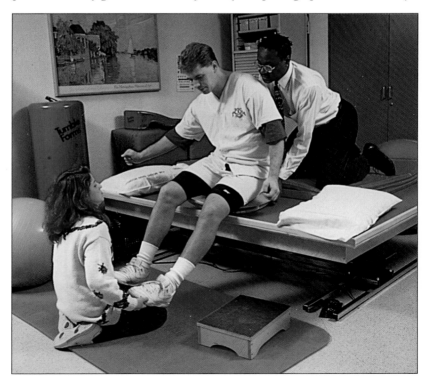

Joanne didn't just lift my spirits; she's half my size, but she could lift my body as well. She never ceased to amaze me. (Vicky Gross)

From the day I went down, I prayed I'd be able to hold Ashtin again.

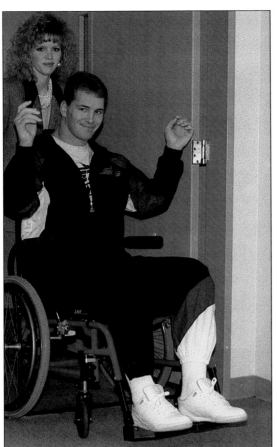

Angela was behind me every step of the way, including the moment I entered my first press conference at Mount Sinai.
(Keith Torrie/*Daily News*)

When we met in February, Mike Utley said, "If you're not out of that wheelchair in two weeks, I'm gonna kick your butt." I believed him.
(Gerald Herbert/*Daily News*)

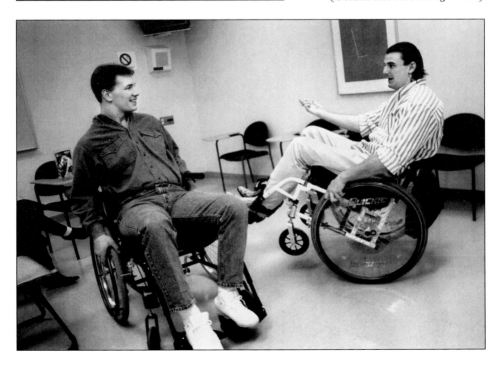

Walking unassisted into my "farewell" press conference, with hundreds of cameras flashing, was an incredible experience. (Gerald Herbert/*Daily News*)

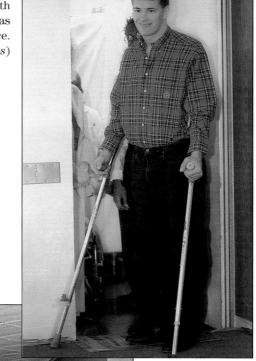

Brothers in arms: Jeff, me, and Marvin (with my empty Quickie) the morning I left Mount Sinai.

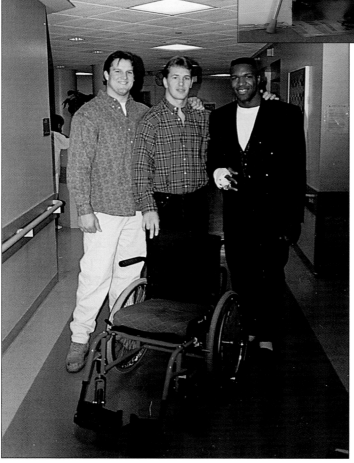

The birth of my second daughter, Haley, added to the joy of returning home.

I'll always be a New York Jet. (Dan Farrell/*Daily News*)

The doctors talked to me about the drug, explaining its untested nature, what it might be able to do, and about the unsure question of side effects. I remember Jim Nicholas telling me in detail how the drug worked, how it oxygenates the damaged nerves, how the decision to use it was totally up to Angela and me but that we had to decide soon, because for Sygen to be effective, the treatment has to begin within seventy-two hours of the injury. It had already been forty-eight. The clock was ticking. If we were going to start it, it had to be by the next day.

Angela had the authority to decide for me, and at first that's what she planned to do. But this was a big burden for her to shoulder herself. The word "experimental" made her extremely nervous. You just don't *know* what the side effects are of an experimental drug. You're taking a chance. There had been no side effects to speak of in the studies, but no one could be definite yet. The drug was too new.

Angela was wrestling with the weight of this decision when Steve Nicholas made a suggestion. "Let *Dennis* make the choice," he said. "He's perfectly capable of making this decision for himself. Let him decide, and you support him one way or the other."

In my mind, there was no question. This was a no-brainer. The possibility of side effects didn't compare to the promise of what this drug might do *for* me.

"Let's do it," I said. Angela guided my hand as we scrawled a mark that passed for my signature. So now there was one more item to add to the list for Wednesday's surgery: Start the Sygen.

Only my family and Rick Schaeffer and the doctors knew anything about the decision. The friends and teammates still streaming in to visit me had no idea. Marvin came by Tuesday afternoon with his wife, Tammy, and James Hasty and Marty Lyons and Billy Hampton, Jr. They spent about twenty minutes, and before they left, Marvin leaned down and whispered in my ear.

"Dennis," he said, "the Lord wouldn't give you this cross if you couldn't bear it."

Marvin always had a knack for saying the right thing at the right time.

Then, for the first time since we'd collided, Scott came through the door.

I'd thought a lot about Scott, and I was worried about him. I imagined he might be feeling some guilt, that somehow he was partly responsible for what had happened. I knew Scott so well. He was one of the biggest, strongest men I'd ever played with— he'd been runner-up in the NFL Strongest Man competition in 1988. The monstrous custom-made jet ski he kept at his house in Point Lookout was legendary. So was his reputation as a single guy who'd never get married.

Unlike the other guys on the team, Scott was *from* New York, from Long Island. While several of us rented homes in Point Lookout during the season, Scott owned his and lived there year-round. I stayed with him a couple of times, at the start of the season, when the house Ange and I rented wasn't yet available. She'd stay in Oklahoma until it was ready, and I'd stay with Scott. I remember the first time I cooked a meal for us—some chicken and stir-fry vegetables over rice. He couldn't believe it. All the married guys he knew let their wives do all the cooking. "Dude," he told me, taking his first bite, "you can stay with me anytime you want. This rice is *killer.*"

Beyond all the single stud surface stuff, I knew Scott's sensitive side. I knew how he responded emotionally to things. When you play football beside someone, when you're both out there in the arena, under pressure, you learn and see things about each other that even your families don't know.

And I knew Scott had to be hurting right now.

He hadn't realized it was me he'd collided with down on that field any more than I'd known it was him. He didn't know *what* hit him, I'd learn later. All he knew was he was bent backward by the blow, badly twisting his ankle underneath him and blasting the air out of his lungs. It was only after his cobwebs had cleared and he was being helped off the field that he saw someone else lying on the turf.

"Who is *that?*" he'd asked.

There was definitely some tension on his face when he looked in my hospital room door. But whatever questions he might have had about how I felt toward him vanished as soon as our eyes met. I was *so* glad to see him, and I showed it. When he saw me beaming at him like that, he just lit up. He was Scotty again.

He came over and hugged me, then showed me something he'd brought, something he'd been given to pass on to me.

It was a paratrooper's beret. Scott's accountant, a man named Craig Northacker, had spent four years as a paratrooper with the Eighty-second Airborne Division in Fort Bragg, North Carolina. He'd watched men die after jumping out of airplanes. He'd seen guys wind up in wheelchairs. He'd hurt himself so badly on the last jump of his career—a night jump—that it took him three years to heal. He'd given Scott this red beret to pass on to me as a symbol of the courage and bravery he'd seen among the men he'd served with.

I was really touched. I'd always had enormous respect for men who had served in combat, who knew the experience of being under fire, an experience that was impossible for someone who hadn't been there to understand. I had picked up a book early in the season, when we were losing game after game and things seemed to be falling apart. The book was called *Marine Sniper*. It was an account of a man who had served in Vietnam as a behind-the-lines sniper, and it contained a quote from Theodore Roosevelt that had hit me hard, that seemed perfect for those tough times when outsiders and critics can start circling like vultures. The quote is from an essay Roosevelt wrote called "The Man in the Arena":

> It is not the critic who counts, not the one who points out how the strong man stumbled or how the doer of deeds might have done them better. The credit belongs to the man who is actually in the arena, whose face is marred with sweat and dust and blood . . . who, if he fails, at least fails while daring greatly, so that his place shall never be with those cold and timid souls who know neither victory nor defeat.

That beret was going to stay with me a long time.

After a while, the rest of the room—Marvin, Hasty, Marty Lyons—left, and Scott and I were alone. I could tell there was still some air left to clear.

"Hey," I finally said, "I really blasted you, didn't I?"

Scott reared back, as if he'd stuck his finger in a socket.

"Dennis, I can't *believe* you said that! I was going to wait till you got a little better, then I was going to tell you *exactly* the same thing.

"You knocked the crap out of me. I swear, you hit me harder than anyone ever hit me in my life."

That was it. We broke up laughing, and I could tell a load had been lifted off the both of us.

Finally night fell. Tuesday night. Angela's dad and Pastor McNabb from our church in Mustang had arrived and come by to see me, but now everyone was gone but Angela. It hadn't been three days since the hit, but already it seemed a lifetime ago. I was exhausted. And anxious. And uncertain. The next morning would be my moment of truth. That surgery would set the course for the rest of my life. I had no idea what the doctors would find in there. They didn't either. They couldn't. Almost everything I wanted to know about my condition brought the same basic answer: "We'll have to wait and see." It was the same with the surgery.

Angela and I talked about the surgery, how I felt about the decisions we'd made. I felt fine, I told her. Then I told her something else.

"Ange," I said, "I'm glad God chose me for this because He knows I have the strength and faith to get through it."

Ange leaned down, in tears, and hugged me.

"I'm glad, too," she said. "I'm glad God chose me to go through it with you."

Then she left. And I turned my thoughts toward the next day. I knew better than to expect a miracle. The doctors had told me exactly what they planned to do. They were always careful, exasperatingly careful, not to get my hopes up too high.

But hope is a funny thing. It has a way of lifting itself if you let it. And I could feel it surging in me as I laid there. I knew I would never play football again. That was over. But walking, being well again, and right away. I found myself imagining that somehow, with this surgery, the wires would suddenly start firing again, that I'd wake up after this operation and my limbs would be back.

I was hoping for that.

12

Seven hours.

That's how long I lay on the operating table that Wednesday as the doctors opened my neck and got a firsthand look at what until then they had been able to see only through X-ray machines—my shattered spine.

They came in first through the front of my neck. What they saw was more debris than they'd imagined, tiny chips of bone too small even to appear on the scans. They cleaned out those chips, along with the rest of the damaged disc between the fifth and sixth vertebrae, which had burst from the impact.

Meanwhile, they opened my right hip and cut out a piece of that bone, the *iliac crest*, and inserted it through my throat, grafting it at the spot where the damage had been done.

Then, to stabilize that spot, a small steel plate—a cervical spine locking plate—about two inches long and made of titanium was attached to my fifth and sixth cervical vertebrae with four titanium screws, two for each vertebra.

Next they turned me over, opened the back of my neck, and attached two more plates, one on each side of my spine. These plates, longer but thinner than the one in front, were screwed to the fourth, fifth, and sixth vertebrae. They used three screws on the right side, but could use only two on the left because the bone was cracked where the third screw would go.

Meanwhile, an IV line was started to a steady supply of Sygen, which I would continue receiving for the next thirty days.

Then they stitched and stapled me up and rolled me into a tenth-floor recovery room. The metal in my neck was now a permanent part of my body—three plates and nine screws. Toss in a little baling wire and Tabasco sauce and we'd be on the road.

The procedure went "perfectly," according to Dr. Camins. He said he'd gotten up for this surgery the way an athlete gets up for a ball game. Going in, he felt the same sort of tension and adrenaline I did before a kickoff. He'd had to prepare himself physically as well as mentally, as had the whole six-surgeon team. Seven hours is a long time.

But it had gone off without a hitch. Blessedly, the halo vest was off. They'd removed it during the procedure, an indication of how stable my neck was now, with those plates in it. It was a fantastic relief having that halo off. I was so horrified I'd have to live in it the way Marcus had. I could move my head now, tilt it from side to side. Now I just had to put up with a soft neck collar. I felt pain from the stitches front and back, but that was all right. This was a step. I was excited, eager. Okay, I thought, I've got that out of the way. What's next?

The same questions came flooding out again. When will I be able to sit up? Hold my daughter? Hunt?

When will I be able to walk?

Again, no answers. The doctors' concerns were more immediate. They were monitoring my liver enzymes, tending to the ulcer on my tailbone, watching my blood pressure and other vital signs and checking a dozen other charts only they understood. Elliott Hershman, the Jets' head physician, was the only one who would come even close to a solid reply when I asked about walking. He was more frank than the others. He would say what the others would not. Nobody ever told me then or in the months ahead, "You'll never walk again." Nobody came out and said that, but some of them thought it. They couldn't help but think it.

Dr. Hershman, though, was candid when I asked him that night, "Will I be able to walk again?"

"It could be years," he said, looking through his round, owlish glasses, "before we know."

Years.

That word hit me as hard as my collision with Scott. I appreciated Dr. Hershman's honesty more than I could ever say. But those words were hard to hear.

Years before they'd even *know* if I could walk?

The fantasies I'd had the night before evaporated like so much steam. The surgery was finished, and I was still flat on my back, my body still unfeeling, still virtually inert. My biceps on both arms were working, as well as my right triceps. That allowed me to raise my right arm, just as I'd done when I'd first tried to unsnap my helmet back on the field. But I couldn't control the arm any better than I had then. It flopped aimlessly when I lifted it. Gravity was controlling where it went more than I was. And my hands were totally limp. My fingers felt dead.

They'd taped a suction tube to my right hand, to help empty my mouth when I threw up. If I felt the urge to vomit, I was supposed to raise that tube to my mouth and let it suck out the mess. Easier said than done. I spent half the time poking myself in the face with that thing, jabbing around the general area of my mouth, trying to guide the tube with an arm that wasn't getting the signals my brain was sending it.

Below my shoulders, besides my arms, I had no movement at all. That was where the doctors were most intently studying me, from my chest down to my toes. Especially my toes. If I was ever going to walk again, that's where I'd have to show at least some sign of voluntary movement, down there, down in my feet. The next four to six weeks were going to be crucial. If at the end of that time I hadn't shown any motion yet, the bets would be off that I'd ever walk again.

No one seemed ready to bet that I would. At least not the doctors. Not at that time.

It was so hard lying there like that *after* the surgery. The doctors had taken their shot, they'd stabilized me, gotten me pretty much out of harm's way. But I was still paralyzed and now there was no event to aim at, no operation to look forward to, no hope that the doctors' skills and scalpels alone could give me back my legs. Now it was turned over to me. Any hope for recovery was in my hands. And the Lord's.

I was still as helpless as I'd been the day before. It was deflating, depressing. I was totally dependent, which is a nightmare for a Type A personality like mine. I had to ask for *everything*, from whichever nurse or attendant happened to be in the room. Could you prop that pillow under my shoulder? Could you wipe my nose? May I have a drink of water? Could you turn me a little bit this way? A little bit that way? Can I have something to eat?

Eating and drinking were a story in themselves. My bowels were paralyzed. So was my bladder. I couldn't urinate, I couldn't have a bowel movement, not on my own. The catheter took care of my urine, but my solid waste was more of a problem. They tried suppositories and enemas in the first few days, but generally those things didn't work. Gas built up in my bowels, and I began to feel bloated, as if my insides were going to burst. That was very painful. It was a pain I had to live with for some time, and even when I was eventually able to have bowel movements, it wasn't *me* having them. It was someone else doing it for me. I couldn't even take a dump for myself.

The nurses and attendants were wonderful. Jessie and Golding, Hugh and Beres, they were with me around the clock. One of them was always there to brush my teeth in the morning, take care of my hair, give me sponge baths now and then. My dad went out and bought some waterless shampoo spray to comb through my hair. I was still filthy from the game, and I'd be wearing some of the sweat and dirt from that Sunday for a long time to come. A bath or shower wasn't even in the forecast right now.

It was hard to get adjusted to this routine. I couldn't help thinking, Is this going to be my day, every day, for the rest of my life? Is this what it's going to be like? I was constantly asking myself those questions. I was worried.

And I was humiliated. I'd prided myself on being a protector and provider for Angela and Ashtin. Now, all of a sudden, after all those years of being the husband and the father, the man of the house, now I provided nothing. Now it was Angela who had to provide for me, to do things neither of us had ever imagined having to do for the other.

I remember Ange putting her head on my chest the day after the surgery and saying, "Mmmmmm, Dennis, that sounds so good."

"*What* sounds so good?" I asked.

"Your heart," she said. "The beating of your heart."

She didn't show it, not to me or to the waves of friends and visitors she faced coming to and from my room every day, but she was feeling the strain, too. She didn't tell me then, but Ange had begun bleeding Thursday morning. Even as she lay there with her head on my chest, she had an emergency appointment the next day with an obstetrician.

But I knew nothing. Angela didn't want to give me something else to worry about.

I had no idea either of how broadly my story was being broadcast by television, radio, and the newspapers. But I was starting to realize that a lot of people knew I was lying in that hospital, and that they wanted me to know they cared. The room was so full of flowers it looked like Hawaii. So many cards and telegrams were taped to the walls, there wasn't room for any more. I got gifts and cards from a lot of famous people—Gloria Estefan, who'd gone through her own spinal cord injury, sent a basket of candy—but the hundreds of cards and letters that came from people I'd never heard of meant just as much. Cards like the one sent by a little boy in New Jersey. His words were written in crayon, next to a drawing of a football player wearing a Jets helmet. "Dear Dennis," he wrote, "I'm a Giants fan, but I hope you get better anyway."

I also got a message that afternoon from Milagro Guzman, the mother of Jessica, the young girl whose school I'd visited after she was murdered. Mrs. Guzman called the Jets front office and asked them to let me know she was praying for me. I couldn't believe she'd taken the time to think about me after all she'd gone through herself.

A large number of police officers were slipping in, too, stopping by to tell me how they were all pulling for me and praying.

I was pretty flabbergasted that so many people were coming or calling or writing to tell me how I'd touched or helped them sometime in the past and now they wanted to do what they could for me. I never thought I was overly involved in the community. I never kept track. I just did it. I'd hear about something or someone, it would affect me, and I couldn't help but respond. Person to person, that's what it's all about. Who keeps track of things like that? But then you wind up in a situation like this, and suddenly all those people reach out to you, and you realize how many there are. It's an amazing feeling, all that connectedness. It's really overwhelming.

I had the beret Scott had brought me hanging where I could see it, and I had my memory bag, too. Marvin had grabbed it from my locker and brought it in. I couldn't squeeze it in my hands now—I couldn't squeeze anything—but just having it with me helped.

Late that day, the question I'd asked Angela in the ambulance, about whether I got the sack, was finally answered. It was funny, because throughout the years, Scott and I would often fight and argue over who should have gotten this sack or that. Two guys hit a quarterback close to the same time, there's often a gray area about who gets the credit. Scott was always telling me I was stealing his sacks, and vice versa.

That's how it went with this one. They originally gave Scott credit for sacking Krieg on the play that put me down. But after looking at the films, the Jets petitioned the league to change the ruling. That Thursday, they did. Greg Robinson came by to tell me the news.

So I had my first sack of the year—and the last of my career.

Funny how my four years as a pro began with a sack against Kansas City—in that preseason game my rookie season—and ended with a sack against the same team. Funny too that an accidental collision with my own teammate became the center of a national debate on the subject of spearing.

It was basically one man who raised the issue, a surgeon named Joseph Torg, who heads the Sports Medicine Center at the University of Pennsylvania. Dr. Torg, whose center studies football neck injuries, watched the tape of my collision with Scott and told a reporter, "Byrd was aiming with his head."

Spearing. Leading with the head down and using your helmet to make a tackle. Not only is it illegal in football at any level, but it's insane. The odds for hurting both yourself and the man you're tackling that way are sky-high. Anyone who knows this game knows that. You'd have to be crazy to put yourself at risk like that. I'm not saying there aren't crazy people out there playing this game, but I'm not one of them.

Yes, I was leading with my head on that play. You almost *always* lead with your head when you're making a tackle. You're *taught* to tackle that way, with your head up, driving nose first into the ball carrier. When you're running, your head is always first. The faster you go, the more you lean forward. The more you lean forward, the further out front of your body your head will go. The key is keeping your head *up*. First, if the head is up there is no danger to the ball carrier of being speared by the crown of a helmet. Second, if the head is up, your own spine is curved, diffusing the force of the compression when you make the hit.

My head was down when I hit Scott, but it's not because I was aiming at anyone. It was a combination of physics and reflex. The physics of my body driving low around the corner and stretching out to reach Krieg put me in a near-prone position. The reflex of ducking when Scott's body was suddenly coming at me brought my head down and, unfortunately, straightened my spine. That set it up to receive the full force of the blow, like a battering ram being slammed into a door.

Jim Nicholas dismissed Torg's charge as "nonsense." And it really was. All you had to do was look at the play and you could see it wasn't anything close to spearing, that there wasn't a thing I could do to avoid what happened. Within a couple of days the question died away.

But a lot of people stayed outraged at Torg. Some of them thought I should feel that way, too. But I never did. I was definitely disappointed that someone would make a statement like that, especially someone who's supposed to be an expert on the subject. But I hold no animosity toward Dr. Torg at all. I wish for his own sake that he would have maybe taken a little more time before making that conclusion.

There were many, many people who, in the wake of my injury, especially during that first week, while I lay in bed in Lenox Hill's

ICU wing, used what had happened to me as ammunition to attack this sport. They had an agenda, and they used me as a tool against the game I love so much, and I really want to fire back about that.

First of all, what happened to me was a fluke. A freak accident. I was struck by lightning. The chances of something like this happening are astronomically small. More people dive off poolsides or fall off swings and are paralyzed than are paralyzed playing football. In 1991 there was only one spinal cord injury among every hundred thousand high school football players in America. Among college players that year there were *none*. Those statistics come from Dr. Torg's own studies. As for professional football, there was, of course, one case of paralysis in 1991—Mike Utley's.

Then, a year later, there was mine.

Jim Nicholas has been a doctor with the Jets since 1960, when they were known as the New York Titans. He watched a player for the Titans die that year from a broken neck, a guard named Howard Glenn. Twenty-two years later, in 1982, a Jets offensive tackle named Jim Luscinski broke his neck and was temporarily paralyzed.

And that's it. Nearly seven hundred players have suited up for the Jets over the past three decades, with another thousand trying out in training camps, and three have sustained spinal cord injuries.

The game is dangerous, especially at this level. I don't deny that. It's played by tremendously gifted athletes with tremendous strength moving at tremendous speeds and hitting one another with tremendous force. But these athletes are also tremendously trained. They are protected by highly advanced equipment. And they're intelligent. They know what they're doing.

Beyond that, most of them love this game just as much as I do. They *choose* to play professional football, and most, like me, feel extraordinarily blessed to have that choice.

I heard that some critics portrayed me as a poor country boy from Oklahoma who wasn't smart or sophisticated enough to realize the risks of the game, who was somehow taken advantage of by the dark forces of football that used me as fodder to make their own fortunes. That's so ridiculous it's hardly worth responding to. How dare somebody who doesn't know the game and who doesn't know *me* presume to speak for me or my feelings? And how dare they use what happened to me to attack the game I love?

I never stopped loving this game, not before I had to leave it behind and not after that. I loved it even as I lay in that ICU room that Friday morning, knowing my teammates were somehow trying to gather themselves to play another game that weekend. I felt no bitterness whatsoever. I had no regrets, no second thoughts.

Bruce Coslet was asked some of these same questions at a press conference late that week. His response was one I would have given if I'd been there.

"To play this game, you have to play it on the edge," he said. "You throw your body around. That's what Dennis was doing. He was hell-bent for leather on that play."

Ninety miles an hour with my hair on fire.

13

L ate that Friday morning, they were getting ready to move me from the ICU to the hospital's orthopedic wing when Angela came in with something in her hand and a look of relief on her face.

"Whatcha got there?" I asked.

"This is your new baby," she said. And she showed me a black-and-white sonogram picture that had been taken that morning. The doctor had told her she was seven weeks pregnant. There was a heartbeat. The baby was alive. But there was still some concern about her bleeding, which I'd known nothing about until then. The obstetrician wanted to see her again in a week.

We clipped that picture up next to our posters on the IV rack. Angela was a lot more radiant now than she'd been the day before, but this was all taking a tremendous toll on both of us. She told me she'd begun to ask herself if she was as strong as she thought she was. She'd been telling friends from the beginning that I was going to walk again. Now it looked like that might not happen. The questions about the baby just made things worse. She said she'd begun to feel doubts for the first time about whether she could handle this. She'd been able to push them away with prayer, but she hated having even a glimmer of doubt.

It made her feel disloyal, she said. Disloyal to me, and disloyal to God.

I told her everything was going to be all right. I was as worried about the baby as she was, but right then I was more worried about her. I loved her so much. I could see what she was going through, and I felt so helpless, unable to even take her in my arms to make her feel better. She had to come to me and lean her head against mine, all the while with the words of the verse from Matthew running through my mind, " . . . nevertheless, not as I will, but as thou wilt."

In the afternoon they moved me up a floor, to the orthopedic section. The ninth floor—Nine Uris, they called it. They talked about keeping me there for two weeks before I'd be ready to leave the hospital for a rehabilitation center. Meanwhile, they didn't waste any time. Now that I was out of intensive care, they were ready to get my rehab going in earnest.

I'd actually been going through rehab since the day after the ambulance brought me in. That's one of the basic principles of a "model system of care" for spinal cord injuries, that physical therapy needs to be initiated as early as possible, so the body isn't allowed to deteriorate. Muscles that are allowed to atrophy, joints that are allowed to lock, blood circulation that's allowed to slow down all mean there's that much more work to do once the patient arrives at the rehab center. Estimates are that a healthy person who's confined to a bed loses about twenty percent of his muscle strength each week. For someone with a spinal cord injury, the loss is even greater.

So from the beginning, Lisa Cervone and Randi Strauss, two of Lenox Hill's physical therapy staff, were working on my joints, shifting my body every two hours, moving my fingers and toes, flexing my elbows and shoulders, my ankles and knees, pulling my heel cords and hips, stretching my legs out and back, side to side, putting me through an exhaustive series of what they called range-of-motion exercises. Hamp, our equipment manager, sent over a pair of Jets high-top sneakers. They were great, providing support for my feet, holding them up rather than having them droop down off the end of the bed.

It was Randi and Lisa's job to stretch me out and keep me loose until I could begin doing those things for myself. There was no telling when that would be.

Once I was moved to the ninth floor, Randi and Lisa began doing something else with my body, and I thought it was going to kill me. I'm talking about the tilt table.

It had been only five days since the accident, but for those five days, I had been flat on my back. One of the priorities now was getting me back to the point where I could sit in an upright position. There'd be no moving from that bed, not even into a wheelchair, until I could be raised to a sitting position.

But that can't be done immediately. It takes time for the body's circulatory system to adjust to flowing vertically again. Just getting vertical is a gradual, painstaking process.

And I mean painstaking. That Friday they put me on a tilt table for the first time. It's exactly what it sounds like—a table that tilts. Five nurses carefully lifted me onto it, then Randi and Lisa strapped me down and slowly began raising it.

They didn't get far. They'd hardly begun tilting me up before I got dizzy. I felt nauseated. I started to pass out. "I've got to go down," I said. "I've got to go back *down.*"

An angle of thirteen degrees is all I reached that first time. They told me how great I was doing, and I was lying there thinking, Right. Great. I haven't done anything but endure the ride. I'm just *lying* here. I can't move anything. I'm paralyzed.

I was exhausted, too, as worn out as I'd ever been on the football field, even during the toughest two-a-days. I was thirsty, just dying for a drink of water, which they couldn't give me because I'd just throw it back up. It wouldn't stay down. The best they could do was give me these little-bitty ice chips. And even those had to be carefully divvied out. I remember begging, actually *begging* for those ice chips. I never craved anything more in my life.

Marvin came by that afternoon, along with Tam. He was still shook up about all this. His eyes were red. I could see he'd been crying. He'd looked like that all week, just drained.

We were talking about the stuff Randi and Lisa were doing with me, and I said something Marvin found fascinating.

"It's weird," I said. "It's like this is my body, but at the same time it's not. I'm *in* it, but it doesn't feel like mine."

Marvin didn't know what to say to that. We started talking about the team getting ready for the game Sunday, and I had the same feeling about that. I was part of the team, but I wasn't.

Cary Blanchard had come by that day to show me a hat the team had made up, with the ichthus symbol stitched on the crown and my number 90 inside it. He said the Islanders hockey team had worn the symbol on their helmets during a home game earlier in the week. And the Jets would be wearing it on theirs Sunday.

They put in a conference call to me that afternoon, all the guys at the other end of the line in Weeb Ewbank Hall at our practice facility, and that just made those mixed feelings of connection and separation more acute. It was wonderful to be able to joke with the guys, just like always. I think it made them feel better; I know it made *me* feel better. But at the same time it was painful, realizing they were there and I was here, and that was the way it was going to stay.

I continued to get more calls than they could count down at the hospital's switchboard. The number was definitely more than I could answer. Some, there was no question I would take. When David Fritts, a hunting companion and my best friend back in Oklahoma, was on the line, I picked up right away. David's a welder as well as a world-class coyote caller, and I remember him saying he was going to get me back out on that prairie with him if he had to build me a special dolly to do it. He was serious, and I was ready to take him up on it. I could see us rigging up one of those sip-and-puff rifles—they work on the same principle as a sip-and-puff wheelchair, controlled by blowing through a mouth tube. We talked about connecting one of those to an all-terrain vehicle and rolling me out across the range. I had to get back out there. I never doubted I would. And neither did David.

The hospital staff was working that Friday evening to rig up a phone system with a headset I could wear, to make it easier to handle the calls. I could operate it by pushing my head against a pad laid on my pillow, answering that way, then listening through

a speaker and talking through the headset microphone. I was trying it out that night with my sisters, who had had a terrible time
trying to get through to me, and suddenly one of the hospital
operators cut in and told me Bill Clinton was on another line,
waiting to speak to me.

Right. Ha-ha.

"Could you tell him I'm on the line with my sisters?" I said. And
I went back to our call. I didn't give the Clinton thing a second
thought. I'd been getting crank calls all week from people telling
the operator they were teammates or friends or someone famous,
so they could get through.

A minute later my dad came in with a small card in his hand.

"Son," he said, "that really *was* the president . . . or the president-
elect. He left this number."

I couldn't believe it. I called the number right away—my dad
dialed it for me—and sure enough, a secretary came on the line,
and in a couple of seconds Bill Clinton came on the line.

"Hi, Dennis," he said. "I wanted to call and tell you I've been
thinking a lot about you lately. And I want you to know I'm praying for you."

"Thank you very much," I said. "I'm praying for you, too. The
way things are going, you need it more than I do."

I didn't really know what to say. I mean, what do you say to the
president of the United States? Especially on the spur of the
moment. We talked for about ten minutes. I told him I'd never
talked to a president before, and he told me he hadn't talked to
many football players. He knew Keith Jackson, he said, since
Jackson's from Arkansas. But that's about it.

Finally, he wished me luck.

"I wish *you* luck," I said. "You're the one who's inherited the
problems."

I hadn't voted for Bill Clinton. I didn't share his point of view on
some key issues. But I respected his sincerity tremendously, especially after that phone call.

It was early the next morning, Saturday morning, that I did
something I hadn't done since being carried off the field the Sunday before.

I moved my toes.

It actually had happened for the first time on Thursday, just a microscopic movement, a flick in my right big toe. Steve Nicholas had been there and thought he saw it, too. But I couldn't reproduce it, I couldn't make it happen again, so the doctors wrote it off as an involuntary reflex, a withdrawal response, although Steve maintained it was genuine.

By Friday, though, I could feel the impulses inside the toes of my right foot. I couldn't move anything, but I told Steve I could *feel* the nerves firing. Something was happening down there. There was no doubt about it. This was not the totally dead feeling I'd had up till then. I'm sure the doctors believed *I* believed I was feeling those nerves. They see a lot of people in my situation who believe what they *need* to believe. Hope and fear can be a strong combination. I had no doubt the nerves were sparking, but the doctors' attitude was, "We'll believe it when we see it."

Saturday they saw it.

It was about 7:30 in the morning, and Dr. O'Leary was giving me the once-over, asking me the usual questions, pushing and poking me in the usual places, telling me to try to move this, try to move that. Finally, he came to my right foot. He asked me to try to move the toes, which I did. And suddenly, almost imperceptibly, the big toe . . . moved. You could hardly see it. It was like the flick of an eyelash. But it definitely moved.

Dr. O'Leary asked me to do it again, to make sure it was voluntary.

Then again.

Then he went through the ceiling.

"*It's a miracle!!!*" he shouted.

And he was out the door, racing down the hall to make some phone calls.

Steve Nicholas was across the hall, examining a ninety-four-year-old man with a hip fracture. He came over to see what all the fuss was about.

"Hey, bud," I said. "Watch this."

And I wiggled the toe.

Steve couldn't believe it. He was ecstatic. "Oh my God," he said.

He had his right hand on the top of my foot and this big grin on his face.

"So is this good?" I asked.

"Good?" he said. "If you had done this two months from now, we would have been thrilled."

Steve rushed out to call Bob Reese over at the Jets complex, where the team would be coming in soon for morning practice before leaving for Buffalo, where we'd be playing the Bills Sunday.

I dialed Angela, who was still at the hotel. Mindi Blanchard had spent the night with her. They were getting set to come over about ten. I asked her how she was doing, what was going on. We chatted for a couple of minutes, then she asked me what was happening here.

"Oh, nothing much," I said. "I moved my toe this morning."

She went crazy, screaming and yelling. She hung up the phone and rushed right over. By the time she and Mindi got there, I was moving the foot itself, just a hair.

Jim Nicholas came in about then. From the start of the week, he'd been making a football analogy, telling me I was backed up against the goal line, that I was fighting my way out a yard at a time. When he saw my toe moving, he told me I'd just completed a bomb. I was out to midfield now. But even that wasn't good enough for him.

"Well, son," he said, "now that this right side's working, we've got to get that *left* side going."

Now I was psyched. *Something* was happening, as if a massive logjam was breaking up. Maybe just a little, maybe just a single log was loosening, but something was shifting.

At about ten o'clock, Pete Carroll and Greg Robinson sneaked by the hospital on their way to the airport for the flight to Buffalo. They said the guys were really pumped up, that they'd been practicing with a purpose all week long, and now they were sky-high from the news about my toes.

"I've got better news than that," I told them, and I moved my foot for them, ever so slightly. Pete and Greg couldn't believe it. We talked for a few minutes, then they asked if there was any message I wanted to relay to the team.

I did want to say something, but I didn't want to make any profound speech. I didn't want to say anything cheap or hollow. I just wanted to make a simple statement, to let them know how I felt. And it wasn't much different from how I would have felt if I'd been right down on the field with them. I asked Pete and Greg to tell the guys that when it got to the fourth quarter, when everyone was sucking wind and exhausted, I'd be watching them. I'd have my eyes on each and every one of them.

By the time Pete and Greg got to La Guardia to meet the team for its 1:00 P.M. flight to Buffalo, there was more news waiting for them.

I'd "fired" my right quad—the quadriceps muscle in the lower thigh, just inside the knee.

It was only a twitch. You could hardly see it. But like what had happened with my toes and foot, this was the spark that could start a fire. I was no medical doctor, but I knew if a twitch is there, it means the nerves are intact from the brain to that point. The highway is open, at least partially. *Something* is there, and if something is there, that means *more* might be there. If you can fire the quad, you can eventually extend the knee. If you can extend the knee, you can *stand*, which would have been fantastic news in itself, even if I could stand on only one leg.

And if you can stand, maybe you can walk.

That entire week, from the moment I had arrived at the hospital, I had resolved that I was going to let what had happened to me be a witness for the Lord, that I was going to let this tragedy be a blessing to other people's lives through my strength and perseverence, through how I dealt with a paralysis that could well be permanent. I knew I had to trust in the Lord, and that's what I did. That's what I prayed for—strength and wisdom and courage.

Then that toe moved. And the moment it did, I knew what I had to do now. I knew my calling. I knew I had to do more than accept and work with what I'd been left. I knew I had to take it back. *Take it back.*

Once that toe moved, then the quad, I spent every waking moment training all my willpower, all my physical and mental strength, on those two places in my body, straining to fan those faint little flickers into something more. I'd lie there flexing that quad over and over and over until it was so fatigued I couldn't flex any more. I did the same with my toe. I couldn't touch it, I couldn't even *see* it, but I could lie there looking up at the ceiling and put every ounce of effort, put my whole *being*, into that right big toe.

I was trying so hard the doctors actually told me it wasn't safe. They said something about pushing so hard that the fatigue might actually do some damage. But I didn't pay much attention to that.

The way the guys felt about all this news, they could have flown up to Buffalo without the plane. I thought a lot about them that afternoon, and about the game. You spend four years getting conditioned to a certain routine, it's hard to shake quickly. I wasn't on the plane with my teammates, but I had Buffalo on my mind, just like they did.

The Bills. Of all the teams in the league, this was our archrival. Obviously there's the intrastate aspect, two New York teams. But there's so much more than that.

First, they're in our division, and things are always more intense against teams in your division. I always got worked up for Miami, for example, but more so for the Bills, probably because they were the team to be measured against in the AFC East, if not in the entire AFC.

And their fans were the toughest I'd ever seen. All opposing fans are rough to some degree, but the Bills fans take it to another level. Sometimes it seemed as if they had nothing better to do up there in Orchard Park than curse and throw things—wadded-up cups, hot dogs, anything they could get their hands on. The only fans who give Buffalo fans a run for their money are the Patriots' fans, but that's because they're mad at *everybody*. Their team was worse than *we* were. Patriot fans were as hard on their own guys as they were on us.

We had never beaten the Bills since I'd joined the Jets. We came close several times, but it seemed that every time the game was on the line, they'd get a break and we'd bite the dust again. It was like a curse. I remember a game two years before, when we were ahead with nineteen seconds to go. I drew a bead on Kelly, had him completely cornered, and somehow he ducked under me and threw a touchdown pass to beat us. I've got a big blown-up photo of that play framed in my rec room at home. There I am, in mid-air, rising above Kelly with my arms outstretched, about to swallow him whole. You'd never dream he got away. You'd never dream the Bills could beat us ten straight times, that it would have been five years since they'd last lost to the Jets. But that's where things stood as the guys flew up to Buffalo that Saturday. We were seventeen-point underdogs. They were on their way to the Super Bowl, and we were 3-9. We were riddled with injuries. We were emotionally and physically drained. No way in the world were we supposed to win.

That night I thought a lot about Marvin. I knew he was lying in his hotel bed 450 miles away, thinking about me. This would be the first time in three seasons that we didn't fall asleep the night before a game in the same room. I know Marvin had to have cried that night, all by himself, which is the way he would spend game nights the rest of the season—alone. Bruce wasn't about to assign Marvin a new roommate.

Late that night I asked a nurse to turn on the TV. It was tuned to ESPN. They were doing something on the NFL, and then there it was, a replay of my collision with Scott. That was the first time I'd seen it. It struck me how *fast* I was moving, that even in slow motion I was a blur. And I could see the power I was putting into that charge, planting my right foot and really *driving* just before the hit.

It didn't bother me, seeing that collision. It didn't shake me up or send chills down my spine. I could see exactly what had happened, that Scott had come from the other side on a stunt and wound up at the same spot as me, with neither of us knowing the other would be there. What really struck me most as I watched that replay was the same thing I'd thought about the instant after the collision. "Man," I said to myself, "what a hit."

Sunday morning I woke up hoping yet another part of my body would be moving, that those twitches I'd had the day before would keep spreading. They didn't, which was kind of a letdown. I didn't understand then the peaks and valleys I had yet to face, the roller coaster ride I was in for. There is no straight line to recovery from a spinal cord injury, but that's a fact I had yet to truly realize. I'd learn, though. The months ahead would teach me.

What stood out most that Sunday morning was seeing Joe Namath walk into my room.

I'd met Joe Namath my rookie year. We were playing the Rams in Anaheim, and I was out on the field early, as usual, testing it with my cleats. I was down around the south end zone, looking up the field, when I felt a hand on my shoulder and heard a voice.

"Hello, Dennis," he said as I turned around. "I'm Joe Namath."

All I could think was, Holy smokes, this is *Joe*, Joe *Namath*. I towered over him, and yet I felt like a kid standing next to a giant. Broadway Joe. He was the same figure to me that he was to every kid—a legend, bigger than life. I couldn't believe he had walked up and was talking to me. And he knew my *name!*

Now he was here, in my hospital room, and I was dumbstruck again. Sure, I was a professional athlete myself. There were trading cards with my picture on them sold in stores. People asked for my autograph when I went out to eat. But Joe Namath, Joe DiMaggio—these guys are supernovas, the most known sports figures in the *world*. And here was Namath, visiting me in a human, emotional way, person to person.

He shuffled in much like Leon Hess did, with his hands in his pockets, almost shy. He'd waited for everyone else to be gone, just like Mr. Hess did. He just wanted to visit a little bit by himself.

I remember saying to him that he probably knew hospitals pretty well, since he'd been in a few himself. That broke the ice and he started telling me about hurting his famous knee for the first time, back in 1965, the year before I was born. Then he told me how Jim Nicholas's mother, Julia had given him a St. Jude medal just before Jim operated on his knee. He said he wore that medal during every game after that, that he had kept it ever since.

And now he took it off and handed it toward me.

"I want you to have this," he said.

I raised my head up, and he slipped the medal around my neck. He was incredibly solemn about what he was doing. I could tell he was really moved. And so was I. I vowed to myself that that medal would stay around my neck from then on.

It was business as usual the rest of the morning, with Randi and Lisa really working me out on the tilt table. We had it up to twenty degrees by then, and they kept me on there twenty minutes. By the time they got me back in bed, I was wrung out, throwing up, not having a good day at all. Mercifully, I fell asleep.

When I awoke, I asked Hugh to turn on the TV. The game was already into the third quarter. Angela and her parents and Mindi were watching over at the hotel, and when they heard I was awake, they all came over.

I'd missed the pregame prayer the Buffalo crowd had had for me, the moment of silence before the national anthem, the TV cameras showing a plane flying over Rich Stadium pulling a banner that read "GET WELL DENNIS BYRD."

I had no idea Leon Hess had come into the locker room before the game and given the guys a pregame speech. That's just not the sort of thing he does. But that day he did. He talked about the team being a family, then he talked about me. "Adversity is a part of life," he said. "You have to overcome it. We're all in this together. I don't care if you come off the field 100-0, as long as you give it everything you've got for Dennis."

I could see the guys were wearing the ichthus and my number on their helmets, and I could see some of the *Bills* wearing it, too! Thurman and Kelly and their safety, Mark Kelso. Jim Ritcher and Kent Hull and most of the rest of their offensive linemen. I was overcome. As much as we had this intense war in the trenches, as much as we battled each other between those sidelines, those guys were still able to show the brotherhood they felt with me. They really had class.

I had hardly woken up before some technicians started wheeling in the equipment to take X rays.

"Hold on a second, guys," I said. "We're not doing anything until I've watched the rest of this football game."

We were ahead 17-10 when the fourth quarter began. I'd been down on that field so many times, I could almost feel it, lying there in that hospital bed, the wind whistling over that frozen turf, the cold cutting you to the core, the deafening roar of 76,000 Bills fans. The gusts were blowing forty-five miles an hour that afternoon, pulling the temperature on the field down to three below zero. Snow was piled on the sidelines, as it usually is in Buffalo in December.

It felt so familiar. So did the touchdown pass Kelly threw five minutes into that final quarter, tying the game at 17, which is where the score was when the Bills got the ball on their own nineteen with just under two minutes to go. That felt familiar, too. I couldn't help thinking, Here we go again. The clock ticking down. Kelly driving them up the field. It had happened like that so many times.

But not this time.

On second down from his eighteen, Kelly lofted a pass to the left sideline, toward his wide receiver, James Lofton. He never saw Brian Washington, our safety on that side. I couldn't even raise my arms as Bee-Dub—that's short for "BW"—cut in front of that pass and took it in for the score. I couldn't jump up and cheer the way I wanted to as I watched Marvin there in the end zone, waving toward the camera, waving toward *me*, flashing the signal I always gave Ange from the sidelines, the thumb, forefinger, and pinky extended on one hand, sign language for "I love you."

I couldn't leap up the way I wanted to, but I was dancing as I lay there in that bed. I was *dancing*.

And when Bill Pickel threw Kelly down with a minute to go, stripped the ball, and fell on the fumble, I cried.

And then it was over. We'd won. Incredibly, we'd won. The guys were leaping all over the field. Marvin had played the game of his life—he wound up with the defensive game ball—and now he had a group of our guys, along with some of theirs, kneeling together in a small circle down on the field, in prayer.

The guys called me up from the locker room. Hasty told me he wished I could have been there. I told him I *was* there. When Scott came on the line, he told me they'd all been thinking of the message I'd sent them, that my eyes would be burning on them in that fourth quarter. "You were here with us," Scott said. "You *were* with us."

Less than four hours later, Steve Gutman came into my room with Jim Nicholas and Pete and Greg. They'd flown straight back from Buffalo, and they had the game ball with them. There'd been no doubt who should have it, they said.

I'd earned three game balls during my career with the Jets, but none of them would ever be as special as this one.

So that's how the day ended. The curtain had come down on a week that was probably more trying than any this football team had ever been through. My teammates had pulled off a miracle that afternoon.

Now it was time to turn back to fighting and praying for a miracle of my own. Jesus Christ had been with me during the past ten days more than He had ever been with me in my entire life.

I knew I would need Him even more in the days ahead.

REBIRTH

14

onday, the day after we beat Buffalo, was the day I finally
got to see Ashtin.

The Jets had gotten a room for her and my mother-in-
law at the same hotel where they had a room for Angela. Ashtin
had been told that Daddy had hurt his legs playing football, that
he couldn't walk and that he was in the hospital. We hadn't
wanted her to see me in the halo vest—we didn't know how she
might take that. And after the surgery I was still a pretty scary
sight, especially to a two-year-old. The staples running down the
front of my neck looked like a hideous zipper. I was physically
wasted, essentially unwashed, still in a lot of pain, and nauseated
most of the day. It would have been frightening for Ashtin to see
me like that. But now, after more than a week, I'd improved
enough that we decided it was okay. I didn't know how she felt,
but *I* couldn't wait any longer.

I heard her before I saw her, calling "Daddy!" as she rushed up
the hall.

"Daddy! Daddy!"

Then she peeked around the door, saw it *was* Daddy, and came
running into the room and scrambling up onto the bed. I asked
her what I always did when we greeted each other. "Where's my

kiss and hug?" She gave me them both, then got down to business. She had her little doctor bag with her, the one I'd bought her two weeks before, and she didn't waste any time. She opened it up and went to work, taking my temperature, checking my blood pressure, listening to my heart.

Then she climbed into my lap and curled into the crook of my left arm. I couldn't move that arm, but I could cradle Ashtin in it and I could caress her with the outside of my right hand. I could kiss the top of her head as she lay there. And I could have no doubt that this was one of the sweetest moments of my entire life. The Bills game, as monumentally special as that was, couldn't compare to the sensation of having my little girl cuddled beside me again.

After a while, she turned to me with a familiar request.

"Tell me a story, Daddy."

"Which one, darlin'?" I asked.

"'The Two Bears,' Daddy. Tell me 'The Two Bears.'"

I'd made up a story for her once about two bears. From then on, whenever she wanted to hear the story of Goldilocks, she'd call it 'The Two Bears.' No matter how many times I tried to tell her this one was *three* bears, she'd still ask for two.

By then the doctors and Angela and I were well into the process of deciding where I would go to begin my rehabilitation. I was hearing anywhere from three to five months in terms of how long I'd need to be at a rehab center. I was hearing two years in terms of how long it would be before I would be walking, *if* I would be walking. Right now I couldn't even be moved from my bed into a wheelchair. My body couldn't handle that upright position.

There are a lot of excellent rehab centers around the country, but we were basically considering four: Craig Hospital in Denver, where Mike Utley had done his work; Marc Buoniconti's Miami Project, in Florida; the Rusk Institute of Rehabilitation Medicine at New York University; and Mount Sinai.

Each of those places had its strengths, but the idea of being anyplace but New York was hard for me even to imagine. This was where my circle of support was, the city that embraced both me and my teammates, who knew and loved me. I knew I needed them as much as any therapy the doctors could offer. I'd always considered myself a leader among my teammates. All the way back to high school, I'd invited them to lean on me. Now I needed to lean on them. I needed them near me.

Of the two New York facilities, Mount Sinai seemed to have the most going for it. Dr. Ragnarsson directed its rehabilitation department and he'd been seeing me already for a week now. Dr. Camins was on the staffs of Mount Sinai and Lenox Hill, so it would be easy for him to keep working with me in the months ahead.

Dr. Camins and Dr. Ragnarsson had taken my parents and Rick Schaeffer over for a tour of Mount Sinai the day after my surgery. Mom and Dad were impressed, although it had hit Mom hard seeing the condition of a lot of the patients there. Stroke victims. Amputees. When they showed her their wheelchairs and talked about how what they did there would help me learn to live life in a chair, she broke down. That was hard for her to take. It was like a glimpse into the future, a very jolting glimpse.

Tuesday, Randi and Lisa got me ready by putting me into a huge padded reclining chair with wheels—you could call it a wheelchair. I had to lie there for thirty minutes, leaning up at an angle of about twenty degrees—about the angle of a fully reclined La-Z-Boy—feeling very faint.

My condition was quadriplegic. I could move the toes in my right foot, flex the ankle, and tighten the right thigh muscle, meaning I could make a contraction there. But I was light-years from being able to use the muscle to lift my leg. I could do the same things, to a much lesser degree, with my left leg. That would be the pattern throughout my rehab, the left side lagging behind the right by two weeks or more. Right now, I had nothing to show on the left side but the slightest flexing.

That was my status as they loaded me Wednesday morning for the move from Lenox Hill to Mount Sinai. I was leaving a week earlier than they had expected when I'd arrived. All during my stay it had taken four or five people to move me, and that's how many came into my room that morning to transfer me from the Clinitron onto a gurney. Again sandbags were tucked on both sides of my head. Again my body was strapped down as I was taken down the elevator and rolled out through the same emergency room doors I'd entered ten days before.

I remember feeling the cold as they took me out to a waiting ambulance. This was the first fresh air I'd breathed since the day I'd arrived. It was bitter cold. December cold. I could feel it on my face and shoulders.

They lifted me into the back of the ambulance, just as they'd done at the stadium, and Angela climbed in with me, just as she'd done before. It wasn't a long drive, but about halfway there I got very claustrophobic. I asked the EMT riding with us to unstrap my head, and he did.

And then we arrived.

I was terrified. I had all these dark visions of what a rehabilitation ward was going to be like. I kept imagining the worst scenes from *Born on the Fourth of July*, where Tom Cruise plays the paralyzed Vietnam veteran who goes through torturous treatment in a VA hospital. All I could think of was being brutally belted to a tilt table like him and having them flip me over and flip me back.

Beyond the sheer terror, I was also scared the way a kid going to his first day of kindergarten is scared. I had gotten comfortable at Lenox Hill with Hugh and Beres and Goldie and the other nurses. They were familiar to me. They were what I knew. These people had shown me warmth and compassion. And now I was being turned over to strangers in a strange place. I didn't know what to expect.

When we stopped, it was at the Upper East Side of Manhattan, almost to Harlem. That's where Mount Sinai Medical Center has sat for the last century and a half. The buildings around me looked dark and grim as I was unloaded and rolled into the hospital, up to my room on the ninth floor, the room that would be my new home.

It was snowing. I could see it through my window. My room was on the north side of the building, so I couldn't see the sun, even if it was out. You never saw the sun, not on this side of the building, not in the winter. And winter was just beginning.

All of the outside world that I'd see for weeks to come would be through that window. It became like a painting to me, a still life of dark brick buildings, rusting metal fire escapes, shadowy rooftops, and, in the center of the scene, an old water tower perched on top of the apartment house directly across from my room. At dusk that water tower would be silhouetted against the blues and purples of the winter sky. Then, at night, there was the glow of lights from the windows across the way. There was one room I could see perfectly from my position in bed. The television was on in that room every night, the glimmer from its bluish light flickering on the walls.

Dr. Ragnarsson was there when I arrived, as he would be almost every morning, when he made his rounds. He was almost fifty years old, but he looked younger. And he spoke with an Icelandic accent. He grew up in Reykjavík, where he still had a home, but he'd been in the United States for twenty years, ever since he came here to become a specialist in physical rehabilitation. He'd had a bad knee injury playing soccer as a boy, and that's what turned him toward making rehab his life's work. Among his previous patients was Roy Campenella, the great Brooklyn Dodger who was paralyzed in an auto accident and just recently passed away. He came to Mount Sinai in 1986 to help set up the hospital's first in-patient rehabilitation department, and by the time I got there, it had grown into a fifty-bed unit. All fifty beds were perpetually filled—with stroke victims, amputees, people with brain injuries. And spinal cord cases.

About a third of the patients in that unit were people like me, people with spinal cord injuries. For those who were paraplegic, the average stay was about two months; for the quadriplegics, it was three to five. That was me, a quad.

Rags—which is what I was calling him before long—answered my questions as best he could, but in the beginning he didn't have anything more specific or hopeful to say than the doctors at Lenox Hill had. I do remember the last thing he said to me and Angela the day we arrived.

"You should hope and pray for the best," he told us, "and always be prepared for the worst."

The rest of that day was a parade of introductions. There were my nurses: Mike, a small, bearded guy who lived in Greenwich

Village; Mary Anne, the most talkative woman I'd ever met in my life; and Rhoda, who had been at Woodstock and spent hours telling me what it was *really* like to be a flower child.

Then there was Jane Walsh, the head nurse, whose job was to teach patients and their families about spinal cord injuries. And Maria Russo, a staff psychologist who was there to help guide Angela and me through the emotional roller coaster that lay ahead of us.

Finally, there were the two people I'd be seeing the most of in the coming months: Lawrence Harding, my physical therapist; and Joanne Giammetta, my occupational therapist. I knew what their jobs were, and I resolved to do everything I could to kiss their butts. These were the two people who were going to be working my body every day, pushing me harder than any coach ever had, possibly pushing me harder than *I* ever had. I wanted them on my side. I didn't want them thinking I thought I was something special because I was this famous New York Jet.

I had no idea what they thought. I had no idea what to expect from anyone. That first day was a swirl of introductions, a steady stream of people in and out of my room. It wasn't until late that night that I had a minute to myself, to try to sort out where I was and what I was doing. I remember lying there, trying to give things a chance to settle down—to settle *in*—when an orderly walked into the room.

His name was James. He said he knew who I was, and he said it didn't make a bit of difference to him or anyone else here that I was a professional football player, a big, bad athlete.

"I seen them *work* down there," he said, talking about the rehab room, talking about the therapists. "I seen people dumped right out of their wheelchairs, layin' there *beggin'* for somebody to put 'em back, and the therapists just standin' there and makin' 'em work their way back up by themselves."

That chilled me. I'd never feared another human being in my adult life, but I was afraid now. I was petrified.

"You're gonna get to where you *hate* these people," James said.

"You're wrong," I answered. "I could never hate these people, because they're going to teach me to walk again."

But inside I was terrified. Inside, I knew that was hope speaking for me more than certainty.

It was faith speaking, as well. And determination. And even obligation. I had cards and snapshots mounted all around my bed, pictures of Ashtin and Angela, of my mom and dad, of Jeni and Dawn and Doug and Dan and my nephews, of Angela's folks, David and Betty, and of her brother, Chris. This was my family. These were the people who knew me best and loved me most. These were the people I was going to walk for.

But no one was talking about walking when I woke up after my first night at Mount Sinai. I was flat on my back, with a right arm I could barely raise, a left arm that was worse, and hands and fingers that could do nothing at all. Absolutely nothing. I was totally dependent on the nurses to brush my hair, give me a sponge bath, shave me, brush my teeth, feed me, empty my bladder with a catheter, empty my bowels with their fingers—all the "Activities of Daily Living" (ADL) that I was supposed to learn to do for myself.

I was dependent on the nurses to turn me every two hours, to keep the ulcer on my tailbone from getting worse and to keep any more from beginning. The only part of my body that I could control with any normalcy was my neck, and it was wrapped in a foam collar, weak from inactivity and wracked with pain and spasms from the surgery. The collar itself was torturous—it was itchy, constricting, and it took away just about the only movement I had, which was my head. When I had that collar on, I could hardly turn my head at all, and it limited my field of vision. Lying on my back with it on, I could see only straight up at the ceiling. If I wanted to look at something—or some*body*—else, I had to strain and lift my head up to peer over the collar. Even that slight elevation of my head—just lifting it off the pillow on my bed— was enough to trigger the dizziness and nausea I'd felt during my tilt-table sessions at Lenox Hill.

The only position in which I felt any comfort at all was flat on my back, but Joanne and Lawrence weren't about to let me stay there. Their first order of business was to get me up and into a wheelchair—immediately.

I didn't have to worry that my name would affect how I was treated, at least not by Joanne and Lawrence. They didn't approach me any differently than they did any other patient they had. They treated me as what I was: a C-5 quad.

Actually, Joanne despised the term *quad*. When she heard me use it, she cut me off.

"Dennis, I *hate* that!" she'd say. "You're not a 'quad.' You're not a 'para.' You're a *person*, a person who's suffered a spinal cord injury."

The hospital itself had me classified "C-5/C-6 quadriplegic motor incomplete" on its charts, but Joanne was right. They don't call cancer patients "cancers." So I stopped using that term.

Joanne is a tiny little woman—five-two and barely over a hundred pounds—but she had this enormous energy and incredible physical techniques. She could do things with my body that a person twice her size shouldn't have been able to do. She was twenty-nine, from New Jersey, and she wasn't afraid of anyone or anything. I wound up getting closer to her than to anyone else I worked with, either at Mount Sinai or at Lenox Hill. She became what my brothers had been for me when I was growing up: both my shepherd and my slavedriver. Lawrence spent hours every day with me as well—he was about Joanne's age, tall and slim, a British native with a strong English accent. We got along great. But as close as I felt to him, it couldn't compare to the bond that grew between me and Joanne.

Joanne told me the first patient she'd ever worked with, when she was fresh out of school in 1986, was a twenty-four-year-old guy in almost exactly the same condition as me. He'd been on a pleasure cruise, had decided to dive into the ship's pool during a party one night, and broke his neck on the bottom. He was wearing a tuxedo when it happened. His was a C-5 fracture, just like mine. I asked her if he was ever able to walk, if she'd ever seen anyone like me walking. She said yes, he eventually was able to walk. It was very labored, not for long distances, and he had to use forearm crutches, but he could walk. Even that image seemed bright to me as I lay on my back in bed.

Joanne's attitude was "get 'em up, get 'em going, none of this static baloney." This was clearly not Lenox Hill, where they'd waited on me hand and foot. Both Joanne and Lawrence made it clear I was going to have to *work* here, at least five hours a day, six days a week, which was fine with me. And I was going to have to get to work right away, which meant getting into that chair. Before I could even think about going down to the rehab room, I had to get into that wheelchair.

It was brutal. The chair itself was a massive black reclining monster, padded, with lots of chrome and large wheels, something like the chair Randi and Lisa had put me in at Lenox Hill, but even bigger. Still, it wasn't big enough for me. My feet stuck out beyond the end, so Joanne had to rig up a couple of extensions made of corrugated cardboard, to keep my feet from flopping off the edge.

She also had to make sure the staff knew how to lift me. It took four or five people to move me from my bed into the chair, and they had to be careful about that sore on my tailbone. If they banged it, it might split open, which would set everything back while they worried about infection and waited for it to heal.

But before they could even put me in the chair, they had to wrap my legs. The dizziness and nausea I'd felt on the tilt table at Lenox Hill is a condition called *orthostatic hypotension*, caused by the combination of weak circulation and a tendency of the blood to pool in the legs. Basically, for most people in a situation like mine, gravity is stronger than their body's ability to push the blood through the veins. So when their body begins to be raised and the legs are lowered, blood leaves their upper extremities and collects in the lower limbs, and faintness and nausea kick in. It's a gradual, grueling process just to be able to eventually sit upright without passing out. For some people, it takes months. Some never get there. They either spend the rest of their lives reclining, or they have a chair with a power release in it, so they can get down quickly when they start to feel sick.

To resist orthostasis and to keep blood clots from forming in my legs—another constant danger—the therapists and nurses put TEDS on me. Thrombo Embolic Dynamic Stockings. I hated them with a passion. They were these tight stockings the nurses pulled over my legs up to just above the knees. They squeezed my legs tightly, to help push the blood back into the upper part of my body. Then, as if that weren't enough, the nurses or therapists would wrap Ace bandages around both my legs, for even more tightness. Joanne would climb right up on my bed, throw a leg up on her shoulder, and have it wrapped and ready to go in two minutes flat. Then she'd do the same with the other one. Amazing.

Just starting at twenty degrees in the chair that first day was a challenge. But Joanne knew what she was doing. She'd put me back down, let me rest a little bit, then get right back at it, pushing it another couple of degrees. Then back down again. And back up. Again and again. It was agony. Tedious and painful. But by the end of the first day, we'd actually doubled the angle we'd begun at. We were up to forty degrees.

And I was dead. By the time they put me back in my bed, I felt like a rag. And now there was another nurse sticking a catheter in my penis, another sticking her fingers up my rectum to empty my bowels—it was beyond humiliating. I was being stripped down to my essence, with no such thing as privacy, no such thing as pride in the sense I'd felt it before, in terms of my conception of myself physically and as a man. I was just a body now. I was still Dennis Byrd, but this body that contained me was something different now. It had been broken, turned into something else. Now it needed to be rebuilt, to be *reclaimed*. I intended to make it mine again, but until then I had to share it with all these people— nurses, doctors, attendants, therapists. It didn't belong just to me anymore.

The posters I had had in my room at Lenox Hill were here now, along with a set of flip cards the Frases, Boyers, and Blanchards had made me, a set of notecards clipped together, each with one of their favorite Bible verses printed on it. I couldn't move my fingers, but I could lift my right hand and push the cards, flipping them over, one by one. It was clumsy, but it worked. I spent hours reading those cards. And every quiet moment I had, all day long, I prayed. I talked to the Lord, asking for His counsel, for His help.

I had an ECU in my room—an Environmental Control Unit—a state-of-the-art device that controlled everything from the lights

to the television to the nurses' call bell to the speakerphone by
my bed. The ECU operated the same way the phone system had
at Lenox Hill, with a little pad placed on the pillow beside my
head. All the machinery around me—including the motor that
raised and lowered my bed—could be operated by pressing my
head or right arm against that pad.

I could see I had the best care possible. The facilities, the staff—
I couldn't ask for anything more. But in a way, all the nurses and
doctors, all the technology, made me feel even more pathetic.
Even at night, I was plugged in—to a pair of "sequential compression stockings," plastic sleeves wrapped around my calves and
pumped with a constant flow of air, to squeeze back that pooling
blood while I slept.

I could handle feeling pathetic, I was truly prepared to handle
anything, with the help of Jesus Christ. But Angela, why should
she have to deal with this, maybe for the rest of her life? I was
determined to walk again. I had no doubt I would. But what if I
was wrong? What if the Lord had other plans for me? What if I'd
never rise out of a wheelchair? I knew I could live with that, but
should Angela?

That night, I told her what I was feeling.

"It's not fair to you," I said. "It's not fair for you to have to be
with me like this forever, for you to have to take care of me like
this. I'd understand if you wanted to leave me."

I had never seen a look like the one that came over her face
when I said those words. It was a mixture of astonishment, disbe-
lief, and anger.

"Dennis," she finally said. "*That's* not fair. I can't believe you'd
say that. I can't believe you'd even *think* that."

Her eyes were full of tears. So were mine. She put her arms
around me, and we both just began crying, openly and without
shame. I realized how carried away I'd been. This person that I
loved so much and knew so well, my companion for so long, the
mother of my child, a woman whose faith in the Lord was as
strong as mine . . .

She was never going to leave me.

15

It was one thing to be moved into the wheelchair, but it was another thing entirely to be taken downstairs to Mount Sinai's rehab room. That was when I realized I was entering a world different from anything I'd ever known, a place unlike anything I'd ever imagined, populated by men and women who were just like I was now—severely physically disabled.

It was Lawrence who pushed me down the first time, the day after I arrived. We rode the elevator all the way to the ground floor, the basement, and that's how it felt. Old. Antiquated. Nothing new or shiny about it. This place was strictly functional, strictly utilitarian. No frills.

Pieces of worn equipment wrapped in old athletic tape sat stacked in corners and against walls as Lawrence rolled me into a room with about a dozen people in it, each working with a therapist, all busy doing something with their bodies. One man was working with a metal walker. A woman was struggling with a cane. A couple of people were lying on elevated mats, trying to learn how to turn over.

There was one boy named Wayne who was wearing a halo vest. He'd been in a car wreck. He was twenty-one.

There was a woman who was paralyzed from the waist down. It

had happened while she was giving birth, during her epidural. The doctor's needle had hit a nerve and *bang*, she was paralyzed—which she didn't realize until later, when the drug wore off and she still couldn't feel or lift her legs.

One girl, a young blonde woman, was missing her left leg. She'd gotten a cut, nothing serious, but it became infected. One thing led to another, and she wound up losing the leg. From a tiny thing like that.

There was a man named Bill who had a serious head injury. He'd been riding a bicycle with his kids one day when he was hit from behind by a car. He wasn't wearing a helmet, and now he was here, walking around all day moaning one phrase over and over and over again. *"Oh, maaan,"* he'd say. That was his response to everything. That was the extent of his conversation, with different inflections.

"Oh, man."

"Ohhhhhh, man!"

"Oh *man*, oh *man*, oh *man!*"

Some people were wailing because they didn't want to work as hard as their therapists were trying to make them. Others were wailing because they *did*, and because the pain was so great. One woman, her name was Zoya, was on a mat, straining with everything she had to move her hip. She'd been beaten nearly to death one night by a gang of muggers who jumped her on a train. They crushed her skull and badly injured her hip. Now she was here, trying to stretch, with the pain of those bone spurs cutting through her. She was screaming as she pushed. But she kept pushing. She knew there was no way around that pain, only *through* it.

Then there was Ken. Ken Rosenblatt, who would become my good friend in the coming months. He was an electrical contractor, in his late thirties. He'd been at work one morning, preparing his payroll, when someone knocked at the door. He opened it and there stood a guy in a mask, pointing a gun at him. Ken tried to grab it, and the guy pushed him down. Ken looked up at the man and pleaded, "Take anything you want. Just please don't shoot me."

The man stared down at Ken for a moment. Then he shot him. He shot him, then he just stepped over Ken's body and took the money. Four thousand dollars. Four thousand dollars for Ken's life.

Now Ken was paraplegic, paralyzed from the waist down. That hurt me, to look at him and think about the fact that he had had no choice. I was here because I'd made a choice, I'd *chosen* to be out on that football field, to take that risk. But a guy like Ken, the only choice he'd made was to earn a living. And somebody just stepped in and took that away from him. Took away his freedom and put him in a prison for the rest of his life, an eighteen-inch-by-eighteen-inch cubicle on wheels.

Waves of feeling were washing through me. Shock. And sadness. And compassion. I'd lived an entire life sheltered from this kind of pain and disfigurement, and now I was surrounded by it. I was part of it. This room was filled with paralysis, amputations, strokes, damaged hearts, damaged minds. And what struck me was how each of these lives had been fine, totally normal, until some tragedy suddenly changed everything forever.

The courage, bravery, and effort—the word "effort" doesn't even begin to describe the intensity I saw in these men and women—were beyond anything I'd ever seen in any football weight room. I was a professional about my body. My body had been my trade. Again, I *chose* that, and I was *paid* for it. These people were being asked to do far more with their bodies than I had ever done with mine, and the only pay they got out of it was the hope of recovery. The only thing that drove them was that dream.

I was eager to start, to start chasing that dream myself, but it wasn't that simple. The biggest problem I had, besides the fact that I was paralyzed, was the severe pain I still felt in my neck, both from the injury itself and from the surgery. It was hard enough trying to raise my sitting level in the wheelchair, but the pain from my neck made it even worse. As much as I'd strain to stay up, my head would start pounding, I could feel myself beginning to vomit, and I'd finally have to tell Lawrence or Joanne to let me back down. I hated that feeling. I hated failing. Hard work was something I had always been comfortable with, and this was no different. It wasn't a lack of effort holding me back. It was just that my body simply was not doing what I was willing it to do. That was frustrating. It drove me crazy. My body had never been a barrier before.

But as frustrating as it was, nothing was going to make me stop pushing against that barrier. I had two cards taped to the wall by my bed. One said, "I can't"; the other said, "Never." These were two phrases I would not allow myself to say or even think. And I didn't.

Joanne rigged up some pieces of foam, slipping them behind my back and shoulders and head to ease the pain in my neck. Then we'd try it again. I'd start to actually turn *white* from the strain, my eyes would get glassy, and Joanne would say, "Dennis, you're bottoming out." I'd say, "No, let's keep going." She'd say, "You're blacking out." And finally I'd have to relent. "Let's go back," I'd say, and, mercifully but maddeningly, I'd sink back. That's what it felt like. Sinking back. I hated that. I wanted to be going forward, not back.

The mat work was just as frustrating. Joanne would get four or five staff people to help transfer me from the wheelchair onto an elevated rubber mat. Now, instead of being on my back in the chair, I was on my back on the mat. I had no muscle strength to speak of, so that's where Joanne began, working on my arms and shoulders with her hands, using progressive resistance exercises. She had me shrug my shoulders while she pushed back against them. She asked me to try to bring my hand to my mouth, again while she pushed against it—that helped with my elbow flexion, with my forearm strength.

Isometric drills served a couple of purposes. They were beginning to build my muscles and helped raise my blood pressure. Whenever I began to feel faint from being upright, Joanne would lower me back down and do one of the resistance exercises to bring my blood pressure back more quickly.

We started trying stomach crunches, too, which were excruciating. The abdominal muscles are a central part of sitting up, of raising and lowering your trunk and simply holding yourself erect. I had no abs at all, nothing. I'm sure some of the doctors doubted I ever would. I could no sooner do a single sit-up than I could stand up and walk. Again, we began with isometrics, Joanne pushing against whatever strength I could muster, which wasn't much at all.

We began working with something called a powder board, which is just that—a wooden board sprinkled with powder to reduce friction as something is rubbed across it. That something was my forearm. We'd put it on this board and I'd try to move my arm back and forth. It was all I could do to move my arm across that smooth, powdered piece of wood. My left arm wasn't strong enough to do even that. Joanne had to pull out a small skateboard, set *that* on the powder board, and that's what I had to move with my left. There was hardly any friction at all, but it was all I could do to budge it.

There was a time when I could bench-press 430 pounds. I was no Scott Mersereau, but 430 wasn't bad. And I could match anyone on squats—I could routinely squat 800. On the leg sled, I could lift 1200 pounds—over half a ton. And now it was all I could do to push a skateboard a couple of inches.

We worked on the mat an hour at a time, taking breaks so Joanne could massage my neck, trying to rub away some of the pain. Then we went back to my room, where Joanne had rigged up my utensils—fork and spoon, toothbrush, hairbrush, cup. She didn't want other people doing for me, no matter how paralyzed I was. She wanted me doing for myself, in any way possible. That's what occupational therapy is about, getting all the independence you can.

Joanne was a bear about independence, from the first day I arrived. I could hardly control my hand, and my fingers were useless, so Joanne slid something called a "universal cuff" over my fingers—a light blue elastic cuff with a leather pocket attached to the palm. She'd slide a fork or a spoon or a toothbrush into that pocket and then, using my bicep and wrist, I could lift food to my mouth or brush my teeth or try to brush my hair. It was painstaking. It seemed like it took hours to do a task that took me seconds before I was hurt. But *I* was doing it, and that was crucial. Joanne rigged up my cup, too, using a Velcro ring with a foam handle I could slide my hand through to lift it to my mouth. It seemed that every time she came in my room that first week, she had another device to help me use my hands. "Miss Go-Go Gadget"—that's what I took to calling her whenever she showed up with that stuff.

It was strange feeling the muscles in my right hand gradually begin to flicker again. Strange and unsettling, because while I could feel them, day by day, beginning to strengthen, it wasn't a strength I could control. They felt out of whack, contracting on their own, having little spasms, curling up instead of straightening. I didn't know what was going on at first, but I soon learned. I soon understood everything there is to know about *tone*.

Tone is essentially the ability of muscles to be controlled, to work with one another, to relax and contract in response to signals from the brain. Tone and strength are two different things. A person's muscles might have strength, but if they are not in tone, if they aren't balanced and under control, then he's got problems.

People with spinal cord injuries often start to feel muscles in their body begin to activate, waking up like loose wires that are suddenly getting surges of power back into them. But there's no switch to control the surges. The muscles tighten up, twitch, go into spasms, or suddenly jerk. They contract on their own, involuntarily. It can be kind of exciting at first, because you're seeing these parts of your body that have been completely limp suddenly starting to *move*.

But then it gets confusing, because the movements are out of control, jerking different parts of the body into cramps, spasms, and intense reflexes. Some spinal cord patients can get spasms so strong their body actually jackknifes right over itself. The person might be working at coming up to a sitting position in a wheelchair when suddenly his abdominal muscles seize into a tight contraction that flexes his body and flips him right out of his chair, like a coiled spring that's suddenly released.

That never happened to me, but I did have these cramps and spasms and curling in my hands that I couldn't understand. I'd ask

Joanne what was going on. I was getting some movement back, but what was all this other stuff?

She told me that was tone kicking in. My finger flexors were coming in and gaining strength, while my finger extensors were still weak. Those two sets of muscles, which are supposed to work together, were out of balance, especially in my left hand, which was pulled into the shape of a claw.

Joanne explained that high tone is no better than low tone. Low tone is a completely flaccid muscle. High tone is a muscle seized up with out-of-control contractions. She pointed out that some spinal cord patients can actually stand on their high tone alone. Their gluteus muscles can be so high-toned that they can lift themselves up to a standing position. Their knees can lock in and they can hold the position. But they can't take a step. They have no control or coordination of the muscles needed to lift one leg, then the other.

Contractions without control are useless. That's what I learned about tone. That's what the cramps and spasms and curling in my hands were teaching me. Again, I was feeling what I'd described to Marvin that day at Lenox Hill—this was my body, but then again it was something I didn't recognize or know at all. Sometimes it seemed like a complete stranger.

Jane Walsh had prepared us for some of this. She came in regularly to talk with Angela and me about what to expect from my body in terms of specifics. She emphasized that there was no straight-line graph, that there were going to be lots of ups and downs. She conducted classes in spinal cord injuries, with groups of patients gathered together. But I didn't want to do anything with a group. I knew that all people would want to do in a group, even well-meaning people, would be to ask me football questions. Attendants did it. Nurses did it. Even doctors did it. I didn't want to talk about football. I wasn't interested in football. I was interested in rehab. *That* was my world now. *That's* what mattered to me.

I talked about this a lot with Maria Russo, whom I resisted seeing at first. Sure, my body was injured, but my mind was perfectly healthy. I figured, "Hey, man, I'm the last person on the face of this earth who needs a psychologist. I'm no loon or anything." But

I found out how useful a person like Dr. Russo could be for just airing out my feelings.

I spent three days a week with her. Our sessions were supposed to go thirty minutes, but many times we'd talk for over an hour. We'd talk about everything. She wanted to know how the physical trauma was affecting me. Was I okay? She knew that regardless of how strong you are emotionally, there are times when you've got questions doctors can't answer. There are times when your heart is hurting or you've got a problem that has nothing to do with your body.

One of the biggest problems Angela and I had was handling the stress from the crowds of people pressing in on us. Friends, strangers, the hospital staff—there were literally dozens of people either in my room or outside the door, day and night. They'd come up to my floor, the nurses would say, "Well, Dennis is sleeping," and they'd just take a seat and wait. For hours! This was incredible loyalty, but at the same time it was really draining for me because it was just so relentless, the faces constantly at my door.

And that's not to mention the media. They weren't a problem for me because they were barred from coming up to my floor or into the rehab unit. I didn't have to face them, but everyone else did. Angela had to sneak in and out of the hospital through back and side entrances to avoid the reporters camped out down in the lobby. Every time a teammate or friend came to see me, he had to run a gauntlet of photographers and reporters. They couldn't come and go without facing an interview. Later on, much later, when I picked up some of those stories and read them, I was amazed at how accurate most of them were, and I realized that was largely because of the information my teammates and coaches had relayed to them.

Still, for some reporters, that wasn't enough. Marvin told me one guy from the *Daily News* tried to talk him into tucking a tape recorder in his coat and bringing it up to tape our conversation. Marvin was disgusted. There was no way in the world he'd do something like that.

The phone was a problem, too. It rang from morning to night. We'd change the number, but that didn't help. I finally stopped answering it unless it was someone who knew the code—one quick ring, hang up, then call right back. That or I had my teammates call in with a beeper code—their phone number followed by their uniform number. That system worked pretty well.

Still, there were times Angela would just say, "That's it. We don't want to see anybody, not even the nurses," and close the door and cut off the phone. We'd feel bad about that, but Dr. Russo said that's exactly what we should do. Just say stop. Just take some control.

Joanne was great about this, too. The first day she came in to meet me, she couldn't believe the crowd in my room. She'd never seen so many people around one hospital bed. Friends, family, hospital staff, Jets personnel, security guards . . . she thought to herself, This guy needs some *space*.

One morning she walked in and there was a doctor by my bed who'd brought eight residents with him to see me. I had no idea who needed to be there and who didn't. But nine did seem to be a lot. Joanne came in, took one look, and just blew her stack. She stormed down to the administration office and said, "Enough is *enough.*" The staff visits seemed to die down some after that.

I really did need time alone with Ashtin and Ange. And they needed some time with me. Ashtin never skipped a beat. It didn't matter to her that Daddy couldn't stand up or Daddy wasn't a football player anymore or even that Daddy's hands didn't work as well as hers did. All that counted was I was her daddy, that I was there for her to climb up in bed with, to lay her dolls against me and spread out their little clothes on my chest and dress them and talk with them and me as if we were all in her playroom back at home.

I hadn't been at Mount Sinai a week when Angela came in with some news about our other child, the baby she was carrying. She had been back to see the obstetrician that day. She hadn't stopped spotting since the week before. They'd taken another ultrasound, and there was still a heartbeat. It was then that the doctor told her they'd expected the worst. They had *not* expected to still see a heartbeat. They were sure she had lost the baby, and they were stunned to see she hadn't. As Ange was leaving, a nurse told her it was a "miracle." All I knew was how overjoyed and relieved I was, both for the baby and for Ange. I knew where that miracle had come from. We both did. The Lord was watching over us. We had no doubt our prayers were being answered.

That Sunday, my first weekend at Mount Sinai, Jeff came up and watched the game with me. It had been only a week since we'd played Buffalo, but it seemed like a year. That Bills game had been a passage for me, a farewell of sorts. Leaving Lenox Hill was, in a way, leaving what I had been before. Watching us play the Colts that afternoon made me realize what was happening. Those were still my teammates out there. They still loved me. They all came out to midfield before the kickoff, along with the Colts, and Marvin led them and the crowd at Giants Stadium in a "Get Well" cheer for me. I was really moved by that. And I hated to see the guys lose that afternoon, *especially* to the Colts.

But I wasn't as wrapped up in it as I'd been the week before. I was in a different place now. I would watch the rest of the games that season, but each time I did, I felt like I was seeing a ship slowly pull away from me, a ship I wasn't on anymore.

Guys go through that feeling when they retire or when they're cut. But it was different for me. I had been just getting started. I was still young. I wasn't even near the prime of my career when, in an instant, that tie was severed. I didn't get cut. I didn't get traded. I left not on my terms, not on the team's terms, but on God's terms.

I would always be a Jet. I knew that, and that feeling would always be precious to me. But I was something else now as well. I was paralyzed. I was in rehab. I was struggling every waking hour to take back my body. That was the entire focus of my life now. That, and my love for my wife and daughter, and my faith in the Lord. Those were the things that would see me through this. And I had no doubt I was *going* to get through it.

I wasn't keeping track of my life by days anymore. Time wasn't measured for me by a calendar. It was measured by the moments that meant something to my body. I can't say what day it was that I finally took my first shower—I know it was sometime during my second week at Mount Sinai—but I can recall every detail of that experience. I can remember them bringing in this old shower chair they had been able to find. It stank of mildew and feces and vomit. As much as they'd scrubbed it before bringing it in, it still stank. But once they'd transferred me into it and Pedro, one of the orderlies, rolled me into the shower stall and turned on the water, I didn't care how bad that chair smelled. The feeling of that cool, glorious stream of water running down my face was one of the most delicious sensations I'd ever felt. Until then, all I'd had were sponge baths. This was the first shower I'd taken since the morning of the game against the Chiefs.

So now there was something else to add to my daily routine. I'd get up every morning at seven, and Dr. Ragnarsson would drop by to check on me. He was already well into his day—he started his rounds about six. One of the nurses, usually Mike, would help me with my Activities of Daily Living stuff, which, by the end of the first week, I was already handling most of by myself, thanks to the gadgets Joanne had rigged up. It was awkward and clumsy and slow—it took me about two hours to get through my morning grooming, dressing (typically I'd pull on a Jets T-shirt and a pair of shorts or sweatpants), and eating—but I was doing much of it myself, which Joanne told me was a tremendous rate of improvement.

I was also able by the second week to roll to one side or the other in bed, which meant I didn't need the nurses to come shifting me every two hours. Now I could change position myself to avoid bedsores. I still had no movement at all in my fingers or thumbs, but my wrists and hands (at least my right hand) were strong enough to use a manual switch now with the ECU instead of the head pad I'd depended on the first week.

I was getting up to eighty degrees in the chair now before the dizziness stopped me. It was about then, during the second week, that Joanne showed up one morning without the usual four or five people to help get me from my bed into the wheelchair.

"All right," she said, "let's get goin'."

"What about the others?" I said.

"We don't need 'em," she told me. "You've got strength now for us to do this ourselves."

I looked at her like she was out of her mind.

"*You're* going to do this *alone?*" I said. I shook my head. "Unh-unh. No way."

"Dennis," she said, "I do this all the time. I've lifted people that weigh a lot more than you. It's technique. It's all *technique.*"

I weighed 255 pounds. How she was going to manage this I didn't know. But there was something about Joanne that made you believe her when she said she could do something . . . or when she said *you* could.

So I let her take over. We got me over to the edge of the bed, then she helped pull me up toward a sitting position, and in one motion rocked me up onto her shoulder and around and down into the chair.

I couldn't believe it.

"No sweat," she said. "That's what we call a stand-pivot transfer. Piece of cake."

My shoulders and arms were getting stronger, and so was my neck, which Joanne had gotten permission from the doctors to begin working on with resistance exercises. I'd lie on my back on the mat and simply try to lift my head while she pressed down on it. The pain was still intense there, so we'd have to stop often so Joanne could massage it. Her approach was holistic, very hands-on, with lots of communication between me and her. And her attitude was very aggressive, lots of "push, push, push," which was a pleasure for me. That's something I knew, something I was familiar with—pushing. My problem was not being able to push as hard as I wanted to. There were some things my body just could not do. There were some things that wore me out much more easily than I would have imagined. I had to deal with something now that I'd never had to face before: limits.

Still, things seemed to be kicking in at an amazing rate those first two weeks. I remember the morning Joanne first got me up into an unsupported sitting position on the edge of the mat. It was only for a couple of seconds, and I needed her help to get there. I was dizzy, slightly nauseated, and I wavered—balance was something I had to relearn like everything else. But I was sitting up. I was *sitting up*, supporting my torso with my abdominal muscles.

Joanne went nuts. She said they don't even *look* for abs in an SCI patient. They weren't looking for them in me. But Joanne's attitude from the start had been, "You never know. You give people a diagnosis, and sometimes they fool ya."

Now she was looking at me and saying, This guy is no incomplete quad. He's a contusion, a *bruise*. She wasn't talking about walking—that was still a universe away—but she wasn't looking at limits either.

We continued discussing tone almost every day. I had a million questions about that alone. Will it go away? When? I'd do something with my arm or my leg, and I'd immediately ask, "Is this *real* muscle?" "Can I control this?" And I'd be thinking to myself, "Can I control my *life* again?"

I was working just as hard in the afternoons with Lawrence, on the tilt table, with Velcro weights, with pulleys. The PT work was particularly aimed at building up the muscles I'd need for transferring myself in and out of a wheelchair and for using crutches to walk. We worked on my trapezius muscles, my deltoids, triceps, and wrist extensors, looking for strength in the arms and in the shoulders and shoulder blades as well, in the scapular muscles.

There was one man I saw in rehab every day, a man named William Moya. He was thirty-five years old, maybe thirty-six, with a wife and two young boys, about five and seven. He was in the room next to mine, paralyzed from the neck down. He'd had a "complete" injury in a car accident—a C-4 injury, one vertebra higher than mine. Like a lot of SCI patients with fractures that high, he had breathing problems and was just getting weaned off a ventilator when I arrived.

They were teaching Mr. Moya to use a sip-and-puff wheelchair, showing him how to guide and control it by breathing into a tube attached to the chair's motor system. It took a lot of effort for him to simply breathe at all, but he was putting everything he had into working on that chair. It was exhausting just watching him.

Yet with all that, every time he saw me, he'd stop and greet me, very gently, very politely. It wasn't easy for him to speak, but he always took the time. He always made the effort.

"It's . . . nice . . . to . . . see . . . you . . . today," he'd say.

Then he'd pause to draw a deep breath.

"How's . . . your . . . little . . . girl?"

Another breath.

"Doing . . . well . . . I . . . hope."

Mr. Moya didn't have to pay attention to anyone else. He had enough to deal with already. But he was always like that, friendly, polite, selfless.

I also met a young man named Josh Praeger, a total stranger who walked into my room one morning. He carried a cane, but he wasn't using it as he came through the door. He introduced himself, said he was a student at Columbia University, and told me he'd been here two years before, going through just what I was going through now. His was a C-4 injury, like Mr. Moya's. He'd been in Israel, he said, sitting in a school bus going through an intersection when a work truck ran a stop sign and slammed into the bus. He was paralyzed from the shoulders down. He had a doctor actually *tell* him he'd never walk again.

It had taken quite a while before he wound up at Mount Sinai, he said. But he'd made it. And he'd made it out. Now he made it a point—he considered it an obligation—to come back and talk to people like me.

Josh came several times, just to stop in and visit. One day, I asked him a question.

"Is it hard?" I asked.

He knew what I meant. Was it hard getting from where I was to where he was.

"Yeah," he said. "It's hard."

"But you can walk," I said.

"Yeah," he said. "I know."

Even Josh didn't want to make me any promises. But the mere fact that he was *there* told me what the doctors couldn't, that there was a chance I could walk again. Josh was saying that to me, simply by coming to see me.

In terms of inspiration, though, there was no one to compare to a man I noticed in the rehab room the first day. He was doing dips between the parallel bars until the veins in his neck stuck out so far I thought they were going to pop.

His name was Bill Cawley. He was about my age, and he'd gotten his injury diving. He dove into a lake and didn't know there was a deck down below. It broke his neck and paralyzed him from the sternum down. His hands were also impaired. He caught my eye right away with his enormous effort between those bars. I mean, this guy was busting his tail. He knocked off thirty dips, with Louie, one of the assistants, holding his legs.

That blew me away. That was the way I had always liked to think *I* worked—in the weight room, out on the football field, in practice or in games. I loved this guy's attitude. We got to talking over the course of the next couple of days. Then one afternoon I took him aside.

"Hey, Bill," I said. "Somebody gave me a copy of the *Terminator 2* videotape. I'm gonna be watching it tonight. Why don't you come up and catch the show with me?"

He was up for it, so I reserved the VCR. They wheeled it into my room that evening, and Bill Cawley and I had a date.

Ange brought in some popcorn, and Bill's mom came by to say hi. Actually, she said more than that. She talked eight million miles a minute. I could hardly keep up with her. Finally she said, "I love you, Bill," gave him a kiss, and left. Ange did the same with me, and then it was just us, Bill and me and the movie.

It had hardly started before we began talking, comparing notes—"This is when I did this." "This is when I did that." I told him how I'd learned to take a candy bar between my hands, hold it up to my mouth and use my teeth to tear off the wrapper.

"So you've discovered your third hand, huh?" he said.

I'd never heard that term.

"Yeah," I said, slowly nodding my head. "I discovered my third hand."

And we both started laughing. We spent the rest of the movie talking, mostly about him. He knew who I was, but I didn't know anything about him. It turned out he was single, college-educated, with a job at a bank. I thought about the fact that I was married, with a wife and child and another child on the way, and I wondered if he'd ever have the opportunity now to have those things. It hurt to think he might not.

Marvin met Bill. So did Jeff. And Cary. I was moving away from the guys as football teammates, but that didn't mean they weren't still close to me. They kept themselves close, all of them, coming in to see me every day. The guys I'd gotten so close to on the football field, the players and coaches alike, weren't about to let me fade away. But it was only natural that guys like Marvin and Jeff and Cary, the teammates I'd been especially tight with before the injury, were the ones who spent the most time with me after it. Marvin and Jeff would come in and actually help dress me. They'd wipe my forehead, help pull on my shirt, help me get into my pants—all the things Angela usually did every day.

I don't think I'll ever forget the first day Marvin came down to therapy with me. He walked into that room and was stunned. You could see it all over his face. He'd never seen anything like this, and I don't think he's ever been the same since. I don't think he was prepared at all for what he saw in that room, and I think it will be with him the rest of his life. Marvin's a man who feels things, and I know he was flooded with feelings at that moment that would stay with him forever.

When I think of Jeff coming by, I think of food. Lots of food. Jeff's a big eater, and every time he came in to watch a game with me or just to sit down and talk, he always brought along a little something he'd picked up at Vincent's—this great Italian restaurant in Garden City—or at Carmine's, another Italian place on the Upper West Side. Manicotti, baked ziti, chicken parmesan, pizza—Jeff would arrive with one of those in one hand and a twelve-pack of Dr. Pepper in the other. He knew Dr. Pepper was my favorite. After a while, so did the nurses—they'd go to catheterize me and have to empty twice the normal amount. That's how they knew Jeff had been there. At first they asked me if he was bringing me beer. I had to convince them I don't drink beer.

Whenever he brought the chicken parm, Jeff would put it on a plate for me and start cutting it up.

"Hey," I'd say. "I can do that. I can *do* that. What do you think you are, my mother or something?"

"Dennis," he'd say, glancing at the fork strapped to my limp fingers, "if *you* do it, the stuff'll be frozen by the time you're ready to eat it."

Despite Joanne's efforts to keep the visitors off my back, we still had to literally wade through a crowd some mornings as we left my room headed down to the basement. My fingers were far from able to grip anything yet, but by the second week my hands were strong enough to push something between them and pick it up—something like the pump Joanne used to inflate the air cushion for my wheelchair. One morning I took that pump between my hands and had Joanne push me out like a squire with her knight, as I waved my weapon at the horde outside.

"Get *back*, get *back!*" I shouted. "*You!* Get *back!* The *Eagle* has *landed!*"

They looked at me as if I was nuts. But they *did* move back.

I had been at Mount Sinai eleven days, not yet two weeks, when my wedding anniversary arrived, December 20. I wasn't in shape to do any shopping, but I knew what I wanted to give Angela, so I sent Jeff out with specific directions on where to find it—a diamond tennis bracelet. And he delivered. When Angela came in my room that evening, I had that bracelet wrapped and ready at my bedside.

As for her, she arrived with her arms full. She had a beautiful basket packed with a bottle of sparkling cider and two glasses. Flowers. And a package of Reese's peanut butter cups. I love Reese's peanut butter cups.

There was more. Ange also had something that went back to that first Monday at Lenox Hill, when she'd been hanging posters and humming the hymn from Isaiah: "They shall mount up with wings as eagles . . . " In her hands was a gleaming sterling silver eagle, its wings outstretched as it takes flight.

I was overwhelmed, but Angela wasn't done. She handed me a gift-wrapped box, helped me open it, and inside was a pair of blue silk boxer shorts and a green polo shirt. She helped me put them on. Then she drew the blinds. On the knob outside my door hung a DO NOT DISTURB sign she'd brought over from the hotel.

I'd had a running joke with the doctors back at Lenox Hill. Every day they'd say, "Get that toe moving. Get that toe moving." And I'd say, "Forget the toe, let's get that other thing moving."

The fact was, I'd never lost sexual sensation or the ability to have an erection. This is something all men with spinal cord injuries wonder about from the beginning—will they still be able to perform sexually? Normally there are two ways to get an erection. One is psychogenic stimulation, which is *thinking* it up. The other is reflexogenic stimulation, or direct physical contact. For most men with spinal cord injuries, the ability to have a psychogenic erection is lost, at least temporarily, while the reflexogenic ability is usually retained, although voluntary control is sometimes a problem. I was fortunate to have retained both abilities. Those particular nerve pathways were wide open, which the doctors said was a great sign.

Angela and I had spent some time cuddling and kissing since I'd come to Mount Sinai. There was no way she could have climbed into that Clinitron bed at Lenox Hill, but here she could actually lie beside me. We definitely knew I was still capable of lovemaking, but we hadn't actually tried it yet. We hadn't had much *opportunity* to try it, living in a fishbowl the way I was.

But this night was ours. And I was glad Ange drew those blinds. Who knows what tabloid might have had a telescopic lens set up in the windows of one of those apartments across the way?

They would have had a field day with this one.

16

Now it was coming on Christmas, and each day it seemed God was blessing me with another gift. So many things I was working on with Joanne and Lawrence were improving at a pace they said they'd never seen before. Every morning Joanne would rush in to see what new development I had to show her, usually a new muscle I could flex. I'd say, "Test it! Test it! Make sure it's *real.*" She'd test it, to see whether this was just tone kicking in or something I could really control. She'd have me twitch on command, and if I could, she'd shout "*YES!*" and do a little dance.

I was close to reaching that magic ninety-degree mark in the wheelchair, and I could stay up forty-five minutes at a time, which had Joanne shaking her head in amazement. Meanwhile, I was building my shoulder and arm strength working with Lawrence in the PT room, where Bill Cawley was always on hand to motivate me with his own effort. That cursed foam neck collar was gone now, and I'd graduated from using the universal ring with my utensils to actually holding my brushes and silverware, thanks to thick foam handles Joanne attached to them. The foam filled my hands, which were now curled into the shape of a grip.

But it wasn't truly a grip. It was a condition called *tenodesis,*

which is common in SCI patients. Without their flexors and ten-
sors, which are paralyzed, the fingers become bent and curved.
Tenodesis is actually a useful position for learning to hold
things—the shape of the hands is ready-made to fit around something thick enough to fill that shape. But there is no muscle
strength or control in the fingers to open and close the hands, to
squeeze, to actually grip. There is no movement. Some SCI
patients never get that movement. The most they get is tenodesis.

I didn't know if that might not be all I would ever have. Neither
did Dr. Ragnarsson. While my entire being was focused on walking, he was looking with a lot of concern at my hands. He was
more worried about the return of function there than in my legs.
He was worried I might have something called central cervical
cord syndrome.

It's a condition that stems from damage to the nerve fibers
located deep in the center of the spinal cord. It's those fibers that
run to the nerves and muscles in the hands, while the fibers that
go to the legs are located on the outside of the cord. In an injury
with the impact of mine, there can be bruising and hemorrhaging
deep inside the spinal cord. The hemorrhaging can damage the
nerve fibers, creating a situation where the hands may stay paralyzed even as strength is returning to the legs.

Dr. Ragnarsson watched my legs starting to gather strength
while my hands stayed limp, and he wondered if I didn't have this
syndrome. He didn't tell me at the time, but every morning, when
he came in to examine me, his eye would fix on this one particular photo we had mounted among the many around my bedside. It
was a snapshot from that Halloween, showing me and Ashtin
carving a pumpkin. We looked so happy. Dr. Ragnarsson's heart
sank every time he saw that picture because his gut feeling was
that I'd never be able to do that again, that my hands would never
be able to carve a pumpkin.

By then, I was worried about my hands, too. I thought about
how I would feel if my legs never came back but my hands did. I
thought I could be happy with that. If I had my hands, then I could
still draw, which I'd always loved to do. I could still shoot. I could
still hold children.

I wasn't sure how I'd feel if I got back my legs but not my hands.

For the time being, I'd lost my hands, and it didn't look like they were coming back. This was one more thing I prayed about. I talked to the Lord about it, about handling the fact that I might not ever have the use of my hands again. I was intent on putting every ounce of effort and determination into getting them back, just as I was straining day in and day out to take back my legs. But if it wasn't to be, I prayed to God for the strength and wisdom to face it with courage.

The doctors all were concerned about how I might deal with feeling recovery in one area of my body and no improvement in another, or how I'd face having a burst of improvement followed by a sudden drop-off or even some backsliding. This was the roller coaster Dr. Russo had warned me and Angela about. Dr. Camins called it "plateauing," and whenever he examined me, he was very careful in how he answered my questions. I'd always ask him, "Am I going to walk?" and his answer was always the same.

"Look, Dennis," he'd say, "every day you're making gains. But we just don't know."

He was being careful, taking the same stance he took when he or Dr. Ragnarsson talked to the press, the same stance all doctors take with situations like mine. They talked vaguely about me perhaps walking in a year or a year and a half, but they quickly added that there was just as much chance it would not happen. I might stay paralyzed from the chest down, only able to use my biceps to do things. There was just no way to know. In the end, every spinal cord case is different. You just have to take them one by one. There were things for me to feel good about, but as for their own feelings, they had a phrase they used with me and with the press. "Guarded optimism"—those words were ringing in my ears by Christmas.

Angela and I were reading a lot from Psalms and Job. Psalms for the comfort and strength it offered, and Job because it spoke so directly to what I was going through. That whole story meant so much to me. Here was this successful, prosperous man who had worked so hard and earned so much, who was so faithful to the Lord, and whom Satan tried to destroy, testing him by taking away everything he had. I could relate to that story in such a complete and perfect way. Job ultimately passed his test. He lost everything, but he was blessed tenfold. He lost everything but his faith.

I had not lost mine. Fear and doubt and depression were constantly beating at my door. I could feel their presence, gathering themselves time and again and making assaults on my faith, but I never let them in. They were never strong enough to break through.

One afternoon, just before Christmas, Angela and Chris were in my room. We had all been reading the Bible together and praying, and now I was lying back resting while they sat nearby, talking to each other. I had my eyes closed. I was dog-tired, as usual, after another session downstairs, and I started sinking down into the gravity of all this. Usually I could keep myself on top of things. My willpower and faith and positive thinking kept me balanced, as if I was perched on top of a big ball. Occasionally, though, one of those things would begin to slip, I'd begin losing my balance, and the ball would start to roll over on me.

That's how I felt lying in bed that afternoon. I'd made a lot of progress, but I was still so far from doing anything close to walking. I couldn't even lift my leg. I could flex some of the muscles, but I couldn't make it *move*. And my hands were so limp. I wondered if I was truly strong enough to handle all this. I wondered if I could take it.

And then a voice came to me, a voice as clear as any I'd ever heard. And it said, *"Be strong, my son. You will walk again."*

I was shocked. I started crying. Angela and Chris looked over and had no idea what was happening. Ange came over and held me, asked me what was wrong, and I told her. Then *they* began crying, too. No moment in my life, before or since, was as strong as that one, the three of us crying together from the bottom of our souls, weeping with joy and awe, knowing that the Lord was with me, that He was with all of us.

The fact was that I had more reason to hope than to despair. Despite the limitations of my fingers, I'd begun to feel the same faint tingling deep inside them, the same microscopic nerve firing that I'd felt just before I first moved my toe at Lenox Hill. No one could see it. *I* couldn't see it. But I could feel it.

In terms of actually using my hands, I still had no finger functions—if I was reading a magazine and I wanted to turn the page, I had to push it with the back of my hand, which more often than not would flip four or five pages at a time. Sometimes it took me as long as fifteen minutes to get to the page I wanted.

But when I felt those nerves beginning to fire, I was convinced it was only a matter of time before something was going to move. I lay in my bed late at night and stared at my forefinger or my thumb for hours, telling it to *work*, actually talking to it as if it could hear me and understand and respond. Hour after hour, night after night I lay like that. I was continuing to work on my toes and feet, tensing the muscles, even trying to lift the feet. But the weight of my heel alone was too much to lift. It would be a while before I could lift that.

But the hands. Something was about to break through with the hands.

Two nights before Christmas, I found myself in a familiar position—holding my hands up to my face and praying for movement, praying for feeling, praying until I was so exhausted I fell asleep. Late that night I was awakened by a buzzing in my hands, in *both* of them. I couldn't move anything, but this was a feeling I'd never had. I remember looking at the clock. It was 3:00 A.M.

The next morning I called my mother in Baton Rouge. Before I could tell her what had happened, she told me she'd awakened in the middle of the night and had prayed for me. I asked her what time that had been. She said about 2:00 A.M.—3:00 A.M. eastern time.

That day I worked hard on my right index finger. I could *feel* it moving, even though neither I nor anyone else could see it. What felt like a tremor was too microscopic to see. But on the following day, Christmas Eve, came an earthquake. The finger moved, and Joanne was there to see it. Like the toe, it was barely a wiggle, just the slightest movement, but Joanne was out of there in a flash to let Dr. Ragnarsson know. And the next day, as she was driving with her fiancé to a friend's house for Christmas dinner,

Joanne heard a report on the radio that my finger had moved! She said that really freaked her out. She hadn't realized until that moment how many people were paying attention to what was happening with me. She had been just like I was, ignoring the outside world and focusing entirely on our days together, what we were doing inside the hospital.

In a way it was strange spending Christmas in Mount Sinai. It certainly wasn't anything I could have imagined a month before. But it was beautiful, too. My room was filled with gifts from the heart, presents that friends and teammates had brought by for Ashtin, and wonderful gifts from total strangers, gifts like a hanging chain of paper origami cranes sent by a Japanese-American church in New York.

We had a small tree, a live Christmas tree, decorated on my dresser. Angela had put tinsel in the window and she and her mom had cooked a dinner of ham, sweet potatoes, a rice-and-chicken casserole, and carrot cake.

The team had put together a video Christmas card for me, and they had sent it over along with word that the Jets had established an annual award for the team's most inspirational player. A trophy was going to be permanently placed in the locker room, and at the end of each season its plaque would be engraved with the name of the player chosen that year by his teammates for uplifting them with his hard work on the field and off. They were calling it The Dennis Byrd Award, and the first name on the plaque would be mine.

I can't describe how much that meant to me. This was an award that would honor the virtues that mattered most to me—effort and inspiration. And it would come from the people who mattered most, the players themselves. Above everything else, certainly above talent, you want your teammates to think you have courage. You want them to know that when that critical moment comes, when it's time to show what you're made of, they can count on you. When I was out on the football field, there were guys on every side of me who I knew I could count on when it mattered most. It meant a lot to me to know that those guys respected me for the same thing.

I ate Christmas dinner with joy that night. Ashtin, Angela, Angela's parents, and her brother were with me. We could see that even with what had happened to me and all that still lay ahead, we were surrounded with an unimaginable amount of love and support, from friends and strangers. I sent out a public statement through the Jets that day, in which I paraphrased Winston Churchill.

"Never before," I said, "has so much been owed to so many by so few."

I knew how many people were praying for me. I prayed for them as well. And I thanked Jesus Christ for blessing me with the love I could feel flowing all around me that day.

The next night I went down to the hospital's atrium, where my night nurse, Geneva, liked to take me now and then if I wasn't too exhausted from the day's work—which was not very often. Geneva was always urging me to get out and around the hospital, to see the sunlight in that atrium, to take in the stars there at night, to do something besides work in rehab all day and crash in my bed at night. Of course I didn't pay attention. I had come here to work, to give everything I had to make myself better. I wasn't here for a vacation.

But this night I said yes. With Geneva's help, I got dressed and transferred into the wheelchair, and she took me down.

It was late. There weren't many people around. And as Geneva rolled me up to the window, I was struck by the fact that I was in this isolated, self-contained bubble. I hadn't paid much attention to the outside world. Now, at this moment, I wondered what the rest of the world was doing.

I could see the Christmas lights twinkling along the Triborough Bridge, linking Queens to Manhattan. I could see the headlights of cars moving like tiny strings of pearls. Up in the sky I saw the lights of an airplane going past, and I thought about that plane being full of people, some going home for the holiday, others leaving home to visit someone they loved. It was all so beautiful. It was all so *alive*.

That feeling stayed with me, and a couple of nights later, just before New Year's, I asked Geneva if we could go outside. She looked at me like she couldn't have heard right. I hadn't been outside the hospital since the day I'd come in, and here I was, almost eleven o'clock at night in the dead of winter, asking to go outside for a spin.

The thought occurred to me that this might not be the safest thing in the world to do. Mount Sinai butts right up against a pretty rough neighborhood. Still, Geneva and I took the chance. She wrapped me up, we took the elevator all the way down, then we rolled out the doors, into the night.

The cold and wind stung my face and neck, and it felt great. I could see my breath. I sucked some of the night air into my lungs and held it there, savoring the cool sensation deep inside. It felt incredible.

Geneva pushed me down the block. Down Madison Avenue. Across Ninety-eighth Street. Then she said, "I think this is far enough." I knew what she meant. Already it was starting to feel dangerous.

We were back inside in a matter of minutes. It hadn't been long, but it was fantastic. The sky. The stars. This was the first time I'd looked up at the open sky—not through a hospital window but at the sky *itself*—since I'd been carried out on the cart at Giants Stadium.

17

With the season over, most of my teammates had left New York and gone home. Only a handful lived in the city year-round, and those who did—guys like Freeman McNeil and Rob Moore—continued coming by to see me. Scott had bought a home down in the Keys that winter, so he was gone. But Marvin was still there—he kept places in Dallas and New York—and Jeff, who normally went back to Virginia in the off-season, rented an apartment near the Jets complex through March. He was rehabbing his knee, so he figured he might as well do it up here and be able to see me.

It was that first week in January that Joanne began working on my hands with something called Functional Electrical Stimulation. It's just what it sounds like, a machine that creates contractions in the muscles by applying an electric current to a specific spot on the skin. Rather than simply sticking the electrodes on my thumbs or fingers, turning the machine on, and watching, Joanne had me do resistance exercises with her while it was on. For example, she would attach the electrodes to my hand, and the stimulation from the machine—a soft, buzzing feeling, not painful at all—would make the hand open up. As it opened, Joanne pushed back against it, making me work with the machine against her own hands. She did that with the fingers and the thumb. With the machine's help, and with Joanne's coaxing, I was beginning to open and close my right hand by the end of the first week of January. I knew it was only a matter of time—about two weeks—before the same would happen with the left.

I was also into a new wheelchair by now, one I could handle myself. My shoulders and arms were strong enough to push the wheels, and I could sit upright, ninety degrees, so I didn't need the recliner anymore. The monster I'd been in for the first three weeks weighed about seventy-five pounds. The chair I moved into at the turn of the year, a fire engine red "Quickie GP," weighed about twenty-six. I felt like I'd been moved from a dump truck into a Miata.

The morning Joanne helped me transfer into it for the first time, I couldn't believe how good that new chair felt. I had to give it a whirl. Joanne was a little concerned that we didn't have the chest strap installed yet, but there was no holding me back. I went wheeling up the hall, Joanne holding on behind. It felt wonderful, so I picked up a little speed. A little too much speed, as it turned out. I came to the corner, cut it too hard, and could feel the thing tipping toward the wall. I had no belt on. No one had taught me yet how to fall out of a chair, how to land, how to get back up—all the things you need to know before you start driving one of these things. It could have been a catastrophe if I'd actually tipped over. Luckily, Joanne was able to right me at the last instant. And I had a newfound respect for my new wheels.

Which didn't mean I toned down my eagerness at being able to get around on my own now rather than having somebody push me. Joanne knew how to use my competitiveness to an advantage in our therapy. She was pretty competitive herself. Once I felt at home in my new chair, she found one for herself, and we raced from my room to the elevator—a distance of about seventy feet. The other staff cleared out when they saw us coming, which was a wise thing to do considering how we went at this. Racing Joanne in those wheelchairs was no different than going against my brothers when I was a kid. It was all-out, ripping down the hall, jostling for position, blocking each other off, yanking lunch-carts or chairs into the way of the other person—anything for an edge—and finally, at the finish line, ramming full-speed into the wall. It was like bumper cars. I doubt this was part of the OT protocol, but it was a blast. And it was great for my upper body.

Even better was getting into the pool for the first time. This was the end of the first week in January, and it turned into a more monumental day than any of us expected.

We went down just after lunch, Lawrence and his boss, Roberta Weiss, head of the physical therapy department, and Joanne, too. I wanted Joanne to be there. Some of the other staff were there, including Dr. Ragnarsson. I rolled my chair up to a mechanical lift, and they transferred me into a harness seat attached to the lift by a chain. The lift then slowly swung me out over the water. I felt like a piece of meat dangling on a hook, but the sensation of slipping into that water was wonderful.

The plan was for me to do nothing more than float that day, with Lawrence and Joanne holding me up as I sat and helping me push my arms against the water, another form of resistance exercise. The water itself wasn't very deep, maybe waist-high if I was standing.

I wasn't supposed to stand. Certainly not that day. But something told me it was time to try. Joanne was there, and Lawrence, too, and there were parallel bars in the water, just like the bars Bill Cawley worked out on in the rehab room.

Lawrence and Joanne floated me between the bars. It all happened so fast I don't think any of us had time to fully realize what I was doing—until I'd done it. With Lawrence and Joanne propping me up, I gripped the bars as best I could. My upper body rose out of the water. My feet found the bottom. My legs locked into place.

And just like that . . . I was standing.

I couldn't believe it. I was *not* supposed to be doing this. The weight of my body, even waist-deep in the water, felt incredibly dense, as if I were made of metal and a powerful magnet was under my feet. You don't have any idea what gravity is really like until you're paralyzed. The muscles are so weak, they can't carry the weight like before. It feels as if you're full of cement.

My sense of balance was just as out of whack. I hadn't been up in this position since I'd gone down on the field. I felt wobbly, as if I were standing on a flagpole.

But what I felt most was awe. And I felt hope flaring so brightly now it was like stepping into the sun. Until then, I had believed I was going to walk again. Now I *knew.*

Joanne did, too. She was studying me intently as I stood there. She could see I wasn't just using my upper body to hold myself erect. I wasn't just hanging there, with my stomach limply sticking out, as it would have if I was depending on the ligaments in my thighs and hips to hold myself up, which often happens with SCI patients in that situation. I was using my gluteus muscles, which Joanne had told me over and over were the key to standing and eventually walking. If the glutes kick in, she'd say, then you're on your way. And my glutes had clearly kicked in. They weren't strong enough to let me walk, but they were strong enough to stand.

I stayed up fifteen seconds. Again, the news spread through the hospital like a prairie fire. Dr. Ragnarsson was amazed, but as usual he was making no promises. "Well," he told me, "you'll be able to sustain *some* form of locomotion, assisted probably with a cane, or with a walker, or with crutches."

I didn't buy the part about the canes or the crutches. Maybe I'd have to use those for a while, but only for a while. Still, Dr. Ragnarsson was right about the fact that I had a long way to go. It had been forty-four days since my injury. I had lost thirty-five pounds, down to a weight of 235. My shoulders and upper arms were coming along great—I could lift forty-five pounds with a machine Lawrence called the "rickshaw," which *looks* like a rickshaw, with two bars attached to weights. You back in your wheelchair between the bars, then you push down on the bars to lift the weights. I was improving every day on that, but as for my legs, it was all I could do to simply push them across the powder board. The weight of my legs was more than my leg muscles could lift.

The weekend after I stood in the pool, Rhoda, my Woodstock nurse, brought me a movie I'll never forget. Freeman McNeil and Rob Moore had been bringing me some pretty far-out stuff from their own collections, movies I'd never heard of. I knew the one Rhoda brought in that Sunday. I'd watched it with my dad when I was a kid. It was called *Papillon*, with Steve McQueen and Dustin Hoffman, the story of two convicts imprisoned on an island penal colony. Through years, through *decades*, through one setback after another, these two men are stuck in this awful place, plotting and failing and plotting again, year after year, to escape this horrible, hopeless situation. Their tenacity was incredible. *Papillon* is French for "butterfly."

I'd seen the movie before, but I saw it through new eyes now. Flight. Freedom. The great escape. I really related to those images, those yearnings. By the end of the movie, I was emotionally drained. And I was more determined than ever to walk out of the hospital.

I understood by now how careful Dr. Ragnarsson had to be, not just with me but with the press, which had been following every report since I'd entered Mount Sinai. I still wasn't reading the newspapers or watching the news much, so I had no real sense of how much the press was paying attention to my progress. I hadn't talked to a single reporter since I'd been hurt. Giving an interview was the last thing on my mind, the last thing in the world I needed to do. My job was to focus entirely on the matter at hand.

But now, finally, it was time to talk to the press. That's what Rick and the Jets and the doctors were all telling me. I was ready, they said, to let the world see for itself how I was doing.

It was a Thursday that I stood for the first time in that pool. The following Tuesday I came through the door of one of the hospital's conference rooms seated in my Quickie, Angela pushing me from behind. And I couldn't believe what I saw.

The room was packed with what must have been more than a hundred reporters. Bulbs flashing, TV lights glaring, pens and pads and microphones and tape players all pointed in my direction. Some guys—the Elways and the Montanas—are used to all this attention. But not me. I'd never faced a crowd of reporters like this in my life. My right foot was tapping up and down, and that didn't have anything to do with nerve damage. That was just *nerves*.

"I don't remember being that good a football player to have this much attention," I told them all, as Angela sat beside me holding my right hand.

I tried sharing what Angela had done for me, and it was hard. I didn't do a very good job of that. I was overcome with a wave of emotion, choked up to the point where I wasn't able to speak at all. Finally, I got my words out, through some tears, and then Angela had a chance to say something.

"We're going to make it through this," she said, "and Dennis is going to walk some day. We're going to just stick together until that time comes, and we're going to rejoice together when it's over. And I know that we couldn't have made it this far without God's strength."

Reporters aren't usually comfortable with the subject of religion. They generally go numb when they hear the words "Jesus Christ" come from an athlete's mouth unless he's using them in vain. But this audience of reporters was actually asking questions about my faith, questions I was only too happy to answer.

"I don't mean to preach," I said, "but I'll take every opportunity that I get to witness. That first week was the darkest time of my life. It was the hardest time of my life, and Jesus Christ was with me more than He ever has been before. He gave me strength.

"I've been in church all my life," I continued, "and after all the things I've learned, all the faith I've built, everything that I've read, I had a choice to either turn my back on Christ or *use* those things that I've learned all my life.

"The choice was easy for me."

The reporters had plenty of questions about the specifics of my rehabilitation, of course, and most of those questions were good ones, sensible and sensitive to what Angela and I were going through. There was only one strange question, and that stemmed more from a lack of knowledge than anything else. A reporter asked me how I would compare the weights I was lifting now to what I'd been able to lift before. The whole room turned toward this guy like, "What planet are *you* from?"

"I couldn't bench-press the NYNEX Yellow Pages right now," I told him.

That got a laugh, then Bruce Coslet added, "That's about all he could bench *before* the accident."

Dr. Ragnarsson had his turn, too. He shared the details of my improvement, but in terms of the future, he was, as always, very cautious.

"More recovery, almost certainly," he said to the reporters. "Full recovery, unlikely."

Someone asked me about my own prognosis for the future.

"I was very fortunate in that my injury was incomplete," I said. "That means that there are a lot of questions that remain to be answered. There are a lot of things that the doctors really don't know about the recovery that I'm going to have. That's where I just rely on my faith in Jesus Christ and keep working hard every day.

"The harder I work down there," I added, "the sooner I get to go back home. No offense," I said, "but I've got a place where I live, and I want to get *back* there."

Two days later, I was back in the pool. Again, a lot of the hospital staff was there. And again, I stood up between the bars. But this time we went a little further. With Joanne and Lawrence helping me, I lifted my right leg, pushed it slightly forward, and set it back down. Then I shifted my weight to that side, lifted my left, and pushed *it* forward.

Walking.

I was walking.

There weren't any shouts or cheers, nothing theatrical like that, but everyone there could feel the drama. I know *I* could. It turned out Joanne could, too. The very next morning, she took me down to the OT gym and sat me up on the edge of the mat.

"Okay," she said, "today you're getting up. Today you're gonna walk."

She left for a minute and came back pushing a food cart, one of the wheeled trays they use to serve meals to patients in bed. Two OT staffers stood by while Joanne set herself in front of me. She told me to start rocking forward—"nose over toes" was the way she put it. When my weight shifted, she said, I should take that momentum and keep going, using my upper body strength and my glutes to push myself up into a standing position. She squatted below me, blocking my knees in case they buckled, and put her hands on my pelvis. When I came up, she said, the cart would be there for me to lean on. The two other OTs would see to that.

I did what she said. I was scared, but I did it. I rocked forward, pushed off, came up, felt a nudge under my glutes from Joanne, and, finally, felt my arms leaning on the cart tray.

I was *up*. My heart was pounding, and so was Joanne's. I was standing up, with no parallel bars beside me, with no water beneath me, just that cart under my forearms. I felt very vulnerable, very shaky. But I trusted Joanne. When she said, "All right now, let's go for it," and put her hand on my right calf to help me lift it up and clear it through, I did as she said.

First the right, very slowly, the cart rolling with me as I leaned on it with my arms.

Then the left. Even more slowly. I had to drag it, like a mummy in an old science fiction movie.

Then the right again.

There were about a half-dozen other patients in the room, each with a therapist, and the entire place was dead still. You honestly could have heard a pin drop. Everyone was staring at us. Greg Robinson and Pete Carroll had come by to see me, but they hadn't expected to see this. They were struck dumb. No way in the world had they dreamed they'd see me *walking*, less than two months after they'd seen me lying on that field. Their eyes were shining with tears.

I could feel my muscles contracting and relaxing, doing what I wanted them to do.

Four steps. Five steps. Six.

By eight I was spent. I didn't have another step in me, but that had been enough. Again, word spread like crazy, and the next afternoon Lawrence had me up between the parallel bars. Now I knew I was going to do it. Angela had been right. I *was* going to walk, and we *were* going to rejoice.

That weekend, January 17, I left the hospital for my first outing—my first *legitimate* outing. By then Angela had taken a class to learn how to help handle my wheelchair—how to go up and down curbs, ramps, and stairs, how to help me make transfers, and how to load and unload the chair into a vehicle. Marvin and Jeff had taken the same class, and so they wheeled me out that Sunday, the three of them, to go watch the Cowboys–49ers NFC championship game at a bar and grill near the hospital.

As much progress as I'd made in the hospital, I was still extremely dependent when it came to moving around in the outside world. Jeff had to pick me up like a baby and lift me onto the front seat of his Bronco. Marvin and Angela sat in the back. When we got to the restaurant, they set up my wheelchair, lifted me out, and rolled me up to the door.

The place was packed. There were steps up front, which meant I'd have to be lifted. Marvin and Jeff could sense that I was uncomfortable with all the attention we were already drawing, so they asked if there was a back entrance to the place and maybe a private table where we might be able to have some seclusion. They were told there was, so we went around back and into an alleyway. The table, it turned out, was on the second floor, up a flight of stairs. Here was Jeff with his bum knee and Marvin with a torn ligament in his finger, and they didn't hesitate. They bent down and lifted me, wheelchair and all, and carried me up those twenty-six steps to the second floor. Ange just about had a heart attack. Meanwhile, I was chiding both of them.

"You guys are gonna drop me," I said, "and then I'm gonna have to do everything all over *again*."

We made it. And it felt magical being there, being out in the real world again. I'd been in the hospital so long, I felt like a visitor here, almost as if I didn't quite belong, like a sailor stepping back on shore after being out to sea.

I got a little light-headed as the evening wore on. Even though I could sit up now, if I stayed in that position too long it started to get to me. I reached for an ice cube and began sucking it.

"What are you doing that for?" asked Jeff.

"It helps keep me from getting dizzy," I said.

"So why don't you just take a drink of water?"

"I've got to be careful about limiting my intake of fluids."

Jeff found out why soon after that. I had to take a leak. So he pushed me into an empty back hallway, guarded the way with his body, and helped with my catheter so I could relieve myself—another blow to his tough-guy image.

That next week, the week before the Super Bowl, Angela and Ashtin and my mother-in-law checked back into another hotel near the hospital. I'd been given clearance by the doctors to spend the weekends with them, but our house at Point Lookout had too many stairs for me to handle. It was quite a commute, too, so the hotel made a lot more sense. Angela was able to take care of my medical needs, the most important of which was giving me my Heprin shots, which I had to have twice a day to guard against blood clots.

Before my first night at the hotel, Dr. Ragnarsson came to give me "the talk"—the rundown on how I might function sexually, how I might not, what to do if things *didn't* function . . . the whole nine yards.

"Doc," I said, "you're a little late. A month late, to be exact."

Now that I was able to visit the hotel, Ashtin could see me in a setting other than the hospital. She was ecstatic to have her daddy with her, and she took to my wheelchair as if it was the best toy I'd ever brought her. She climbed up into it and pushed it around the room by herself. Two and a half years old, and she was handling that chair like a pro.

I'd been working in rehab with a walker and with forearm crutches by now, taking a few more steps each day. But I was still in a wheelchair when I went out. One night toward the end of January, I was sitting on our hotel room sofa when I got the urge to try out my legs in a new setting, with no doctors or therapists around. I pushed myself up to a standing position and made an announcement.

"Hey," I said, "let's go for a walk."

Angela stood on one side of me, her mother on the other. I put an arm on each of their shoulders and we walked into the next room. It was very slow, very deliberate, more shuffling than actually stepping, but we walked, with Ashtin jumping beside us squealing, "Daddy's *yeggs* are better! Daddy's *yeggs* are better!"

That was a first, taking steps without the crutches or the walker.

The next night we went out to a Knicks game—Ange, Jeff, Marvin, and I. The Knicks officials asked me if I'd come out to midcourt before the game, and I said I'd rather not. We took our seats on the sidelines—I sat in my wheelchair—and they still introduced me, which was an honor. The crowd gave me a standing ovation, which felt terrific. Then, just before tipoff, Patrick Ewing broke ranks to come over and shake my hand. Some of the other players, including Dominique Wilkins, did the same. I turned to Jeff and joked, "Man, I should have broken my neck a lot sooner."

But just as memorable as the fanfare at the game was the fact that that was the night I was first able to take a leak by myself, without a catheter. I had had my first bowel movement the night I watched *Papillon*. That was a big step for me, being able to do that for myself and not need the help of a nurse anymore. It was great to get back a little independence, to reclaim a little privacy and dignity. And then, the night of the Knicks game, I transferred to the toilet to have a bowel movement and, for the first time in two months, I urinated. I couldn't control it—when it started and when it stopped—but it was working now. I could feel a sensation that was different than simple bladder fullness. I could feel that sensation of "having to go." I knew it would only be a matter of time before this stabilized, too. What a great feeling.

Things were clicking in at a rapid pace now. The day before the Super Bowl, Scott paid me a surprise visit in the OT room. He'd come back from Florida for a Jets physical and dropped in to see me. He was surprised when they told him to go on down to the rehab room. He hadn't expected to be able to see me actually working out.

He had no idea what he was in for.

When he came into the room, I was sitting on the edge of the mat table. He walked over to me, and I stood up and gave him a hug. That blew him away right there, to see me stand up like that, and to put my arms around him to boot. The last time Scott had seen me, I was flat on my back and could hardly lift my forearms.

"Wait," I told him. "The best is yet to come."

With Joanne on one side of me, my hands resting on her shoulders, and a therapist on the other side in case I stumbled, I began walking across the OT room and toward the elevator doors, seventy feet away. This was far beyond anything I'd done yet, much further than I'd ever walked and with less assistance. Again, the other patients and therapists stopped to watch. I didn't know it at the time, but Scott was walking right behind me, matching my every step with his own, as tears streamed down his face.

We reached the elevator doors, and I picked up the phone and dialed Mr. Hayes, the elevator attendant. "Willie Mays" Hayes, I called him. He was in his fifties, always cheerful, always upbeat. We'd gotten to know each other well, as many times as I rode that elevator.

"Hey," I said when he picked up the phone, "come on down and pick me up."

Mr. Hayes was used to seeing me sitting there in my wheelchair when the doors opened, dead tired and ready for a ride back to my bed.

But this time, when the doors opened, I was *standing* there.

He almost fell over. And as bright as his smiles always were, the one that came on his face at that moment put all the others to shame.

Joanne, who's a pretty tough nut to crack when it comes to tears, didn't show me any. But I later found out that after I went upstairs, she went into her office, closed the door, and bawled like a baby.

As for Scott, he was overcome by the fact that of all the days to drop in on me, he'd picked this one. He felt that it was meant to be. It was a power beyond either of us that had brought us together the moment we collided on the football field, and Scott felt it was the same kind of power that had brought him into the rehab room at a moment like this.

I know he was right.

That Sunday, before the Super Bowl game between the Cowboys and the Bills, I had an outlet even better than a press conference to be a witness for the Lord. I had prayed often during my career, telling God that if I ever made it to a forum like the Super Bowl, I would use the opportunity to share my faith and let people know what Jesus Christ meant to my life. A week before the game, NBC shifted its pregame broadcasting lineup, canceling a feature on Michael Jackson's halftime show and asking me and Angela instead to do an interview with Bob Costas.

We did the interview with Costas speaking by video remote from the Rose Bowl and Angela and I sitting in a conference room at Mount Sinai. I told Costas and tens of millions of viewers that my hands and legs had come back strong and I expected to be walking by myself soon. We talked about some details of my progress, and then I was allowed to speak about the Lord without wondering how it would be edited or whether it would be deleted. This was television, and it was live.

"Without question," I said, "the biggest factor in my life has been my faith in Jesus Christ. That's been able to keep me going whenever the times are really tough.

"It's been a hard two months," I said, "but God's given us the strength every day."

I never got to the Super Bowl as a player, but as a witness for Jesus Christ, I got something even better. I reached more people through that broadcast than I ever would have through a locker room interview. And when the Bills took the field, I was moved to see the same guys who'd worn my number and the ichthus that December afternoon against the Jets still wearing it against the Cowboys.

The Lord does have a way of working things out.

It had not yet been two months since I arrived at Mount Sinai, and now it was just about time to leave, far ahead of schedule and with more mobility than anyone had dared dream of two months earlier. Anyone but Angela and I.

Again, we had several choices of top-notch rehabilitation centers to choose from, including the Miami Project and Craig in Denver. But there was no doubt where I wanted to go, and where Angela and Ashtin wanted to go. We wanted to go home.

As February began, we knew it wouldn't be long. I was still working hard every day in rehab, still trying to strengthen the muscles that had woken up and to awaken the ones that hadn't. I was chomping at the bit, eager to leave. But I still had some work to do. And I still had one person to see.

Mike Utley.

Mike was up in Connecticut, making an appearance for the Special Olympics, and he'd arranged to come down to visit me. Mike
Lupica, the *Daily News* sportswriter, who was doing a magazine
story on Utley, came with him, to interview both of us about our
injuries.

I was both eager and anxious about seeing Utley. I was eager
because there had been so much that had happened to each of us
since the East-West Shrine Game and I was excited about going
over it all, getting out and having dinner and enjoying Mike's company. But I was anxious because I knew Mike had been through a
lot, and that his recovery had been different from mine. He'd
spent seven months in his halo vest. He'd worked as hard at Craig
Hospital as I'd worked at Mount Sinai, but so far only the toes and
arches in his feet and the muscles in his left calf had come back.
When he arrived with his girlfriend and Lupica, he was in a
Quickie chair of his own.

We met in an empty classroom. Mike was already there when I
wheeled my chair into the room. He was wearing cowboy boots,
and his feet were strapped to the chair. Muscle spasms. Tone.

"Hey, Byrd," he said.

We both reached out and shook hands.

"Hey, big man," I said. "Thanks for coming."

We asked for a few minutes alone before Lupica came in and
did his interview.

It was great seeing Mike. He was still the same upbeat joker I'd
first met in Palo Alto. We shot jabs at each other, goofed around
with our wheelchairs, kidded about doing some one-on-one pass
rushes right there, me against him. As we chatted, Mike occasionally popped a wheelie. I could tell he was as glad to see me as I
was him.

We talked about how we both love the game of football and
how neither of us blames the sport for what happened to us. I was
so glad to see Mike felt the same way I did about that.

But then we started talking about the therapy we'd each gone
through, and things began to get a little uncomfortable. I mentioned procedures that Joanne and Lawrence had used with me

that Mike had never heard of. When I mentioned the stim machine Joanne used on my hands, Mike's face kind of dropped. He said he'd never heard of it. He didn't say anything else, but I could tell he was a little jolted, wondering why I'd gotten this treatment and he hadn't.

By this point in my recovery, when I needed to stretch after sitting in one position too long, I'd stand up, just as I was able to do before my injury. But Mike couldn't do that. When he had to stretch, he did it by using his arms to raise himself out of his seat, giving himself what we call a "pressure release," letting the blood flow a little bit.

We both stretched a couple of times during that session, and I was very self-conscious about it. I was also very aware of how I was sitting, how I moved in my seat, how I held my legs and feet. I felt sensitive to Mike's situation, even in terms of the things I said. I felt guilty. I knew there was really no reason to feel that way, but I did. I couldn't help it. And I think Mike was feeling some pangs of discomfort, too, despite the brave and gracious things he said during our interview with Lupica.

"I heard you were getting better," Mike said, "and I prayed I was right about where you were going and now I can see I am. You'll get up and walk, then you'll take a picture of the damn chair just so you'll have it to keep, and then you'll say good-bye to it forever.

"I see where you are with my own eyes now," he said, "and it's just going to make me push myself harder."

Mike truly was wishing me the best, but at the same time it hurt him some to sit there and be compared to me. I knew it did.

That's what Lupica's story was about—comparing the two of us. And I think Mike was as relieved as I was when the interview was over and we went out to dinner. That was great, relaxing and having a good meal and talking about something besides our injuries.

When our meals came, though, I noticed another difference that broke my heart. While everyone else's meal was set on the table, Mike's had to be put on a tray on his lap—his wheelchair wouldn't fit under the table.

"Two Tough Guys." That's what Lupica's story was headlined.

But that wasn't quite right. It should have been "One Tough Guy." I'd been through a lot, but Mike Utley had gone through even more. And I loved and respected him for how he was facing his own journey, with grace and strength and courage.

As for me, it was time to move on to the next stage of mine. It was time to come home.

We set the date for February 12, a Friday. There was one more press conference to attend, this one to say good-bye to the city Angela and I had come to love so much, the city we had made our second home, that had taken us in for four years and that had helped take care of us for the past two and a half months.

Again there was a battalion of reporters and cameramen waiting as I came into the room. I could tell by the looks on their faces that they did not expect to see me *walk* in.

But I did, using my arm crutches, with Lawrence and Angela walking behind me. I'd been on my feet for some time now, but that was in private, with my therapists and with my family. This was the first time the public had seen it, and they were visibly moved. Even the *New York Times*, which rarely goes overboard with emotion, used a dramatic image to describe the moment.

"The scene," wrote Timothy Smith, the *Times* reporter, "held the wonderment of Neil Armstrong's walking on the moon."

Dr. Ragnarsson spoke first, telling the audience I'd made "a remarkable recovery."

"He has regained strength in virtually every muscle that used to be paralyzed," he said. "I think this is truly spectacular.

"I only wish I knew what the specific ingredient in his recovery was," he said. Then he glanced over at me and added that he knew *I* knew the answer to that one.

As for my chances of ultimate recovery, he said, "There are a lot of unknowns. I don't think anybody truly knows."

Then it was my turn. I'd prepared a four-page speech, which was harder to read than I could have possibly imagined.

"I'm very glad to be here standing before you today," I began. "I'm glad to be standing *anywhere* today."

A few nervous chuckles ran through the room.

"Obviously," I said, glancing up, "that was written down."

That brought a roar of real laughter. Then I settled into my speech. Step by step, person by person, I went through each stage of the model system of care I had received, singling out and thanking the people who had helped bring me to this point. It took a long time to get through the list. I choked up as I came to each person. Each name brought back vivid memories of that person's part in my experience. It was like reliving the entire seventy-six-day journey with the people who shared it.

I began on the field, with Bob Reese and Pepper Burruss, who stabilized me at probably the most crucial point in the whole process.

Then I thanked Jim Nicholas, who orchestrated the care that kicked in once I reached the hospital, and Steve Nicholas, who was with me from the field to the emergency room and on through the rest of that critical day.

I couldn't even speak when I came to Dr. O'Leary's and Dr. Camins's names. How can you thank someone who receives you in broken pieces and makes you whole again?

I thanked Dr. Hershman, who was by my side throughout my stay at Lenox Hill, coaching me through the process, explaining what was happening throughout the dizzying swirl of treatment.

Then there was Dr. Ragnarsson, whom I thanked for being there to see me each and every morning—although I did *not* thank him for being there so *early*.

As for Joanne and Lawrence, all I could say was, "Thank God for sending these people my way."

I thanked Rick for the friendship he'd formed with me long before my injury, for the responsibilities he shouldered during it and was continuing to take care of even as I spoke.

Then I thanked Mr. Hess, who had kept making his late-night visits throughout my stay at Mount Sinai. I wanted people to know that not only did he spare no expense in seeing me through my recovery, but he spent more hours of his own time with me than I could count. I wanted them to know that he had treated me like one of his own children and that I'd come to look up to him much the way I'd look up to a grandfather. I said I loved him. And I meant it.

I thanked the people of New York, the people I knew and the

many, many people I didn't, for their thousands of get-well letters and letters of prayer.

Finally, with more fresh tears welling up inside me, I came to the end, to the definition of who I had been when I first came to this city and who I had become as I prepared to leave.

"Four years ago," I said, "I came to New York a young Christian man."

I paused to draw my breath and fight back the tears.

"Now I go home a young Christian man and a New York Jet."

I had to pause again.

"I'm very proud to say that I'm a New York Jet," I said, the tears finally fighting their way out, "and I will be forever."

So that was it. Now it was time to leave. My teammates had been coming in all week to say good-bye. Jeff and Marvin stopped in that afternoon. I was in my wheelchair when they got there, but I stood up when they arrived. Before they left, I got Ange to snap a photo of the three of us standing side by side, Marvin and Jeff and me, with the wheelchair in front of us. The empty wheelchair.

Mike Utley had been right. I *was* taking a picture of that chair so I'd have it to keep. And I *did* plan to say good-bye to it forever.

But not yet. For the time being, I still needed the chair. It would be coming home with me, along with about a quarter-ton of unopened mail the Jets had boxed for me over at the team offices. I had those to bring home, along with more memories and emotions than I knew what to do with.

The next morning, my last morning in New York, I was awakened by a shout at my door.

"Udder check!"

I couldn't believe it. Early in my rehab, Joanne had brought in a videotape of her and her fiancé from that Halloween. They had both dressed up in cow outfits and danced through Greenwich Village Halloween night, yelling "Udder check!" at passersby. A local television news team took some footage and broadcast it that evening. That was the tape Joanne brought in to show me. I loved it. From then on, whenever things were dragging or people in the rehab room were feeling down, I'd pull out that tape and pop it in. *"Udder check!"* It was great. Pure Joanne.

And now here she was, at my door, at seven in the morning . . . dressed in that Halloween cow outfit.

She walked over to the window and pulled the blinds, as if it was just another day.

"Dennis," she said, peering outside, "don't freak out, but it's *snowing.*"

I figured this was part of the joke. Then I looked outside, and she was right. The stuff was tumbling down, so thick I could hardly see the buildings across the street. No way, I thought. No way did I wait weeks and months for this day, only to have the weather wipe it out.

"I can't believe it," I said. "I'm going. I don't care. We're flying out, *today.*"

I put my clothes on, and Joanne took her cow outfit off. Then she handed me a gift. It was a small wooden box, made of separate pieces of wood intricately locked together. You could pull it apart, and the box would fall into a pile of pieces. Put the pieces back together, and it was a solid, single unit again.

"Like you," she said.

I gave her a big hug. Then I handed her a keychain some of my police buddies had given me. It was made from a detective's badge, with the number 90 on it, my uniform number. Joanne put her keys on it right then and there.

It was time to leave. I made my way downstairs, getting snapshots taken with the staff and the other patients I'd come to know so well. I'm usually not much for photographs. But this time it was *me* who wanted the pictures, not somebody else.

I had planned to walk out to the car that would take us to the airport, but the snow was too heavy, the sidewalk too slippery. There was a crowd of reporters outside, and it wouldn't have been a good idea to bite the dust in front of them.

So I went out in the wheelchair, with Angela and Ashtin and my parents-in-law and Rick. I transferred into the back seat, they loaded the chair in the trunk, and we were on our way.

I had planned for us to fly commercial. I wasn't comfortable with Mr. Hess spending even more money to fly us back to Oklahoma in a private plane. But Rick told me Mr. Hess was insisting.

Mr. Hess told me himself that this was something he *wanted* to do, not something he felt obligated to do.

The car took us to Teterboro Airport in New Jersey, just north of Newark, where a small jet was waiting. With a lot of effort I made it up the steps and into the plane. Mr. Hess had hired a nurse for the flight, and there was a seat that fully reclined, allowing me to lie down.

As soon as we were settled in, they cleared us for takeoff. Then we were taxiing down the runway. Then we were in the air.

It had been seven months to the day since I'd left Tulsa to come to training camp. Now, finally, I was headed back.

Now, finally, I was going home.

COMING
HOME

18

O wasso.

It's a word the Osage Indians used for a railroad depot built in the 1890s by the white settlers at a spot in northeast Oklahoma where the Atcheson, Topeka and Santa Fe rail lines ended and Indian territory began. In the century since it was built, that original depot has grown into a town of about eleven thousand people. But the name is still the same.

Owasso.

It means "The End."

It also means "Turnaround."

And it is where I came home to that February afternoon with Angela and Ashtin.

It had been three years almost to the day since Angela and I had first moved into our house, six miles outside of town. In those three years, this place had become as essential to us as the clothes we wore or the food we ate. We had come to love New York, but there was no comparing the six months a year that we lived there with the feeling we had each time we came home to Owasso, to our lake and the trees and that familiar Oklahoma sky.

There was one tree in our back yard that I had noticed when I first looked at the property. It was down the slope toward the lake, a large ash tree. Cut into its bark was a date and a name:

1909
Lt. Hew

I had no idea who Lieutenant Hew had been. But I felt his presence intensely as I ran my hands over the numbers and letters he had carved in that bark more than eighty years ago. I was fascinated that the marks he had made then had endured after all this time. As much as that tree had grown, its bark hadn't been able to cover that date and name. The numbers and letters had actually pushed out, to the point where you could read them with your fingers like braille. I had walked out there many times since we'd moved here, to run my hands over those marks, to actually *feel* their perseverence.

Now, as I came back to this place after where I had been, that feeling was even stronger, that sense of eternal endurance that runs all through this land I love so much, this land that is as much a part of me as the blood in my veins. Just riding out from the Tulsa airport the day we returned, I could feel the strength and wildness and rugged beauty all around me. Being back here, I knew, was going to be as therapeutic as anything a doctor could prescribe.

It felt odd entering my house in a wheelchair. The insurance company had asked what changes I thought we'd need to make before I moved back in. How many ramps would we need? Which showers would have to be rebuilt for wheelchair access? How would the commodes need to be redesigned?

I told them not to worry about any of that stuff. "I worked my entire life to have this house," I said. "I'm not going to start tearing it up now." I didn't plan to stay in the wheelchair long enough to make those kinds of changes necessary.

I could stand and walk now, with forearm crutches, but it took a lot of effort, and it was only for short distances. And I was exhausted when I was done. Still, I resolved to use the wheelchair as little as possible. I used it when I went into Tulsa for my daily therapy session. When I was home, though, I got around under my own strength as best I could.

It wasn't easy. The staircase to our second floor is fourteen steps high, but it looked to me like the World Trade Center. Still, I resolved to climb it the first day I was home, and I did. It took me ten minutes to mount the steps—this for a guy who used to be able to run the forty-yard dash in 4.8 seconds. But I made it. And that meant I could play with Ashtin in her bedroom, which she'd been asking me to do ever since we'd gotten home.

She got me to squeeze into her toy playhouse with her. I might have lost thirty-five pounds since I'd been hurt, but I was still six-five, 235. Getting into that thing was as tough as any of my rehab workouts. Getting *out* was even tougher. And getting back down the stairs was a nightmare. My strength was sapped, and my balance wasn't the greatest, so instead of trying to walk down, I sat down and descended step by step on my rear end.

I was out to find and stretch my limits from my first day back. That Sunday—Valentine's Day—Angela and her parents were in the den talking. They didn't notice me slip away. I picked up my truck keys and worked my way out to the garage and up into the driver's seat of my Bronco. As soon as I started the engine, Angela came bursting out the door.

"Where do you think *you're* going?" she asked.

"I'm going for a *ride*," I said. "See ya."

And I backed out. I knew I had enough control in my right leg and both arms not to be endangering myself or my neighbors. But my *neighbors* didn't know that. One of them, Celeste Alford, was working in her yard as I drove past. She looked up and nearly fell over. She lives on a cul-de-sac, so I passed her again on the way back out. This time I stopped to say hi.

"I don't believe this," she said. "You're supposed to be *para-lyzed*. What are you doing in that truck?"

"Out for a Sunday drive," I said. And I put it in gear.

It was the next day that I began my rehab in Tulsa. With the help of the staff at Mount Sinai, we had chosen Tulsa's St. John Medical Center as the site to continue the therapy I'd been doing in New York. When I wheeled myself into the fourth-floor rehab

room at St. John, it was like entering the set of *Star Wars*. Bright
sunlight streamed through walls of windows, which wrapped
around a sprawling, carpeted room filled with state-of-the-art
equipment and machinery. The setting was a striking contrast to
the basement facility at Mount Sinai. But I knew by now that
looks didn't matter when it came to rehab. What Joanne and
Lawrence and the rest of the staff at Mount Sinai had done with
me was nothing short of miraculous. And the reason for their success—for *our* success—had nothing to do with how shiny or new
the equipment was. It had to do with their knowledge and effort,
and mine.

I quickly found that the staff at St. John intended to push me
just as hard as Joanne and Lawrence had, which was great. Dr.
Annie Venugpol, the supervisor of the department, assigned a man
named Gary Braswell as my occupational therapist and a woman
named Janet Day as my physical therapist. Gary is in a wheelchair
himself, paralyzed from the waist down from an automobile accident nine years ago. After Janet put me through our two-hour
morning routine, Gary would take over for an hour in the early
afternoon.

That was my schedule five days a week, Monday through Friday,
three hours a day. Janet particularly focused on my walking, spending the first forty-five minutes each morning—when I was strongest
and freshest—smoothing my gait, working on my strength and balance, and practicing getting up and down stairs, which was a monumental task. The small six-step riser we used, three steps up and
three steps down, loomed larger than the Skelly Stadium steps had
back when I was running those Alpines in college.

To ensure continuity in my treatment, Rick requested the Jets
to pay for Joanne to fly to Tulsa, observe my rehab activity, and
consult with my new therapists. As usual, Leon Hess was only too
happy to comply. In what seemed like no time at all, I was actually doing bench-presses and squats on a leg sled, the kind of athletic exercising that reporter in the press conference had asked
me about. It was all I could do to bench fifty pounds now, but that
was a long way past the NYNEX Yellow Pages.

In strict medical terms, I was identified now as *quadriperesic*, rather than quadriplegic. This meant my limbs, once paralyzed, were now very weak but functional. My left side was continuing to lag two weeks behind my right. I still had no normal feeling from my shoulders down. I couldn't tell blunt from sharp, hot from cold. I *could* feel a constant burning sensation in my hands and feet, in my lower back and in parts of my legs. It felt like a bad sunburn. It's a nagging, uncomfortable sensation, but it's also a signal that the nerves are activating, which is good. Any feeling is good after you've been paralyzed.

I was also feeling spasms in my legs, especially in my left. By the end of March, I was strong enough to take Ashtin out for little walks, but only for *little* ones. We'd go maybe an eighth of a mile down the road, and it would be time to turn back or Daddy wasn't going to make it. When I did get back, my legs would be wobbly, and I'd need a good rest.

One thing I was able to do now, and I made a point of it, was drop in and visit other patients at St. John, the same way Josh Praeger had dropped in on me. There was one patient in particular, a young guy named David Cane, who had accidentally driven an all-terrain vehicle over a cliff. He'd fractured his C-5 vertebra, like mine, but his was a complete injury, which meant his cord was severed. He was paralyzed from the shoulders down. He was eighteen years old, with a child, a little daughter named Briana. I began making a point of dropping into David's hospital room a couple of times a week, to bring him a book, maybe a videotape, but mostly just to talk. I wasn't there as Dennis Byrd, former New York Jet. I was there as Dennis Byrd, former quadriplegic. And that's what meant the most to David.

The fellowship I shared with the patients I came to know at Mount Sinai—the bond we developed through our common experience, and the lessons they taught me about the strength of the human spirit—is something I'll treasure until the day I die. Before I left Mount Sinai, I knew I wanted to use some of the blessings I'd received to help other people in situations like the one I'd experienced. I talked with Rick Schaeffer about this, and we decided to develop something called the Dennis Byrd Foundation.

It's an organization that's going to help send disabled kids to a specially designed summer camp, a place geared to their needs, fitted to accommodate wheelchairs and crutches. It's going to be built in the kind of open, outdoor Oklahoma-type setting that meant so much to me as a boy and that I thought about so many times as I lay in those hospital beds in Lenox Hill and Mount Sinai. I can't count the hours I spent staring up at those ceilings wanting so badly to be out fishing again, shooting a rifle again, calling coyotes again—just to be *outdoors* again. That's what summer camp is, it's being outdoors in a way a lot of kids have never had the chance to experience.

I know what it's like to have that desire to do something and not have the opportunity or capability to do it. This foundation will give these kids that opportunity. There might be a child who's never shot a bow and arrow before, or who's never handcrafted a leather belt, or woven a basket, or climbed a rope up an obstacle course hill, or paddled a canoe, or fished, or simply had a place where he or she could sit and watch the sun set, then maybe relax around a campfire and have somebody spin a story for them or show them a Native American dance. There are kids who don't know what these things are like, and I'd like them to have a chance to know. Then they can have these memories and visions in their minds for the rest of their lives, just the way I've got them in mine.

It was because of this foundation that I made my first trip back to New York in April. Angela and Rick came with me, and we had some meetings there to announce our plans and to start setting things up. We were invited to attend the Mets opening day baseball game at Shea Stadium. Marvin and Jeff came along, as well as Bruce Coslet and Steve Gutman. Before the game, they had a ceremony at home plate making me an honorary Met. To see those fifty thousand people standing and cheering me the way they did was overwhelming. It was another vivid reminder of how supportive and loving the people of this city have been to me, how open their hearts have stayed and apparently always will stay. When I raised my right hand toward them in the "I love you" sign, they knew what it meant. And they knew that I meant it.

I was almost floating when we came home from that trip. Things couldn't have been going any better. Every day I could see something new developing with my body. Angela's pregnancy was coming along smoothly, with the July due date seeming not so distant anymore. I was getting out to a nearby rifle range once a week with my good friend Mike Stigers, and David Fritts was eager to set up a coyote-calling expedition. Things couldn't have been brighter when, two weeks after we got back from New York, Angela and I were awakened by an 8:00 A.M. telephone call. Angela went to answer it. When she came back, she looked like she was in shock.

"Dennis," she said. "Gus has been shot."

"Gus?" I said. "*Gus* Gus?"

"Yes," she said. "He's been shot in the head. He's in the hospital in Tulsa."

We called a friend to watch Ashtin, then rushed to the car. As I drove, my head was swimming with thoughts.

Gus Spanos. I couldn't believe it. Like a lot of the guys who played football at Tulsa, Gus came to love the town so much that he decided to stay after he graduated. He became a police officer in 1991. That same year he married a wonderful girl named Christie Davidson. They didn't have any kids yet, but it was only going to be a matter of time. Gus was born to be a father. He loved people, and they loved him, especially kids. He was one of the most popular guys on the team when he was playing football, and he was one of the most popular police officers on the force. He had that big, broad personality, the kind of charisma that wraps around you in an instant and pulls you in. He was one of those guys whose happiness was so overwhelming it made you happy, too.

Gus worked a rough neighborhood, on the north side of Tulsa. But he loved his beat, especially the kids he saw on the street every day. Those kids loved him. They called him "G.G.," short for "Gangster Gus." He was one of those police officers who got out of his car, who talked and joked with the people on his beat, who was a *person* to them and not just a man in a uniform. He got to know the people he served, and they got to know him. He was as tough as they come when it was time to get tough, but the rest of the time he was Gus. Just Gus.

And now he was lying in a hospital room with a bullet in his head.

"He's gonna be all right," I thought to myself over and over. "He's gonna pull through." I prayed all the way to the hospital.

When we got to Tulsa Regional Medical Center, we rushed up to his room. It wasn't hard to find. There were more than sixty people jammed outside the door. Police officers. Guys he'd played football with. And friends. Lots of friends.

Dave Rader, our head coach at Tulsa, was there. He told me Gus had been shot in the back of the head. He was brain-dead. They were keeping him alive on a machine to save his organs. There was nothing anyone could do.

The words went right through me. I was devastated. Gus's mom, Fifi, showed me into the room. Gus's brother, Lou, who had followed Gus to Tulsa to play football and was still a student there, was by the bed along with their dad, George. Fifi and George had just flown in from Pennsylvania. The shooting had happened at about two that morning, and they'd gotten a call not long after.

Gus had been making a routine traffic stop. He had radioed a dispatcher that he was pulling over a car just off Cincinnati Avenue, on the north side. Another officer arrived on the scene a few minutes after Gus's call. He found Gus's car parked with its headlights on. Then he saw Gus's body lying on the street about ten feet away. Gus's gun was on the ground nearby, but no shots had been fired from it. Police were now looking for the car Gus had stopped, but so far they'd found nothing.

I stayed that day by Gus's bed, and all that night, too. Just to be there. The machines were going, keeping him alive, and I talked to him. I looked at him. His parents stayed there, too. Fifi had cut my hair whenever she came down to visit Gus. She knew what Gus had meant to Angela and me. We didn't need to say anything. There wasn't much to say. We were all there just to be with Gus.

It was strange to sit there and realize Gus was brain-dead but at the same time to know his *body* was alive. I sat there holding his hand, and it was warm. It was alive. *Something* was still fighting there.

I thought about how Joe Namath had come to my bedside during the biggest struggle of my life and how he had given me a gift, something to help me battle back. Now it was me sitting beside the bed, and Gus, this kid I'd helped to grow up, was the one lying in it.

I reached for the St. Jude medal around my neck, the medal Joe Namath had given me. I pulled it, and the chain snapped. I opened the fingers of Gus's right hand, placed the medal in his palm, and closed his fingers back around it.

The next morning, Friday morning, Danny Tarabrella arrived. He'd driven all night from Pennsylvania. It wasn't long after he got there, just before noon, that they turned the machines off. Gus lived an hour after that on his own. Then he died.

I prayed then, as I had prayed all night, and all the day before. I kept asking a question I'd never asked about myself, and that was, Why? Why Gus? Why like this? Here I was, recovering after battling back against the odds, and here was Gus, having had no opportunity to do what I'd done. I knew what kind of fighter Gus was. Nothing could have kept him down, no matter what the odds. But he had no chance. He wasn't given one.

I asked, Why? And once again Jesus Christ's words came back to me. "Father . . . nevertheless, not as I will, but as thou wilt."

Jesus Christ knew He was going to die on the cross. He knew that. And He knew what He was going to go through before that, that He would be beaten and spit upon, that He'd have His beard pulled out of His face, that He'd be flogged. Yet He never questioned the Lord. He never asked why. So how could I?

Something I noticed as I was leaving, even amid all the pain and anguish filling that room, was the fact that there were quiet conversations going on in the corners, and you could hear Gus's name, and then you'd hear a chuckle and see smiles on these faces that were stained with tears. That was the magic of this guy, that he could put a smile on people's faces even in a situation like that.

Even when he was gone.

19

Six weeks after Gus died, the man who murdered him turned himself in in Oakland, California, ending a nationwide manhunt. In front of a crowd of television cameras, the man kissed his baby daughter good-bye before surrendering to police. Christie Spanos, who never had the chance to have a child with Gus, had to watch that scene on the evening news, like almost everyone else in Tulsa.

That was a month ago.

It's mid-July now, three months since Gus was buried with the St. Jude medal around his neck. I don't think Mr. Namath would mind.

It's been five months since I came home from New York.

It's been nearly eight months since my neck was broken.

I can sit here on my back porch, watching lizards scoot across the rocks that lead down to the lake, watching the breeze bend the trees above me, and I can wonder, Has all this really happened? Was that really me lying on my back in those hospital rooms, my body bolted together, unable to move? Was I really there? Did I really go through that?

I'm surrounded by permanent reminders that I did. There's the foot-long scar down the back of my neck and the five-inch line up the front. There is the five-inch scar on my right hip, where they took out the bone to rebuild my spine.

There are the four small scars where the screws went in my head for the halo vest. They'll be there forever.

So will the screws and plates in my neck. When Angela and I were back in New York in April, I visited Lenox Hill, and Dr. O'Leary showed me the X rays of my neck. I could see the screws he and Dr. Camins had put in to fasten the plates. Each one jutted out at a different angle.

"Man," I said to Dr. O'Leary, "a carpenter would be *ashamed* of that work."

He looked at me with a rather indignant expression, insulted that I'd compare his work to rough carpentry. Then he carefully explained *why* the screws were angled. As he and Dr. Camins had driven each one through the bone, they'd had to dodge nerves, blood vessels, and arteries. They were working around things you can't even see with the naked eye, and they were doing it with the same size screws I'd use on a plank of wood.

I gave Dr. O'Leary my humble apologies.

That metal inside my neck is there forever, like Lieutenant Hew's carvings in that ash tree. Bone will eventually grow around the plates and screws, the way bark has grown around the letters and numbers, but it will never cover up what now holds me together. Nothing will.

My wheelchair is out in the garage now. I don't use it anymore, but I'm not getting rid of it. I want it there. I want to see it every time I climb in and out of my truck. I want to remember what it was like not knowing if that's where I'd spend the rest of my life.

There's about a quarter-ton of mail out there, thirty cases of letters shipped to me by the Jets that I still have to open and read. And I will. It's going to take some time, but I will.

My green Jets jersey is there, too, the one I was wearing the day I went down. It's tattered and torn from the scissors Steve Nicholas and Pepper Burruss used to slice it open. I like that. It looks like it's been someplace.

There are two mementoes I keep in the living room, under glass. One is the paratrooper's beret Scott brought me in the hospital, and the other is my leather memory bag. I'm thinking of taking a screw off the wheelchair and adding it to that bag.

I was filling this house with pieces of my past long before this injury changed my life. There's a room upstairs where I do the reloading for my rifles. I've always loved doing that meticulous, detailed, fine work with my fingers and hands. That's *always* been therapeutic for me. I get almost hypnotized during the process of preparing a bullet—cutting the primer pockets, deburring the flash holes, trimming the cases, chamfering the case-mouths, measuring the powder to the nearest half-grain. I get lost in the *exactness* of it, just as I get lost in the precision of model-making. Now those things have become OT exercises for me, helping develop dexterity in my fingers.

I've got models I built long ago mounted all around that room. I've got two coyotes mounted as well, and a beautiful Tom Turkey. I've got a rusted kerosene lantern from Granny's old place sitting on a table by the sofa, a lantern just like the one Jeni used to hold as we all huddled down in that storm cellar.

And I've got photographs, moments of myself and my teammates when I was a Jet. The walls of the room are painted Jets green, and covering them are pictures of my teammates and coaches, an action shot of me and Marvin hugging in midair after a sack, a shot of me collaring Marino, another of me taking down Troy. The photo of me soaring in on Kelly for that sack that he somehow sidestepped to throw the game-winning pass is up there, too.

One evening, early in the summer, I was up in the room when something opened up inside and it all rushed in, all the memories and all the sorrow. I had been reloading some shells, I was finished for the night, I'd put everything away, and I dropped down on the sofa to catch my breath. I started looking at the pictures, reminiscing about each of those moments, and each moment brought up another, and pretty soon everything started tumbling inside me, feelings just cascading out of control. For months I'd been totally focused on simply getting my body back. Except for brief moments, which I'd quickly put aside, I hadn't been able to sit back and fully feel the fact that I'd never be with these guys again, that I'd never play football again, that this part of my life was behind me now.

I have always been very unabashed about how much I love the guys I played with, my coaches, and all the other people who are part of that family that makes up a team. These people mean so much to me. I knew they'd still always be there for me, but I also knew I'd never again share the bond of being down on the field together, being in the heat of combat, feeling the incredible high that no one can understand unless they've experienced it.

I do miss it. I miss being on the bottom of a pile, everybody on top of you, and you're lying deep under there just clinging to some guy, hanging on as tightly as you can because when they finally pull everybody off, you want them to know that *you're* the one who tackled him.

As I sat there on that sofa that evening, I was swept by the realization that it was all over. Those pictures were all I had. I'd regained the ability to walk. I'd battled back so far, but the fact was that there was nothing I could do that would ever get me back on the football field again. And that crushed me. More than the halo vest, more than anything I'd gone through in all these months, that devastated me. I'd understood from the moment they'd lifted me off the turf that my career was finished. But knowing something in your mind is one thing. Feeling it in your soul is another. Until now, I hadn't really allowed myself to feel it.

I started to cry. And I kept on crying, harder and harder, from a very deep place. All these emotions just came pouring out in the form of tears.

After a while, Ange came up to see how I was doing. She saw me there on the sofa, came over, and took me in her arms, and that's where we stayed for the next forty-five minutes, crying together, with me weeping from the bottom of my soul, totally, completely emptying myself out. That was the hardest I'd ever cried in my life.

It was good to have done that. The psychologists would call it grieving. Mourning. It's a stage everyone is supposed to go through before they can truly leave something behind. They say you have to let yourself feel the hurt. Then you can go about the business of moving on.

I feel like I've done that. I'm not stuck in the past. I have no need to hang on to what I used to be. I've got a shelf filled with videotapes of my games as a Jet, but I've never had the urge to take them down and look at them. No video could be as vivid as my memories. I can call on them whenever I want, but I'm not clinging to the past. I have no need to relive anything. My years as a New York Jet are a part of my life I've already lived, a wonderful part of my life. But my life is still going on. I'm only twenty-six years old. I've still got sixty or seventy years to go.

I do think about the guys. Almost every day I think about them. When May arrived, I was wondering what they were doing up in minicamp. Now it's July. In two weeks they'll all be reporting for training camp. I think I'm going to go up, as a matter of fact, and it'll be great. It'll be great to sit back on the sidelines with a glass of iced tea and watch the guys dying out there, and be able to rub it in. Training camp is *not* fun. But watching should be.

That's something I'm looking forward to. I've got so much to look forward to. My body has continued to improve at what the staff at St. John tells me is an amazing rate. By June I'd moved from quadriperesis to *hemiperesis*, meaning only my left side was severely weakened. My right side had improved to "slightly impaired." And now, in mid-July, the hemiperesis label is already behind me. My sense of feeling still has not returned to normal. I still cannot tell if I'm being touched by something blunt or sharp, hot or cold. I still have that sunburn sensation almost constantly.

But my muscular strength and control get better every day. When I'm fresh, I can walk without even a limp. I'm benching over a hundred pounds, and I can lift 250 on the leg sled. Janet's got me up on the exercise bike now, and I can do six minutes on that. I can go five on the Stairmaster.

These are things they wouldn't have dreamed I'd be doing six months ago. I remember walking between the parallel bars one day in January, struggling to take a step, and I asked Lawrence if he thought I'd be jogging by, say, October.

"Jogging?" he said. "You'll be *walking* by October. But jogging? I don't think so."

"You're on," I said. "Dinner for the winner at the restaurant of his choice.

"Buddy," I added, "I'm going to make you take me to the poshest restaurant in this city. And you're paying."

I told Tom Brokaw that story when he interviewed me for an NBC News story. He told me he wanted a piece of that action. So I guess I'm going to have two bets to collect come October.

There are some things I'll never be able to do again. Like play football. But there are also things I can do that I've never done before. I used to be in tremendous football shape, but I wasn't in the kind of condition to, say, run a marathon. That's something I'd like to do. That's something I know I *can* do.

I told Angela not long ago that I'd thought hard about what would be the greatest physical obstacle I could dream of to take on and overcome, a goal I could achieve that would prove to myself that I've worked hard enough. I told her I thought climbing Mount Everest might do the trick.

"Dennis," she said, "don't you think that's a, ummmm, *lofty* goal?"

But I was serious. I *am* serious.

I do have a long way to go. There are still days when I'm frustrated by what I can't do, when my body reminds me in graphic terms of what has happened to it. The other night I drove out to see David Fritts at his place, over an hour away, far out in *Boga Cheetah*. We were going to go coyote calling. I was well on my way, already in the middle of nowhere, when the truck began making some strange noises. I pulled over and found the front tire about to fall off. A couple of lug nuts were missing, and the rest were loose. Apparently someone had tried to steal it and given up.

I pulled off on a slope, a spot covered with rocks and pieces of shale. I was reaching under the hood to get out the lug wrench when I lost my balance. My knees buckled and I went down hard, *roached* by a bunch of little-bitty rocks. Here I was talking about climbing Mount Everest, and a little bit of gravel had put me flat on my back.

That really angered me. That's not the only moment I've had like that, but I manage to keep them in perspective. I know someday I'll go back and kick that rock around a little bit.

Meanwhile I've got other things to look forward to besides what I can do with my body.

First, beyond anything else, is my family, which has now grown by one. Even as I sit here, Angela is inside the house nursing our new baby, Haley Lauren Byrd. She was born July 9, at three in the morning at St. John, the same hospital in which I'm doing my rehab. Ashtin is beside herself that she's got a little sister now, and Angela and I thank the Lord that they're both such healthy, happy little girls.

I'm looking forward to watching my daughters grow, day by day. And I'm also looking forward to working again. My major in college was communications, and I've always enjoyed and respected the spoken word as well as the written one. This fall I'll have the chance to try my hand at broadcasting—I'll be doing commentary for about a half-dozen NFL games on CBS television. I'm not sure where that might lead, but I'm eager to find out.

Beyond that, I've thought about doing some writing for the outdoor and hunting magazines I've always loved to read. I can't think of anything I'd rather write about than the outdoors.

The fortunate thing about my situation is I *have* a choice about how I'm going to make a living now that my injury and my first career are behind me. A lot of people in my situation don't have that choice. They face incredible medical expenses with nowhere near the opportunities for making an income that I have. And they have nowhere near the financial stability I've got with Rick's guidance. From the beginning of my professional career, Angela and I have done wise things with our money. The financial security we built during my four years with the Jets gave me the peace of mind that money was not going to be something we had to be overly concerned with. Even with that, if the Jets had not stepped in and taken care of my medical costs—which Mr. Hess assured us they would, from the day I was injured—things would have been pretty rough for us. I can only imagine what it's like for people without that kind of support.

I wish I could say all it took for the recovery I've had was effort and willpower and an undying determination to overcome odds. But it's not that simple.

Neither is it enough to simply call it a "miracle." I cringe a little when I hear that word. It's tossed around so loosely these days that it's begun to lose its meaning. There *are* such things as miracles. They do happen. But there is nothing simple about them. There was nothing simple about mine.

The reasons for my recovery were a mixture of medicine and miracles, of divine love and human faith and, yes, of endless hours of sweat and pain and tears.

In terms of hands-on medical attention, from the moment I went down on the field to the day I left Mount Sinai Hospital, all the way up to this moment, my case has been a textbook example of what a model system of care can do. Ten years from now, I hope the treatment I received will seem archaic. There is that much still to learn about treating spinal cord injuries. I pray the doctors and researchers will continue to discover new and effective ways to deal with this condition, and I pray the public will give them the support they need.

The word "miracle" was used loosely—*far* too loosely—to describe the drug I was given to treat my damaged nerves. Sygen was headlined in newspaper stories as a "mystery" drug with possibly miraculous powers. The fact is that no one will ever know what part Sygen played in my recovery. Dr. Ragnarsson has made that point over and over again, and I feel the same way. It's impossible to say how much or how little it had to do with the feelings that returned to my nerves. What I do know is that at best, Sygen was just one ingredient in the recipe for my recovery.

Just as crucial was the love and support I received from the tens of thousands of people who responded with cards and letters and phone calls and prayers. Knowing you're not alone is so important to making it through an ordeal like this. I know there are people who go through a situation like mine feeling that they *are* alone. I wish they knew they aren't.

I had my teammates with me, which meant more than I can ever say. The love I have for them, and they for me, is for a lifetime.

The Jets organization, of course, supported me immensely, both materially and in spirit. And they supported one another. After I was released from Mount Sinai, Mr. Hess presented a gold Tiffany wristwatch to each of the Jets trainers and doctors who had helped get me through that fateful November day. Engraved on the back of each watch is my number, 90, the Jets team logo, and the numbers 11.29.92.

It's gestures like that that show the kind of family the Jets organization considers itself. Knowing I belonged to that family gave me constant comfort while I was in the hospital. It's comforting even now, and it always will be.

Angela and I are fortunate in that we allow God to guide us in our decisions. Financially, things would be painfully different had we not met Rick Schaeffer, our agent, attorney, and close friend.

I had my athletic and physical training to thank for my recovery as well. That helped enormously in terms of understanding what pain is, what effort and determination are, what it means to push and push and, when you feel like collapsing, to push some more. Never give up. I'd learned that lesson on the football field, and I used it every minute I was in the hospital and rehab rooms.

I had my love of the land behind me, the sense of independence and solitude, of isolation and endurance that I'd developed during countless hours out on the prairie. When I found myself immobilized, strapped in a bed and unable to move anything but my eyes, I was able to call on the calmness and quiet strength I'd absorbed from the land I grew up on.

Then there was my family and Angela's. Our parents made us who we are, so in that sense they've been with us all along. And of course they were at my bedside when it counted most.

As for Angela, there is no way I will ever adequately be able to express my feelings for her. I loved her from the bottom of my heart before any of this happened. Now, after these past eight months, my heart is much deeper than it ever was. And no one has filled it as much as she has.

Finally—and this is the "specific ingredient" Dr. Ragnarsson referred to at that final press conference—there is my faith. They say you're always tested where you think you're strongest. What better way to test a professional athlete than through his body?

I could easily have been destroyed by what happened to me. I could easily have been broken, just fallen apart. In every material sense, I was weak and vulnerable. But there is a verse in 2 Corinthians about that very thing, about weakness:

> And He said to me, "My grace is sufficient for thee, for My strength is made perfect in weakness."

I had *become* weakness, and I became it in an instant. Suddenly. As suddenly as a clear April afternoon turns into a tornado. As suddenly as a coyote appears in a breeze-blown stand of buffalo grass. As suddenly as a bombshell explodes on a war-torn beach. As suddenly as a gunshot to the head ends a good man's life on a dark city street. As suddenly as a collision on a football field changes one man's life on a gray November afternoon.

Only in this weakness was I able to completely lay my entire life at Christ's feet, holding nothing back, putting it all in His hands. He would have to fight the battle for me, and He did. Every place where Satan attacked me, every apparent weakness, turned into a blessing, a gift.

I feared that my wife would leave me, but she is beside me now as never before, with a love that has been tested by fire.

I feared I would never hold my daughter again; I hold her today and she holds me back with the love of a little girl who knows she will never lose her daddy. And she has a little sister now who will hold me the same way.

I feared I might be abandoned, forgotten; instead I have been embraced and honored more than I ever could have dreamed. I've continued to be uplifted by the dozens of letters that still arrive in the mail each week from people I've never met who want me to know how much they care. How can a man ever show his gratitude for so much love and support? And I've been overwhelmed by awards like the Father of the Year honor I was given in May in New York, the honorary doctorate I received at the graduation ceremonies at Fairleigh Dickinson University, and the Jim Thorpe Award presented to me just this week. At each ceremony, I made a point of acknowledging the hundreds of thousands of men, women, and children who have gone through the same experience as mine with much less attention and perhaps less support. It is they who know and who helped teach me the true meaning of courage.

I feared I would never have my legs beneath me again; they are there now, and they will only get stronger. There could be no better answer to what Satan tried to do to me than to walk out onto the Giants Stadium turf in September for the Jets' opening day game.

I'm going to take that walk. I always knew I would. Even when the fear was strongest, I still believed from the bottom of my heart that someday I would walk back onto that field. I didn't know when, but I knew I would. And now I will.

People ask me time and again if I ever asked, "Why me?" during these past eight months. When I hear that question, I think of what Arthur Ashe had to say when he was asked the same thing before he died of AIDS-related pneumonia early this year.

"If I say 'Why me?' about this," he said, "then I've got to say 'Why me?' about all the *good* things that have happened in my life."

That's precisely how I feel. When I look back and remind myself of where I've been, of where I was only a matter of months ago but, more than that, of where I was *years* ago, of all the blessings I've received throughout my life, with so much life still *ahead* of me, how could I possibly ask "Why me?"

That's the miracle. That's the magic. It's knowing that all of life is a blessing, that the Lord is with us even if we falter, He is with us even if we fail, He is with us when we break, and He can help to make us whole.

I've always believed that.

And I always will.